U0960243

澳洲私校语言入学考试(aeas)满分词汇宝典

澳洲游洋学院教学委员会　编

天津大学出版社
TIANJIN UNIVERSITY PRESS

图书在版编目(CIP)数据

澳洲私校语言入学考试(aeas)满分词汇宝典 / 澳洲游洋学院教学委员会编. —天津：天津大学出版社，2019.6（2022.11 重印）
通往澳洲顶级私校的第一本权威用书. 澳洲当地顶级学术师资倾力打造
ISBN 978-7-5618-6425-8

Ⅰ.①澳…　Ⅱ.①澳…　Ⅲ.①英语－词汇－高等学校－入学考试－澳大利亚－自学参考资料　Ⅳ.①H313

中国版本图书馆CIP数据核字(2019)第112513号

AOZHOUSIXIAO YUYAN RUXUEKAOSHI (aeas) MANFEN CIHUI BAODIAN

出版发行　天津大学出版社
地　　址　天津市卫津路92号天津大学内（邮编:300072）
电　　话　发行部:022-27403647
网　　址　www.tjupress.com.cn
印　　刷　廊坊市海涛印刷有限公司
经　　销　全国各地新华书店
开　　本　169mm×239mm
印　　张　18.25
字　　数　340千
版　　次　2019年6月第1版
印　　次　2022年11月第2次
定　　价　45.00元

前　　言

游洋教育作为AEAS(Australian Education Assessment Service，澳大利亚教育评估服务机构)考试培训和教育的行业领军学校,在教学研发上一如既往地走在行业前沿。继过往推出的把握AEAS考试核心的模拟题研发,现在更创行业之先,为大家带来更加实用的学习资料。

1. 游洋aeas词汇宝典的权威性

在aeas词汇宝典的编撰工作中,编者以大量全面的AEAS官方题库为依据和指导,钻研官方题库对各年级考生词汇储备要求,精准定位各年级必备的核心词汇。同时,编者横向参考澳大利亚全国统考NAPLAN(National Assessment Program—Literacy and Numeracy,全国评估项目——读写和计算)对各年级学生的词汇储备要求,通过科学严谨的研究分析,进而确立了对我们词汇宝典的词汇范围。同时,本着有效、权威的编撰宗旨,编者参考了比较权威的英语词典《科林斯大词典》中界定的必备英语词汇。因此,这套词汇宝典不仅涵盖了AEAS考试的必备词,同时也能有效地帮助学生为极具挑战性的私立学校学习打下必备的词汇基础。

2. 游洋aeas词汇宝典的内容

帮助学生在情境中学习和记忆单词是游洋aeas词汇宝典编撰的目的之一,让学生掌握单词的各种用法,了解在AEAS考试的各个单项都能应用的篇章素材更是游洋教育编写此书的初衷。这套书籍中的文章涵盖了从家庭日常,到校园生活,再到青少年的生活见闻等题材,每一篇文章都准确契合AEAS考题的话题范围。

在词汇呈现方式上,编者在行文中特意尽量使用主动语气,使学生尽可能学习词汇(尤其是动词)的原本形态,进而使学生能为相应的动词派生词打下基础。另外,编者刻意在篇章中穿插了很多核心词汇的派生词,力求使学生通过“多见面”这种方式轻松掌握关联词汇。

3. 如何使用游洋 aeas 词汇宝典

游洋 aeas 词汇宝典每个单元包含一篇短文，必备词汇表以及词汇填空练习。那么对于备考学生和家长，应该如何使用这套词汇宝典使它发挥到最大效能呢?

对于词汇量中等偏上的学生可以先读文章，大概理解篇章内容后再参考词汇表进一步学习词汇在篇章情景中的用法，最后利用填空题做自我检测。

对于词汇量较小或者年龄跨度大的学生来说，可以先浏览词汇表，大概认识单词后，再通读篇章，然后在篇章情境中进一步学习单词是如何使用的，最后再用填空题做自我检测。

4. 预期的学习效果

游洋 aeas 词汇宝典选取了各年级的必备词汇，学生如果能熟练记忆和运用其中的词汇，不但能从容应对 AEAS 考试，而且能帮助学生积累在私立学校学习的必备词汇基础，进而自信从容地展开私立学校学习历程。

另外，编者建议家长和学生在开始用填空题做自我检测前，可以把练习复印几份备用。带学生做完第一遍后，间隔两周再拿出来让学生重做一次，这种定期复习的方式能更有效系统地帮助学生加深对新词汇的记忆。

编者

2019 年 5 月 1 日

Contents

A 游洋 aeas4-6

词汇宝典

Passage 1

My Home

My home is in a quiet eastern area. Big trees grow around my home and there is a park across the street. There are five people in my family, and we live together. My home is lovely. Our front door faces south. A kitchen, a living room, a study, two toilets and four bedrooms make up my home. This house fits our big family very well.

Once you get in my home, you can walk along the hallway to the living room and the kitchen. We also have a tall cupboard and a large fridge in the kitchen. We put many cups, glasses, bottles, and plates inside the cupboard. There is also a first-aid chest in the cupboard. So it's handy for accident at home. When I want to drink some juice, I can always find it in the fridge. That's why I think fridge is the most useful invention in the world. We put a bin at the corner of the fridge; that's the place we throw away rubbish.

The design of these rooms is special and it makes our house look beautiful. I love my bedroom best. I put everything in order, so my bedroom seems very tidy and neat. In my bedroom, there is a desk against the wall and a bookshelf above the desk. It is my favorite place to stay. I study, play and sleep there.

We have a big TV in the cozy living room; my family always spends nighttime there. We often watch news and films on TV. My father and I like playing games, but my grandma and grandpa read books when they have time. I love my home.

必备词汇：

<u>名词</u>

area [ˈeərɪə] 区

corner [ˈkɔːnə(r)] 角落

home [həʊm] 家

family [ˈfæməlɪ] 家庭
place [pleɪs] 地方
wall [wɔ:l] 墙壁
book [bʊk] 书籍
bin [bɪn] 垃圾桶
design [dɪˈzaɪn] 设计
game [geɪm] 游戏
heart [hɑ:t] 心;内心
juice [dʒu:s] 果汁
meat [mi:t] 肉
rice [raɪs] 米饭
rubbish [ˈrʌbɪʃ] 垃圾
tree [tri:] 树
time [taɪm] 时间
vegetable [ˈvedʒtəbl] 蔬菜
cook [kʊk] 厨师
father [ˈfɑ:ðə(r)] 父亲
mother [ˈmʌðə(r)] 母亲
grandpa [ˈgrænpɑ:] 祖父
grandma [ˈgrænmɑ:] 祖母
people [ˈpi:pl] 人
kitchen [ˈkɪtʃɪn] 厨房
toilet [ˈtɔɪlət] 洗手间
bedroom [ˈbedru:m] 卧室
room [ru:m] 房间
study [ˈstʌdɪ] 书房
bottle [ˈbɒtl] 瓶子
bookshelf [ˈbʊkʃelf] 书架
cup [kʌp] 杯子
cupboard [ˈkʌbəd] 柜子
desk [desk] 书桌
fridge [frɪdʒ] 冰箱
glass [ˈglɑ:s] 玻璃杯
plate [pleɪt] 盘子
table [ˈteɪbl] 桌子
TV[ti:ˈvi:] 电视

形容词

big [bɪg] 大的
best [best] 最好的
Chinese [ˌtʃaɪˈni:z] 中国的
favorite [ˈfeɪvərɪt] 最爱的
free [fri:] 自由的
great [greɪt] 很好的
large [lɑ:dʒ] 大型的
lovely [ˈlʌvlɪ] 温馨的;可爱的(a lovely kid)
my [maɪ] 我的
neat [ni:t] 整洁的
quiet [ˈkwaɪət] 安静的
round [raʊnd] 圆形的;圆的
tall [tɔ:l] 高的
tasty [ˈteɪstɪ] 可口的;美味的
tidy [ˈtaɪdɪ] 干净的
yummy [ˈjʌmɪ] 好吃的;可口的
cozy [ˈkəʊzɪ] 温馨的;舒适的

动词

is [ɪz]/**are** [ɑ:(r)] 是

can [kæn] 能够
cook [kʊk] 煮饭;烹饪
drink [drɪŋk] 喝
eat [i:t] 吃
find [faɪnd] 找到
grow [grəʊ] 生长;成长
have [həv] 有
love [lʌv] 热爱
play [pleɪ] 玩耍
read [ri:d] 阅读
sleep [sli:p] 睡觉
stay [steɪ] 停留;保持
study [ˈstʌdɪ] 学习
want [wɒnt] 想要
watch [wɒtʃ] 观看

介词

above [əˈbʌv] 在……上面
against [əˈgenst] 倚靠;靠着
always [ˈɔ:lweɪz] 总是
around [əˈraʊnd] 在……周围
in [ɪn] 在……里面
from [frəm] 从……哪里
there [ðeə(r)] 那里
often [ˈɒfn] 常常
where [weə(r)] 那里
two [tu:] 两
five [faɪv] 五

短语

living room 客厅
be good at 擅长
make up 组成
throw away 丢弃
put...in order 把……放整齐
in my heart 在我心里

Passage 1 配套单词填空练习

1. I have a c________ corner in my bedroom.
2. It is a bad thing to t_____ ______ rubbish anywhere.
3. I love the d________ of the new iphone.
4. Doctor Tim is our f_________ doctor.
5. I got an ice cream from the f________.
6. Children g________ fast, they will be big soon.
7. My f________ story book is Harry Potter.
8. Fried chicken is very t_______, so I love eating them.
9. My mum always asks me to keep my room n________.

10. I don’t like eating v______________
11. You can find food in the k_________.
12. Please put your things in o________.
13. The plate is r__________, just like the shape of sun.
14. Be q_________, the baby is sleeping.
15. Look a_________ to see if you can find the book.
16. I don’t want to s________ at home; I want to go out.
17. There is a light a________ the table.
18. Please put r____________ in the bin.
19. Do you want some icy j_________?
20. My grandpa is standing a________ the wall now.
21. I live in a quiet a_______, I love this place.
22. I have a l_________ cat.
23. I find some glasses in the c___________.
24. I want to be f________ like a bird. It can fly anywhere it wants.
25. What do you want to d_______, juice or water?
26. My house is really t________, because I grandma cleans it often.
27. Can I use your t________?
28. Lily is g________ at reading; she can read very fast.
29. Look, that is a very t_______ tree.
30. This is a l__________ area.

Passage 2

Friends in the Garden

Dear children,

Do you know there are many tiny friends in the garden? Busy bees, cool bugs and pretty butterflies all come to the garden in the beautiful spring. These are insects in the nature.

If you look closely, you can see bees buzz around flowers, some bugs look cool and some look strange, and butterflies usually dance around flowers. I guess they like the smell of flowers. I am curious about bees, although many people are afraid of them. They have got scary stings at the end of their bodies. Their bodies are yellow and black, their heads are smaller than their tummies, their wings are the smallest, but they can fly very fast. I wonder how these little wings carry the heavy bodies. Is it amazing?

But I never think about touching bees because I fear they would sting me. Bugs are in different sizes; some are big, while some are tiny. Ants are busy looking for food; spiders always make webs in a shady tree. Butterflies are the prettiest; some have spots on their wings, but some have waves on their wings. When bees and butterflies dance around flowers, it is a fantastic view to see. When spring arrives, it is a wonderful idea for you to get into your garden to enjoy the amazing of these little lives.

With regards,

Garden lover

必备词汇：

名词

bee [biː] 蜜蜂
body [ˈbɒdɪ] 身体（bodies）
bug [bʌg] 昆虫；虫子
butterfly [ˈbʌtəflaɪ] 蝴蝶
children [ˈtʃɪldrən] 孩子；儿童
color/colour [ˈkʌlə(r)] 颜色
creature [ˈkriːtʃə(r)] 生物
flower [ˈflaʊə(r)] 花
friend [frend] 朋友
head [hed] 头；头部
idea [aɪˈdɪə] 主意
insect [ˈɪnsekt] 昆虫
garden [ˈgɑːdn] 花园
kind [kaɪnd] 种类
life [laɪf] 生活
lives [laɪvz] 生命
nature [ˈneɪtʃə(r)] 大自然
web [web] 蜘蛛网
smell [smel] 气味
spring [sprɪŋ] 春天
spot [spɒt] 斑点
tummy [ˈtʌmɪ] 肚子（tummies）
view [vjuː] 景观；风景
wave [weɪv] 波浪；波纹
wing [wɪŋ] 翅膀

形容词

amazing [əˈmeɪzɪŋ] 令人惊讶的
black [blæk] 黑色的
busy [ˈbɪzɪ] 忙碌的
big [bɪg] 大的
cool [kuːl] 酷酷的；凉爽的
curious [ˈkjʊəriəs] 好奇的
different [ˈdɪfrənt] 不同的
fantastic [fænˈtæstɪk] 极好的；惊奇的
heavy [ˈhevɪ] 重的
little [ˈlɪtl] 小的；少的
pretty [ˈprɪti] 漂亮的；美丽的
prettiest [pˈrɪtɪst] 最漂亮的
small [smɔːl] 小的
smaller [sˈmɔːlər] 更小的
smallest [ˈsmɔːlɪst] 最小的
strange [streɪndʒ] 奇怪的
tiny [ˈtaɪnɪ] 小的
yellow [ˈjeləʊ] 黄色的
wonderful [ˈwʌndəfl] 精彩的；极好的

动词

arrive [əˈraɪv] 到来；到达
buzz [bʌz] 嗡嗡叫
carry [ˈkærɪ] 负担；运送
come [kʌm] 来；到来

dance [dɑ:ns] 跳舞
enjoy [ɪnˈdʒɔɪ] 欣赏；享受
fly [flaɪ] 飞
guess [ges] 猜测
have[hæv]/**has** [hæz] 有
know [nəʊ] 知道
like [laɪk] 喜欢
look [lʊk] 看
see [si:] 看见
wonder [ˈwʌndə(r)] 想知道

副词

closely [ˈkləʊslɪ] 仔细地(look closely 仔细看)
fast [fɑ:st] 快
very [ˈverɪ] 很(very fast 很快)

数量代词

many [ˈmenɪ] 很多
some [səm] 一些
one [wʌn] 一个

短语

get into 进入

Passage 2 配套单词填空练习

1. We can find little c__________ in the garden.
2. Spiders are a kind of i__________.
3. When the spring a__________, we can see flowers in the garden.
4. If we are looking for ants, we need to look c__________, because they are so tiny.
5. Tim is a c__________ boy; he wants to lot all things about cars.
6. Butterflies are the p__________ creatures; they look so pretty.
7. There is f__________ view from my bedroom window.
8. Lucy's exam result is a__________; she did not get such good result before.
9. I can't g__________ the result of the game.
10. Do you have any i__________ about animals' life?
11. I can hear bees b__________ in the garden.
12. Do you e__________ yesterday's party?

13. There is a strange s__________ in the kitchen.
14. My dog has s______ on its body, so we call it Spotty.
15. When there is wind, we can see big w_________ on the sea.
16. Some bugs look very s___________, for example, they have tiny eyes but big bodies.
17. There are many c_____________ playing outside.
18. We always have w___________ time at school.
19. Some butterflies are really p__________.
20. I need to c________ bags to school everyday.
21. My t_________ felt sick, is that because I ate something bad?
22. I hope I have w__________, so I can fly anywhere.
23. I have many things in my bag, so my bag is really h___________.
24. How f_________can you run?
25. Ants are really t__________.
26. I only have l_________ free time everyday, because I have much homework.
27. There are different l_______ in the world.
28. Many people have very busy l__________.
29. Some b_____ look really strange, I don't want to touch them.
30. Which c_________ do you like, red, blue or green?

Passage 3

Go to the Library

There is a library near my home. It is free to join the library, and you just need to fill out a form on spot. The library will mail the library card to your home address. I can borrow books from the library and I like reading books about animals. The librarians are very nice. They know everything about books. The library is huge and has two levels. Children's books are on the first level, but books for people at my dad's age are stored on the second floor. There are all sorts of children's books, cartoon and picture books.

When I get to the library, I always look for new books, because new books interest me more. Today, I spot a book with an awesome picture of a tiger on the cover; it looks so vivid that my eyes open wide with surprise. I take it down from the shelf and begin to read it on spot. The tiger's yellow fur and black stripes look scaring, but I am not frightened, I want to know more about it.

The book is called "Save Tigers". It says many tigers live in jungles, but they will lose their home soon. This is because people cut down trees in jungles, so the jungles become smaller and smaller. The living conditions of animals become poor, some animals even have died out. I want to know more, so I ask the librarian if I can borrow this book. He replies yes. I cannot wait to find out the end of the story.

Normally, I can keep this book for a loan period of 3 weeks. If I cannot finish reading the book before the time limit comes to an end, I can renew it for another two week. This means I have plenty of time to finish the book.

必备词汇：

名词

age [eɪdʒ] 年龄
animal [ˈænɪml] 动物
cartoon [kɑ:ˈtu:n] 卡通；漫画
book [bʊk] 书籍
cover [ˈkʌvə(r)] 封面
end [end] 结尾；结局
floor [flɔ:(r)] 楼层；地面
fur [fɜ:(r)] 皮毛
help [help] 帮助
jungle [ˈdʒʌŋgl] 丛林
level [ˈlevl] 楼层；等级
library [ˈlaɪbrərɪ] 图书馆
librarian [laɪˈbreəriən] 图书馆管理员
picture [ˈpɪktʃə(r)] 照片；图画
sorts [sɔ:t] 种类
stripe [straɪp] 条纹
tiger [ˈtaɪgə(r)] 老虎
condition [kənˈdɪʃn] 状况；条件

动词

cannot [ˈkænɒt] 不能
call [kɔ:l] 把……称为；打电话
cut [kʌt] 砍；切
borrow [ˈbɒrəʊ] 借
find [faɪnd] 找到
keep [ki:p] 保留
know [nəʊ] 知道
live [lɪv] 居住；住
lose [lu:z] 失去
read [ri:d] 阅读
renew [rɪˈnju:] 续借；更新
reply [rɪˈplaɪ] 回答
say [seɪ] 讲述；说
save [seɪv] 拯救
spot [spɒt] 注意到
store [stɔ:(r)] 存储；保存
take [teɪk] 拿
wait [weɪt] 等待

形容词

first [fɜ:st] 第一的
frightened [ˈfraɪtnd] 吓到的；受惊的
huge [hju:dʒ] 巨大的
interesting [ˈɪntrəstɪŋ] 有趣的
nice [naɪs] 友好的
second [ˈsekənd] 第二的
scaring [skeərɪŋ] 吓人的

副词

normally [ˈnɔ:məlɪ] 一般而言
near [nɪə(r)] 在附近；接近
soon [su:n] 不久；很快

代词

everything [ˈevrɪθɪŋ] 一切；所有事情

more [mɔ:(r)] 更多

thing [θɪŋ] 东西；事情

短语

loan period 借阅期

get to 到达

ask for 询问；请求

come to an end 结束

cut down 砍倒

look for 寻找

live in 居住在……

plenty of 许多

on the spot 立刻

die out 灭绝

Passage 3 配套单词填空练习

1. Some schools have a_______ limit for students, for example, 7 years old for grade 1.
2. You borrowed these books for 20 days, now you need to re__________ the books.
3. When will they r_________ your call?
4. I want to s__________ wild animals.
5. Some animals like tiger have f______.
6. Lions and tigers live in j_________.
7. I can borrow books from the l_____________ near my home.
8. How long did you w_________ for your friend?
9. What is l_________ period for these books, two weeks or three weeks?
10. My T-shirt has s_________, so I call it a stripy T-shirt.
11. The living c_________ of many animals are bad.
12. Which l_________ do you live in?
13. I feel so f_____________ every time when I see a snake.
14. There is a h_______ cloud in the sky.
15. The spider looks really s__________.
16. Do you know the e_________ of the story?

17. My sister likes reading p__________ books, because she don't know words.
18. Jimmy is always the f________ student to arrive at school.
19. My brother s_______ something moving in the garden.
20. I need a place to s_________ my old books.
21. My parents will come home s________.
22. The f________ is wet, so you need to be very careful.
23. I cannot find the c________ of the book, so I cannot return it to the library.
24. Some c________ books are really interesting, they have funny images.

Passage 4

My Daily Routine

At weekdays, I start my day in almost the same way. I get up at 7 o'clock in the morning and then I get dressed. After the breakfast, I get into the car and buckle the belt. My sister sits beside me in the car. When we are ready to leave, my mum drives us to school. I have three classes in the morning, and two classes in the afternoon.

During breaks, I rush to the playground; I always scan the playground to find my friend Timmy. He is skinny but full of energy. He likes climbing monkey bars. When we play on the monkey bars, we need to grip the bars firmly, if not, we may fall from the bars.

Our lunch break comes at 12:30pm and it is followed by a long break. We sit in the canteen to eat our lunch and talk about funny stuffs. Timmy always shares jokes, and I like share with him the silly fight I had with my sister.

I finish school at 4 o'clock in the afternoon. Once the bell rings, I fly out of the classroom. I wait for my mum to come to pick me up. As the playground is next to the street, so we can hear clearly the traffic noises. Most parents are in a hurry when they pick up their kids from school.

My mum usually picks me up early. On our way home, I share my school day with my mum. She loves listening to my story. Sometimes, I have a rough day, I just want to stay silent and say nothing.

When we get home, my mum cooks simple dinner and I start to do my homework. Sometimes, I find the homework is very difficult; then I will ask my elder sister to help me. She is quite patient and brilliant at answering hard questions. With her help, I can finish my homework perfectly. My sister says it is a good idea to revise the hard questions, so I can do better next time.

My family usually has dinner around 7 o'clock in the evening. After dinner, we talk for a while or watch TV. As bath takes longer time, so I would just have a quick shower. Then, I write a dairy before I go to bed. I go to bed at 9 o'clock at night. I'm a sound sleeper; this means I fall asleep very quickly.

必备词汇:

名词

weekday [ˈwi:kdeɪ] 工作日
afternoon [ˌɑ:ftəˈnu:n] 下午
breakfast [ˈbrekfəst] 早餐
class [klɑ:s] 课
morning [ˈmɔ:nɪŋ] 早晨
belt [belt] 腰带;皮带
school [sku:l] 学校
way [weɪ] 方式;道路
break [breɪk] 休息
stuff [stʌf] 东西
joke [dʒəʊk] 笑话
fight [faɪt] 打架
sister [ˈsɪstə(r)] 姐妹
traffic [ˈtræfɪk] 交通
noise [nɔɪz] 噪声

动词

start [stɑ:t] 开始
buckle [ˈbʌkl] 扣住;扣上
leave [li:v] 离开
drive [draɪv] 开车;驾驶
play [pleɪ] 玩耍
rush [rʌʃ] 冲;奔向
scan [skæn] 扫视;扫描
grip [grɪp] 抓住
fall [fɔ:l] 落下;跌下
ring [rɪŋ] 打铃
finish [ˈfɪnɪʃ] 结束;完成
follow [ˈfɒləʊ] 跟随
share [ʃeə(r)] 分享
fly [flaɪ] 飞翔

形容词

daily [ˈdeɪlɪ] 日常的;每日的
same [seɪm] 一样的
ready [ˈredɪ] 准备好的
skinny [ˈskɪnɪ] 皮包骨头的;很瘦的
funny [ˈfʌnɪ] 可笑的;滑稽的
silly[ˈsɪlɪ] 可笑的;愚蠢的
early [ˈɜ:lɪ] 早的
silent[ˈsaɪlənt] 沉默的;安静的
rough [rʌf] 艰难的;粗暴的

副词

almost [ˈɔ:lməʊst] 差不多
firmly [ˈfɜ:mlɪ] 牢牢地

clearly [ˈklɪəlɪ] 清楚地

介词

beside [bɪˈsaɪd] 在……旁边

during [ˈdjʊərɪŋ] 在……期间

短语

monkey bar 攀爬架

get into 进入;陷入

get dressed 穿衣服

talk about 谈论

fly out 冲出

wait for 等待

pick up 接

in the same way 以同样的方式

finish school 放学

full of 充满

for a while 一会儿

next to 邻近;紧靠

in a hurry 匆忙

Passage 4 配套单词填空练习

1. We always do housework on w ________ because we are busy working on weekdays.
2. The fridge is f ________ of fruits, there is no space for other things.
3. What did you do d ________ your holiday?
4. Tom didn't have b ________ , it's 10 o'clock and he feels hungry.
5. Can you wait me for a w ________, I am nearly ready.
6. My parents will p ______ me up , so I don't need to go home by tram today.
7. There is a heavy t ________ jam during peak time.
8. Have you f ________ your homework ? Not yet.
9. My grandparents know what happens everyday, they like reading d ________ news.
10. The post office is n ______ to the library, it's hard to miss it.
11. We thought he was s ________ but actually he is very clever.
12. He told a f ________ joke and everyone laughed.
13. It's a ________ 10 pm, let's go back home before there is no public transportation.
14. Lucy and lily are good friends, they have s ________ hobbies.

15. Can you speak louder? I can't hear you c __________.
16. We should not f ________ with each other, let's be friends.
17. We have four c ________ today, biology, geography, English and music.
18. Why are you in a h ________? I am late for school.
19. The bus l _______ at 6:30, we'd better get up at 6 o'clock in the morning.
20. Mary used to be fat, but now she is s ________.
21. There is an old saying that goes like this : "the e _______ bird catches worms."
22. I have remembered this word f _________ and I will not forget it.
23. The little is always s ________ while her brother is always noisy.
24. Let's put all these s ________ in the store room.
25. My neighbor is decorating his house, which makes a strong noise.
26. If you drink beer or other alcohol, you can not d ________ your car, because it's too dangerous.
27. In the class, we t _______ about endangered animals.
28. The printer doesn't work, but you can use the scanner to s _______ you document.
29. He lost balance and f _______ down.
30. When we have good things , we should s _______ them with our friends instead of enjoying them by ourselves.

Passage 5

My Neighbor—The Hanson Family

The Hanson family lives on the right side of our house. Mum says they are good neighbours.

Mr. Hanson is a short man. He often pulls a funny face when he rests under the shade in front of his house. His wife Mrs. Hanson is a friendly woman in her middle age. Mrs. Hanson often leans against their front door and watches kids playing on the street.

They have a son called Mark and a daughter called Grace. Grace is a pretty girl and she often babysits my younger sister when my mum is sick.

Grace has a soft voice. She often sings songs to my sister when she takes care of her. After they play for a while, Grace usually spells words with my sister. After the spelling, Grace would teach my sister to count simple numbers. Grace is good at studying, so she often gives us exam tips. According to Grace, there is no trick to get high score except hard work and making great notes.

Mark loves playing basketball. He is a great player. He even represents his school to play in several matches. He has a basketball net at his backyard. I can hear him practising basketball every afternoon. I guess Mark will have a match towards the end of the term. Mark often says their team members support each other. Everyone brings great value to their team. I know he wants to win the match badly with a great total score.

必备词汇：

名词

neighbor [ˈneɪbə(r)] 邻居

shade [ʃeɪd] 树荫

wife [waɪf] 太太

voice [vɔɪs] 声音

song [sɒŋ] 歌

number [ˈnʌmbə(r)] 数字；个数
tip [tɪp] 小建议
trick [trɪk] 诀窍；花招
score [skɔ:(r)] 分数
note [nəʊt] 笔记
player [ˈpleɪə(r)] 比赛者；玩游戏的人
match [mætʃ] 比赛
backyard [ˌbækˈjɑ:d] 后院
end [end] 结束；终点
term [tɜ:m] 学期
value [ˈvælju:] 价值

动词

rest [rest] 休息
babysit [ˈbeɪbɪsɪt] 照看（小孩）
spell [spel] 拼写
count [kaʊnt] 数数；计数
give [gɪv] 给予
represent [ˌreprɪˈzent] 代表
hear [hɪə(r)] 听见；听到
practise [ˈpræktɪs] 练习；实践
support [səˈpɔ:t] 支持
win [wɪn] 赢得

副词

recently [ˈri:sntlɪ] 最近
towards [təˈwɔ:dz] 在；朝向
badly [ˈbædlɪ] 很；非常

介词

except[ɪkˈsept] 除了……之外
with [wɪð] 以……；包括

形容词

short [ʃɔ:t] 矮小的
friendly [ˈfrendlɪ] 友善的
pretty [ˈprɪtɪ] 好看的
sick [sɪk] 有病的；生病的
soft [sɒft] 温柔的；柔软的
simple [ˈsɪmpl] 简单的

短语

hard work 勤奋
basketball net 篮球网
team member 队友
lean against 斜靠在……上
bring...to 带来
on the right 在右边
pull a face 扮鬼脸
in front of 在……前面
in middle age 中年
take care of 照顾
for a while 一会儿
according to 根据；按照
be good at 擅长
each other 相互

Passage 5 配套单词填空练习

1. This machine is s ________ to operate , it's not complicated.
2. He is tall while his brother is s __________.
3. Where have you been? I haven't seen you r _________.
4. There is a pear tree in our school b __________.
5. Tony likes playing guitar , he p ___________ every day.
6. She just moved into the house next door, so we are n _________ now.
7. My cousin is g _______ at history, he can remember lots dates and events.
8. Mary was s ________ so she was absent from school yesterday.
9. My pet dog has fluffy and s ________ hair.
10. The majority of students s __________ this idea, then let's carry it out.
11. Different color of the uniform r ____________ different grades.
12. T _________ notes is important, it can help us to remember important information.
13. The little boy who always p ______ a face is naughty.
14. My sister thinks this sweater is ugly but I reckon it p ________.
15. I will go on holiday next month , can you help me to take c _______ of my cat?
16. Friends should help e _______ other.
17. He is the champion who w _______ the competition.
18. My uncle is a f ________ man , he always be nice to everyone.
19. It's sunny today, you can see s _________ under the tree.
20. My little brother can c ________ from 1 to 100.
21. After my reading teacher gave me some t ______, I can find answers easily now.
22. Did you h ________ the sound?
23. Hard working b ________ good luck to us.
24. There is a lake in f ________ of the village .
25. The director changed the film plot a __________ to this story.

26. I am too tired, let’s have a r ________.

27. My parents g ______ me a bicycle as my birthday present last year.

28. Mr. green is in his m ________ age, he is 48 years old.

29. The two teams are having a m _________ now.

30. We should not play t ________ on our peers.

Passage 6

Children's Book Club

Do you enjoy reading? Are you ready to laugh your pants off? Come along and join our local children's book club. You can delve into the exciting world of children's books. Our expert of children's books will guide you through many copies of books. You will be given the opportunity to discuss your favourite books as well. Famous writers also join us for some events. There you can go behind the scene of how the books were created, and engage in reading activities that you can treasure forever.

In addition, the club also holds a book fair every year, so the little readers can buy books at a bargain price. At the book fair, some new writers display or release their new books. Another exciting thing about the book fair is the lucky draw. Everyone can have a go at the lucky draw. The club officials will announce the winner on the last day of the fair. The prize is a couple of books.

I like the book fair, because there are many books available for purchase. New books cost much money, so my parents encourage me to save some money for the books. I saved my pocket money for the whole year, so I can buy as many books as I can.

必备词汇：

<u>名词</u>

pants [pænts] 裤子

club [klʌb] 俱乐部

world [wɜ:ld] 世界

expert [ˈekspɜ:t] 专家

copy [ˈkɒpɪ] 一册；一本

opportunity [ˌɒpəˈtju:nətɪ] 机会

event [ɪˈvent] 活动

scene [si:n] 情景

response [rɪˈspɒns] 反应；答复

fair [feə(r)] 市集

bargain [ˈbɑ:gən] 便宜货

price [praɪs] 价格
official [əˈfɪʃl] 官员
winner [ˈwɪnə(r)] 获奖者
prize [praɪz] 奖品
purchase [ˈpɜːtʃəs] 购买

动词

guide [gaɪd] 引导
create [kriˈeɪt] 创造
treasure [ˈtreʒə(r)] 珍藏;珍视
hold [həʊld] 举办
display [dɪˈspleɪ] 展示;展出
release [rɪˈliːs] 发布
announce [əˈnaʊns] 宣布
cost [kɒst] 花费
encourage [ɪnˈkʌrɪdʒ] 鼓励
save [seɪv] 节约;存钱

形容词

local [ˈləʊkl] 本地的;当地的
another [əˈnʌðə(r)] 另一个
exciting [ɪkˈsaɪtɪŋ] 令人激动的
lucky [ˈlʌkɪ] 幸运的
last [lɑːst] 最后的
available [əˈveɪləbl] 有的;可以得到的
whole [həʊl] 全部的;整体的

副词

through [θruː] 通过;自始至终

短语

book fair 书市
lucky draw 抽奖活动
come along 前来
delve into 徜徉;深入研究
engage in 参与
laugh one's pants off 放声大笑
go behind the scene 跑到幕后
as well 也
in addition 另外;此外
have a go 试一试
as many as I can 尽量多
a couple of 两个;几个
the whole year 一整年

Passage 6 配套单词填空练习

1. I like English, my brother likes it as w ________.
2. How much time did you spend on your homework everyday? A c ________ of hours.
3. Our principal a ________ the news that our school library will be refur-

bished next year.

4. My parents always support and e __________ me.

5. There is a book f _______, lots of books are on sale, let's go and buy some.

6. This museum d ________ a great range of ancient stuffs.

7. This bag only c ________ 10 dollars.

8. The winner deserves a p ________.

9. A great number of products are on sale now, many customers are p _______ in the department store.

10. Look! The CD only costs 2 dollars, it really a b __________.

11. They are not l ________, they come from foreign countries.

12. I'd like to go to your birthday party, but unfortunately, I am not a _________ next Friday.

13. When will our school h ________ the sports meeting ?

14. Don't focus on this part only, you should analyze the passage as a w _________.

15. Scien tists are d ________ into that experiment.

16. He is an e ________ of computers, he can solve all kinds of computer problems.

17. The p _________ of that car is high, I can't afford it.

18. If you can work effectively , it will s _______ plenty of time.

19. Many students e ________ in this competition.

20. I called you three times this morning, but you didn't r __________.

21. There is a football c _______ in our school, do you want to join it?

22. To join the library, you need two passport photos and in a _________, you need to show your student card.

23. The children are so curious about the stage that they go b ________ the scene to have a look.

24. This museum opens almost the w _______ year, except on Christmas.

25. I'm not good at it, but I'd like to h _______ a go.

26. The baseball match is really e __________, all of us are excited.

27. He has two sons, one is a lawyer, the o _________ is a football coach.

28. My dream is to travel around the w ________ to meet people from different countries.

29. It is a great o ___________ to have a speech in front of school assembly.

30. This t __________ is precious, we should cherish it.

Passage 7

To Recycle

This term, my school gave us a school project of protecting our earth by recycling rubbish. Our teacher taught us to sort out different types of rubbish before we can recycle or reuse them again. Recycling can happen in our daily life.

If we find glass bottles or jars, we can try to use them as vases for flowers. We can even fill the bottles with water and use them as drinking bottles. If we find a cardboard box, we can put it into the recycle bins. We can save trees if we reuse paper.

Let's look around our home and see if we can find something else for recycling. I guess you may find plastic bags to reuse. Yes, you may find some juice cans. If you figure out that juice cans are made of metal, you can also reuse it or put it into the recycle bin.

必备词汇：

名词

project [ˈprɒdʒekt] 项目；计划
earth [ɜ:θ] 地球
rubbish [ˈrʌbɪʃ] 垃圾
type [taɪp] 类型
recycling [ri:ˈsaɪklɪŋ] 回收
glass [glɑ:s] 玻璃
bottle [ˈbɒtl] 瓶子
jar [dʒɑ:(r)] 罐子
vase [vɑ:z] 花瓶
cardboard [ˈkɑ:dbɔ:d] 纸板
box [bɒks] 盒子
bin [bɪn] 垃圾桶
can [kæn] 易拉罐
metal [ˈmetl] 金属

动词

recycle [ˌri:ˈsaɪkl] 回收
protect [prəˈtekt] 保护
reuse [ˌri:ˈju:z] 再次利用
happen [ˈhæpən] 发生
find [faɪnd] 找到
fill [fɪl] 填满，填写

形容词

else [els] 另外的

plastic [ˈplæstɪk] 塑料的

短语

sort out 分类

put into 放入

look around 四处瞧瞧

figure out 弄懂;弄明白

made of 由……做成

Passage 7 配套单词填空练习

1. People live on e _________, may be there are other creatures live on other planets.
2. There's no container for the flowers, I need to buy a v _______ to put flowers in.
3. There are different t ________ of animals in the zoo, we can go and observe them closely.
4. Plastic bags and b ________ should be recycled to protect our environment.
5. To make this handcraft , we need c ________, glue and scissors.
6. When leave the classroom , we should take away the r ________ and throw them in the trash bin.
7. Where is my school uniform? I can't f ________ it.
8. It is our responsibility to p __________ the environment.
9. The accident h __________ last night.
10. Books are m _________ of woods.
11. I haven't f __________ it out, can you explain it to me ?
12. My umbrella isn't here , I must have put it somewhere e _______.
13. I need to buy a j _____ of jam.
14. R ________ household waste is good for our environment.
15. Disposable chopsticks cannot be r __________. It's a waste of resources.
16. Before you join the club, you need f ______ in this form.
17. P _______ your book into your school bag in case you forget to bring it.

18. There is no b _______ around, I can't throw away my litter.

19. The librarian is s ________ out books.

20. I received a b _______ on my birthday, when I opened it , there was a present inside.

21. Heavy m _________ pollutes the soil.

22. We should recycle and r __________ materials.

23. If we reuse paper we can save t _______.

24. After the party , there were juice c _______ and cola bottles everywhere.

25. G ________ bottles are fragile, if you drop them on the floor, they will be broken easily.

26. Many people use p _________ bags in their daily life.

27. He is the p __________ manager.

28. I love spring, all the f _________ blossom , they are colorful.

29. L ________ around your room , it's messy and dirty.

30. It's hard to g _______ which team will win, they are both great.

Passage 8

My Typical Day in School

School is fun for most kids. I like going to school. My school is new and has three large buildings, and a playground. We have classes in the buildings. I have nice classmates, and amazing teachers. I am studying four subjects this term. They are English, arts, music and math.

I always pay much attention in class. In English class, our teacher teaches us to describe things or people. We learn words from a story. In music class, our teacher divides us into small groups. Then we can play different musical instruments. Some students play guitar, while others beat drums. Currently, I am learning drum. It can be quite noisy in the music class. In arts class, we can draw pictures and fold paper toys. In math class, our teacher explains hard questions to us. I'm a top student in math, but my best friend Luke feels bored in math class. Luke and I are like brothers, so I'm happy to help him with math after class. I don't want to see him fail his final math exam.

When we have breaks, we can run, jump and play in the sand pit. In hot days, we sit under the trees, but in cold days, we run several laps to keep our body warm. When we feel tired, we can sit round in a circle to have a nice chat. It is common to see girls playing with skip rope, but boys chase each other.

必备词汇:

<u>名词</u>

building [ˈbɪldɪŋ] 楼;建筑

class [klɑ:s] 课;课程

subject [ˈsʌbdʒɪkt] 科目

art [ɑ:t] 艺术

music[ˈmju:zɪk] 音乐

math [mæθ] 数学

group [gru:p] 小组

guitar [gɪˈtɑ:(r)] 吉他

drum [drʌm] 鼓

picture [ˈpɪktʃə(r)] 图画
toy [tɔɪ] 玩具
question [ˈkwestʃən] 问题
brother [ˈbrʌðə(r)] 兄弟
exam [ɪgˈzæm] 考试
break [breɪk] 休息
lap[læp]（操场）圈

动词

describe [dɪˈskraɪb] 描绘;描写
divide [dɪˈvaɪd] 分开
beat [bi:t] 击打;敲击
draw [drɔ:] 画画
fold [fəʊld] 折叠
explain [ɪkˈspleɪn] 解释
fail [feɪl] 失败
jump [dʒʌmp] 跳
run [rʌn] 跑
chase [tʃeɪs] 追赶;奔跑

形容词

typical [ˈtɪpɪkl] 典型的
most [məʊst] 大多数的
large [lɑ:dʒ] 大型的
nice [naɪs] 友好的
noisy [ˈnɔɪzɪ] 喧闹的
hard [hɑ:d] 困难的
top [tɒp] 拔尖的;顶尖的
bored [bɔ:d] 无聊的
final [ˈfaɪnl] 最后的
hot [hɒt] 热的
cold [kəʊld] 寒冷的
warm [wɔ:m] 暖和的
tired [ˈtaɪəd] 累的
common [ˈkɒmən] 普遍的;常见的

副词

quite [kwaɪt] 很;非常
even [ˈi:vn] 甚至

短语

musical instrument 乐器
sand pit 沙坑
skip rope 跳绳
help with 帮助
have class 上课
in a circle 围成一圈
keep warm 保持暖和
pay attention to 集中注意力

Passage 8 配套单词填空练习

1. What's your favorite s __________? History.
2. He has been working for 10 hours, he is t ______ and he need have a rest

now.

3. This movie is q _________ exciting, we like it very much.

4. It is c _______ today, the highest temperature is only 6 degrees.

5. It is h _______ outside, I'd like to have a glass of chill mineral water.

6. There are loads of people in the park , it's n ________. Let's go to the library to enjoy the quiet atmosphere.

7. Students should pay a ________ to what the teachers say in class.

8. What kind of musical i __________ do you like? I prefer violin.

9. In last PE class, we s ________ rope.

10. Can you d _________ the picture? Tell us what it's about.

11. When you take notes, you can d _______ pictures to help you memorize things.

12. The car r _______ so quickly that it collided with the van.

13. If you f _______ the exam, don't be frustrated, keep working hard, you will succeed sooner or later.

14. When I was little , there were full of dolls and t ________ in my bedroom.

15. The zoo is pretty large, it will take us a whole day to visit all the sections.

16. I don't understand the meaning of this word, can you e _________ it to me please?

17. After class, students come out of the school b _________ and go back home.

18. Reading teacher gave us ten q __________ to answer.

19. At first the little boy was quite interested in the book, but soon he became b _______.

20. It is a c _________ design, we can see it everywhere.

21. He f ________ the letter and put it in an envelope last night.

22. After the f _______ exam, we finished this semester.

23. Our team is united, we always h ______ each other.

24. It's cold outside, please wear a scarf to keep w _______.

25. Students are sitting in a c _________ and enjoying the picnic and games in

the park.

26. When we meet someone for the first time, we say “n ______ to meet you”.

27. Jade is a t _________ student who always wins school scholarship.

28. After an intensive period of work, you should have a short b _________.

29. They have a lot in common, including appearance, so we all think they are b ________.

30. Teachers have d ________ students into different groups according to ability.

Passage 9

Actions Your Body Can Do

Do you ever wonder what actions your little body can do?

Your body may be small, but it can do many kinds of actions. Your legs can shake, your hands can wave, your head can nod, and your body can wiggle!

Now, do you feel amazed by your own body? Your body can do even more things. Let me go on:

You can breathe.

Your brain can think.

Your eyes can observe.

Your ears can listen.

Your nose can sneeze.

Your mouth can speak.

Your arm can hug.

Your knees can bend.

Your feet can hop, while your ankles can turn.

Your tiny fingers can tap, while your tiny toes can tiptoe.

When your brain thinks, ideas pop into your mind. If you think harder, you will become smarter. When you read a story, your brain also works quietly to understand it. But if you think too hard, you may lose yourself in the story.

When your hands write, your ideas come to life on paper. You can make stories when you write it down. One word after one word, you build up a chain of words. These words make up a story! It is brilliant!

必备词汇：

名词

action [ˈækʃn] 行动；行为
kinds [kaɪndz] 种类；类型
leg [leg] 腿
hand [hænd] 手
head [hed] 头部
nose [nəʊz] 鼻子
arm [ɑ:m] 手臂
knee [ni:] 膝盖
feet [fi:t] 双脚
ankle [ˈæŋkl] 踝关节
finger [ˈfɪŋgə(r)] 手指
toe [təʊ] 脚趾

动词

wonder [ˈwʌndə(r)] 好奇；猜想
shake [ʃeɪk] 摇摆；摇动
wave [weɪv] 挥动；挥舞
breathe [bri:ð] 呼吸
nod [nɒd] 点头
wiggle [ˈwɪgl] 扭动
think [θɪŋk] 思考
observe [əbˈzɜ:v] 观察
sneeze [sni:z] 打喷嚏
speak [spi:k] 说话
hug [hʌg] 拥抱
bend [bend] 弯曲
hop [hɒp] 单脚跳
turn [tɜ:n] 转动
tap [tæp] 敲击
tiptoe [ˈtɪptəʊ]（垫着脚尖）走
understand [ˌʌndəˈstænd] 理解；明白

形容词

amazed [əˈmeɪzd] 惊讶的
smart [smɑ:t] 聪明的
brilliant [ˈbrɪlɪənt] 精彩的；聪明的

短语

go on 继续
pop up 冒出来
in...mind 在脑海里
lose oneself in 陷入
come to life 有了生命
write down 写下来
build up 造出
a chain of 一串
make up 组成；构

Passage 9 配套单词填空练习

1. He is a b _________ child, because he learns things quickly.
2. People should take a _________ to save water.
3. She felt a __________ when she heard of the news.
4. My parents took me to the zoo and taught me to o _________ different kinds of animals.
5. After a short break, we w _________ on reviewing our lessons.
6. The reason why I can't stop s __________ is that I catch a cold.
7. If you know the answer, please nod. If you have no idea , please s _______ your head.
8. I saw some pictures of dinosaurs' footprint, I think they had huge f ________ .
9. Mom was not carefully enough when she was cooking, she cut her f __________.
10. The teacher speaks so fast that I can't w ________ down what he says.
11. When spring comes, everything c _________ to life again.
12. He fell down from the ladder and hurt his a _________.
13. Female students m ______ up 40% of our school faculty.
14. When he heard the song, he lost h _________ in memory.
15. The line isn't clear, can you s ________ louder?
16. A fox has four l ________.
17. Before you answer the question, you 'd better t _______ it over.
18. The chimpanzee's a _______ are really long.
19. If snakes died out , it would cause a c ________ of problems in our eco system.
20. He w ________ his hands in the crowd in order that his classmates can see him.
21. My sister is having a cold with running n ________.
22. Jimmy fell off his bicycle and broke his right l _______.

23. I w ________ what the result is.
24. To b ________ up our strength, we need go to fitness center regularly.
25. Before they say goodbye, they h _______ each other.
26. Go along this street and the first b ________ you come to is the museum.
27. My pet dog is s ________ , it can understand my words.
28. The book fair sells a various k _______ of books.
29. In the countryside , we b __________ fresh air and eat green vegetables.
30. My dog always w ________ its tail when it feels happy.

Passage 10

Zoo and Animals

In the past, animals lived in the wild. But now many of them live in the zoo. I usually visit zoo at weekends to learn about animals. Monkeys act silly and they often add lots of fun to my trip. Be careful, they can take away your food without you noticing it. Giraffes look elegant, and they often chew up leaves quietly. Birds fly freely in the air, and chirp up in the tree. Hippos swim happily in the pond. I don't like crocodiles among all animals, because they often sneak around and that is scary. I worry that they will attack me from behind my back. Small paths in the zoo lead to different animal places.

Direction signs are everywhere, so I can find my way easily. I love visiting the Australian animals most. Kangaroos hop around behind the fence. Koalas are lazy, they even do not move around. Possums look clever; they can climb huge trees without effort.

I learn valuable things from my visits to the zoo. I learn that wild animals are in danger, because humans cut trees in the forest, they have no place to live. I learn that humans affect animals' homes by burning down forests. But I think we can change these bad things. It is certain that wild animals still have a chance to survive in the wild, so they will not go extinction.

必备词汇：

<u>名词</u>

zoo [zu:] 动物园

monkey [ˈmʌŋkɪ] 猴子

trip [trɪp] 行程

giraffe [dʒəˈrɑ:f] 长颈鹿

leaf [li:f] 树叶（leaves）

hippo [ˈhɪpəʊ] 河马

pond [pɒnd] 池塘

crocodile [ˈkrɒkədaɪl] 鳄鱼

path [pɑ:θ] 小路；小径

direction [dəˈrekʃn] 方向
sign [saɪn] 指示牌
kangaroo [ˌkæŋgəˈruː] 袋鼠
koala [kəʊˈɑːlə] 考拉熊
fence [fens] 篱笆
possum [ˈpɒsəm] 负鼠
humans [ˈhjuːmənz] 人类
forest [ˈfɒrɪst] 森林
place [pleɪs] 地方
chance [tʃɑːns] 机会;可能
extinction [ɪkˈstɪŋkʃn] 灭绝

动词

visit [ˈvɪzɪt] 参观
add [æd] 增添
notice [ˈnəʊtɪs] 注意到;留意到
swim [swɪm] 游泳;游水
worry [ˈwʌrɪ] 担心
attack [əˈtæk] 攻击
climb [klaɪm] 爬;爬上
cut [kʌt] 砍伐
affect [əˈfekt] 影响
change [tʃeɪndʒ] 改变
survive [səˈvaɪv] 生存;存活

形容词

careful [ˈkeəfl] 小心的
elegant [ˈelɪgənt] 优雅的
lazy [ˈleɪzɪ] 懒惰的
valuable [ˈvæljuəbl] 宝贵的
wild [waɪld] 野生的
certain [ˈsɜːtn] 确定的

副词

easily [ˈiːzəlɪ] 轻易地

介词

without [wɪˈðaʊt] 没有
behind [bɪˈhaɪnd] 在……后面

短语

the wild 野外
chew up 嚼碎;咀嚼
chirp up (鸟)叫
sneak around 鬼鬼祟祟地走
hop around 跳来跳去
chop down 砍倒
in the past 在过去
learn about 了解;学习
be careful 小心
take away 拿走
in the air 在空中
in the tree 在树上
behind my back 在我背后
lead to 通往;导致
without effort 毫不费力地
in danger 身处危险

Passage 10 配套单词填空练习

1. In the zoo, students learn how animals s _________ threats and protect their habitats.
2. The soldiers have been a _________ by their enemy.
3. When we go across the road, we must be c _________ in order to avoid cars.
4. Look! There are a great number of birds in the t _______.
5. I like outdoor activities, such as hiking and c _________.
6. Jess has problem in memorizing history information, so she w ________ about the history exam.
7. In the picture book of animals, we saw g _________, their necks are really long.
8. Many workers are cutting down trees in the f _______, which destroys animals' habitat.
9. There are lots of smoke in the a _______, we'd better wear a mask.
10. With autumn coming, the l ________ on the tree fall on the ground.
11. It is noisy here, let's go to a quiet p ________ to study.
12. The weather report says there is a c _________ of rain today.
13. Water is a kind of v __________ resource, people need conserve it.
14. Children are excited because they are going to v ________ dinosaur museum.
15. Tommy is l ________, it's 10 o'clock in the morning, he still sleeps in .
16. Some of the students think animals should live in the w _______ rather than in the zoo.
17. It's too easy for Mick to complete this task, he has done it without e _________.
18. My father likes s __________, he goes to the swimming pool almost everyday.
19. It is a h _____ on and hop off shuttle, which runs every 10 minutes.
20. The car accident has l _______ to traffic jam.

21. According to the news, there are many animals in d ________.
22. If you want to be a dentist, you must l ______ about abundant dental knowledge.
23. We didn't n _________ the timetable so we missed the exhibition.
24. My pet parrot c _________ early in the morning, which wakes me up everyday.
25. The number of wombats is really low, which may cause wombats e _________.
26. If you want to make progress, you 'd better c _________ bad habits.
27. Logging companies c _______ down trees to make profit.
28. My grandma is an e ________ old lady, I have never seen her angry.
29. The machine is not complicated , you can operate it e ________.
30. Be quick! Or you will be left b ________.

Passage 11

Four Seasons

The turning of four seasons occurs every year. The weather is warm and fine in spring. The sky is clear and air is fresh. Trees begin to grow leaves, grass turns green, and flowers pop out everywhere. The lovely weather in spring allows us to do many things outside. We can have a picnic in the park, climb hills, or have a walk in the bush. Spring is the time to put thick clothes back to the wardrobe. We just need to wear thin sweaters, pants or skirts.

The temperature rises quickly, and soon summer comes. It is often sunny and hot in summer days, but sometimes rain pours down heavily. I only wear T-shirts, shorts and sandals in summer. But I have to wear a hat and sunglasses when I go outside. We often go swim in a swimming pool, or just play water on a beach. I can play with sand, look for little fish in the water, or chase after my dog. My home is stuffy in summer, so I like spending my day in the garden. There are bush fires in summer in Melbourne, so we do not go camping in summer.

Autumn follows summer. Crops become ripe for harvest in autumn. The weather cools down. Cool wind is blowing most of the time in autumn. I need to put on a jacket or a coat to keep myself warm.

Winter is the coldest season. It sometimes snows in my city and all things are covered with snow. If that happens, we can build a snowman, or skate on ice. But I need to wear my gloves and thick clothes. I love winter best, because Christmas is in winter. I write greeting cards to my family and friends, and I also receive lots of presents for Christmas.

必备词汇：

名词

turning [ˈtɜ:nɪŋ] 转变
season [ˈsi:zn] 季节
weather [ˈweðə(r)] 天气
spring [sprɪŋ] 春天
summer [ˈsʌmə(r)] 夏天
autumn [ˈɔ:təm] 秋天
winter [ˈwɪntə(r)] 冬天
picnic [ˈpɪknɪk] 野餐
hill [hɪl] 小山
bush [bʊʃ] 丛林
clothes [kləʊðz] 衣服
wardrobe [ˈwɔ:drəʊb] 衣橱
sweater [ˈswetə(r)] 毛衣;汗衫
skirt [skɜ:t] 裙子
shorts [ʃɔ:ts] 短裤
sandals [sændlz] 凉鞋
hat [hæt] 帽子
sunglasses [ˈsʌnglɑ:sɪz] 墨镜
temperature [ˈtemprətʃə(r)] 气温
beach [bi:tʃ] 沙滩
crop [krɒp] 农作物
harvest [ˈhɑ:vɪst] 丰收
jacket [ˈdʒækɪt] 夹克;外套
coat [kəʊt] 上衣;外套
snow [snəʊ] 雪
snowman [ˈsnəʊmæn] 雪人
ice [aɪs] 冰
glove [glʌv] 手套
greeting [ˈgri:tɪŋ] 问候
card [kɑ:d] 卡片
present [ˈpreznt] 礼物

动词

occur [əˈkɜ:(r)] 发生
grow [grəʊ] 生长
turn [tɜ:n] 变得;变化
allow [əˈlaʊ] 允许;使得……能
walk [wɔ:k] 步行
rise [raɪz] 上升
pour [pɔ:(r)] 倒;倾泻
spend [spend] 花(时间);花(钱)
follow [ˈfɒləʊ] 紧接着;遵循
blow [bləʊ] 刮风;吹
snow [snəʊ] 下雪
cover [ˈkʌvə(r)] 覆盖
skate [skeɪt] 滑雪
receive [rɪˈsi:v] 收到

形容词

fine [faɪn] 晴朗的
clear [klɪə(r)] 晴朗的；清澈的
fresh [freʃ] 清新的;新鲜的
green [gri:n] 绿色的
thick [θɪk] 厚的
thin [θɪn] 薄的

stuffy [ˈstʌfɪ] 闷热的
ripe [raɪp] 成熟的

副词

heavily [ˈhevɪlɪ] 重重地;猛烈地

短语

swimming pool 游泳池
bush fire 丛林火灾
pop out 突然出现
put ... back 放回去
play water 玩水
pour down(雨)倾盆而下
look for 寻找
chase after 追赶
spend my day 打发时间
cool down 凉爽下来;变冷

Passage 11 配套单词填空练习

1. The rain p _______ down suddenly, he got soaked in the rain.
2. Two dogs are c ________ after each other in the park.
3. On her birthday, she received lots of p ________.
4. It is cold out there, if you want to go out , please put on your warm c ______.
5. I love winter, because I like ice s _________ so much.
6. Autumn is a season full of h __________.
7. My parents don't a ________ me to play outside unless I finish my homework.
8. It's windy today, the wind blows h _________.
9. In winter, heavy snow c ________ the ground, everywhere you can see is white.
10. The weather is fine and the air is c ________ today, let's go hiking.
11. School group will enjoy a b _______ walk through the national park to see different trees.
12. I plan to s ________ 3 days in Sydney and 4 days in Melbourne during my holiday.
13. In summer, the leaves are green, while in autumn, they are yellow.

14. The sun r ________ early and goes down late in summer.

15. When you go ice skating, remember to wear your t _________ jacket to keep you warm.

16. The van p _______ out all of a sudden, then the accident o _________ yesterday.

17. Shall we turn on the air conditioner? It's hot and s _______ in the room.

18. Mom, have you seen my biology book? I have l ________ for it everywhere, but I can't find it.

19. With autumn coming, most of the fruits are r _________.

20. Jimmy forgot to bring his g ________, now his hands are numb with cold.

21. The little boy is too excited , we must do something to make him c _______ down.

22. This piece of paper is really t ________, it is nearly transparent.

23. After dinner, our family like to have a w _________ in the park.

24. We will have a p ________ at the back of the museum tomorrow because there is no restaurant near it.

25. My grandma watches w _________ forecast everyday, she always tells me what to wear next day.

26. We should g ________ more trees to protect our environment.

27. The t __________ is 32 degrees today, it's hot and stuffy.

28. We are going surfing next week, don't forget to prepare your shorts, hat and s ___________.

29. You'd better wear sneakers instead of s _________ in PE class.

30. I have sent her 3 emails but she said she didn't r __________ them.

Passage 12

Go to Market

We have a Sunday market in my city. My parents like taking me there. We are able to buy lovely salad and fresh fruits there. Many market stalls sell vegetable and bread. The stalls are quite small and have simple covers above their benches. Stall owners display all sorts of food on their benches, so customers can choose them easily. My family likes vegetable such as cucumber, carrot and pumpkin. We also buy diary products like aged cheese or yoghurt there. The market is run by our local city council. The city council grants licence to farmers to set up a stall in the market.

It's a fact that vegetable and fruit at the Sunday market are fresher than those in super market, because farmers just pick them from their farms before they go to the market.

The food prices at the market can be higher, but the food is fresher. So we would rather pay a little bit more for the fresh food. Most stalls accept cash or card for payment. This makes it easy for customers to pay their shopping there. After we finish shopping, we treat ourselves with some fresh snacks like a salad roll. We love shopping at the market. It is a wonderful experience for me.

必备词汇:

名词

market [ˈmɑːkɪt] 市场;集市
salad [ˈsæləd] 沙拉菜
fruit [fruːt] 水果
stall [stɔːl] 小摊档
bread [bred] 面包
cover [ˈkʌvə(r)] 顶棚
bench [bentʃ] 台子
owner [ˈəʊnə(r)] 主人
customer [ˈkʌstəmə(r)] 顾客
cucumber [ˈkjuːkʌmbə(r)] 黄瓜
carrot [ˈkærət] 胡萝卜

pumpkin [ˈpʌmpkɪn] 南瓜

product [prɔdəkt] 产品

cheese [tʃi:z] 芝士

yoghurt [ˈjəʊgɜ:t] 酸奶

supermarket [ˈsu:pəmɑ:kɪt] 超市

farmer [ˈfɑ:mə(r)] 农场主;农民

farm [fa:m] 农场

council [ˈkaʊnsl] 委员会

license [ˈlaɪsns] 执照

price [praɪs] 价格

cash [kæʃ] 现金

card [kɑ:d] 银行卡

payment [ˈpeɪmənt] 付款

shopping [ˈʃɒpɪŋ] 购物

snack [snæk] 零食

experience [ɪkˈspɪəriəns] 经历

动词

be able to 能够

sell [sel] 卖

display [dɪˈspleɪ] 展示

choose [tʃu:z] 选择

grant [grɑ:nt] 授予;发放

pick [pik] 摘

pay [pei] 支付

accept [əkˈsept] 接受

finish [ˈfɪnɪʃ] 完成

treat [tri:t] 对待;款待

形容词

aged [eɪdʒd](指物)发酵的;(指人)年老的

wonderful [ˈwʌndəfl] 精彩的;极好的

短语

diary product 奶制品

salad roll 沙拉卷

all sorts of 各种各样的

it is the fact that 事实上

set up 设置

would rather 宁可

a little bit 一点点

Passage 12 配套单词填空练习

1. I would r __________ stay at home than go outside, it's too hot out there.
2. If you don't have your driver l _________, you can't drive the car.
3. We usually make p _________ lanterns on Halloween.
4. He sent the invitation to me but I didn't a _________ it.
5. Gorge is an old c_________ in our shop, he comes nearly every day.

6. Mom says we should eat more vegetables, such as carrots and c _________.
7. There are cucumbers tomatoes and lettuce in the refrigerator, let's make a s ______ for dinner.
8. The p _______ of that smart phone is too high, I don't think I can afford it.
9. Lucy's father is the o _______ of the farm, he owns many cows and sheep.
10. I like diary products, milk, cheese and y ________ and so forth.
11. Martin had some b ________ and a bottle of milk for breakfast this morning.
12. Let's go to the s _________ and buy some snacks.
13. He is a member of city c __________.
14. I don't have enough cash, can I pay by credit c _______?
15. Tim is on a diet, he only eats vegetables and f _________.
16. Before we go to the market, we should write a s _________ list, in case we forget something.
17. Samples of all ages are d _________ in that museum.
18. The p ________ of this company are of excellent quality, so the company has a great reputation.
19. The exhibition was so w __________ that when it finished, everyone applauded.
20. The department store sells all s ______ of products.
21. The most pleasurable e ________ of the event is the fireworks display.
22. My little parrot is a ______ to speak simple words.
23. I haven't decided which school I will choose.
24. Some people t ________ their pets like humans.
25. I s ______ up the computer so that I can work at any time.
26. There are three types of p _________ in our shop, which is by cash, by card or by cheque.
27. She thinks the sun goes around the earth, but it is the fact that the earth goes around the sun.

28. There are a great number of s __________ in the market, selling different products.

29. I haven't f _________ my task so I can't go to the cinema with you.

30. There are a variety of animals in the f _______, such as horses, cattle and sheep.

Passage 13

A Weird Afternoon but Amazing Surprise

When I got at home from school, no one was at home. It was so quiet that I felt a bit uneasy.

I shut the door behind me and called "mum".

No one answered me. I waited and called again. Still no one replied.

I felt weird, because my mum was always at home in the afternoon. I saw no light on. So I walked down the hallway to my mum's room and knocked on the door. No response. I felt my heart beating quickly when I turned the door handle. I peeped into the room quietly and saw no one. I went on to the bathroom and knocked on the door. Again, no one responded. I began to panic.

I suddenly remembered something. A couple of days ago, she said she would miss me if she went away. But she did not say when she would go. This idea gave me a fright. As I was worrying, I got into the kitchen. I needed a cold drink to calm down myself. When I was about to open the fridge door, I saw a note. It read:

"Dear Jo,

I will be away for a few days. Mrs. Lina will take care of you for me.

Wash your hands before you have some snacks.

Don't go and play with Tim until you finish your homework.

BUT, the FIRST thing you must do is: Get into the garden now.

…"

Then, I just peeped through the gap between the curtains at the back window. Wow, I found everybody was there. So I rushed out directly. "Happy Birthday Jo" my mum jumped out from the crowd and hugged me closely. "We want to give you a big surprise!" My mum said. I can't believe my eyes. It is a real surprise to me! I forgot it was birthday!

I considered this as a very successful surprise party.

必备词汇：

名词

afternoon [ˌɑ:ftəˈnu:n] 下午
light [laɪt] 灯
hallway [ˈhɔ:lweɪ] 走廊；过道
handle [ˈhændl] 把手
response [rɪˈspɒns] 回应；回复
idea [aɪˈdɪə] 想法；念头
fright [fraɪt] 惊骇；惊恐
note [nəʊt] 便条
gap [gæp] 缝隙
curtain [ˈkɜ:tn] 窗帘
window [ˈwɪndəʊ] 窗户
surprise [səˈpraɪz] 惊喜

动词

shut [ʃʌt] 关上
answer [ˈɑ:nsə(r)] 回答
wait [weɪt] 等待
reply [riˈplaɪ] 回答；回复
knock [nɒk] 敲门
turn [tɜ:n] 扭动
peep [pi:p] 窥探；瞥见
respond [rɪˈspɒnd] 回应
panic [ˈpænɪk] 感到恐慌
remember [rɪˈmembə(r)] 记得；记起
miss [mis] 想念
wash [wɒʃ] 洗
finish [ˈfɪnɪʃ] 完成
rush [rʌʃ] 冲
believe [bɪˈli:v] 相信
forget [fəˈget] 忘记
consider [kənˈsɪdə(r)] 考虑；认为

形容词

weird [wɪəd] 古怪的；离奇的
uneasy [ʌnˈi:zɪ] 不自在的；心神不宁的
calm [kɑ:m] 冷静的
back [bæk] 后面的
real [ri:l] 真的；真实的
successful [səkˈsesfʊl] 成功的

副词

suddenly [ˈsʌdənlɪ] 突然地
ago [əˈgəʊ] 之前
when [wen] 什么时候
directly [dɪˈrektlɪ] 直接地
closely [ˈkləʊslɪ] 紧紧地

短语

call out 大声叫喊

peep into 往里瞧

go away 离开

calm down 使……平静

be about to 即将

peep through 透过……窥探

consider...as 认为;把……看作

give me a fright 吓我一跳

Passage 13 配套单词填空练习

1. I received the email but I haven't had time to r _________ it yet.
2. Don't f ________ to set up your alarm, or you will be late again.
3. The old man c _________ the little boy as his own grandson.
4. Let's go hiking this weekend. Good i _______!
5. I didn't notice him at the doorway, so he g ______ me a fright when I went out.
6. Mick has been abroad for two years, he m _______ his family and his pet dog very much.
7. He is a s __________ leader, all the members in the club follow his advice.
8. The sunlight is so strong, I think we'd better buy a thick c ________ to prevent it.
9. It's cold outside, they sit c________ together to keep warm.
10. Before we have dinner, we ought to w ________ hands.
11. How long have you been w________? Just half an hour.
12. The h _________ of the front door doesn't work, let's fix it.
13. It is a good manner to k _______ at the door before we enter the room.
14. The interviewer asked him a question but he didn't r _________ it immediately.
15. If you know the answer of that question, please put up your hand d __________.
16. Grandma is angry, we should do something to c _______ her down.
17. The meeting is a _________ to start, Bob is still on the way, I think we should wait for him.

18. It was sunny this morning but s __________ it rained cats and dogs.

19. There is a pear tree at the b _________ of our schoolyard.

20. Alice is in a r _________ because the class bell is ringing.

21. We will meet at our school gate tomorrow a __________, approximately 4 pm.

22. Lucy doesn't review the lesson so she feels u __________.

23. The movie is based on a r _________ story.

24. We used to think Mr. White was w _________, but now we know he is normal.

25. The little kid p _________ into the room because of curiosity.

26. Mom leaves me a n _________ which tells me there are milk and bread in the refrigerator.

27. It is hot and stuffy in the room, shall I open the w __________?

28. There is a car accident and a man is c _________ out for help.

29. The a __________ to this question is simple.

30. He is a boy who never tells lies so I b _________ his words.

Passage 14

My Neighbo(u)rhood

I live in a small town in the countryside. It is a lovely neighbo(u)rhood. There is a large shopping centre near the town square. Local people do most of their shopping there, because it is convenient. On the ground floor, there are banks, the post office, chips shops and grocers near the entrance.

At the second floor, there are clothes shops and pet stores. There are offices in the upper levels. I know a big company runs business there. There is a high demand for freshly prepared food, so the shopping centre provides some cafés shops for customers. Outside the shopping centre, there are many car parking spaces. Customers can park their cars, trucks or vans there.

There is also a hospital opposite the town square. Everyday, hundreds of people visit the hospital. I think it is important to have a hospital nearby. A police station is located not far away from the shopping centre. Sometimes, I can see police officers on the road. I think police officers are great, because they can ensure our streets safe.

必备词汇：

<u>名词</u>

town [taʊn] 小镇

countryside [ˈkʌntrisaɪd] 乡下地区

neighbo(u)rhood [ˈneɪbəhʊd] 街坊邻里

centre [ˈsentə] 中心

square [skweə(r)] 广场；(数学)正方形

ground [graʊnd] 地面

floor [flɔ:(r)] 地；楼层

bank [bæŋk] 银行

chips [tʃɪps] 薯条

shops [ʃɒps] 商店

grocer [ˈgrəʊsə(r)] 杂货铺

entrance [ˈentrəns] 入口

pet [pet] 宠物
office [ˈɒfɪs] 办公室
level [ˈlevl] 楼层;水平
company [ˈkʌmpəni] 公司
business [ˈbɪznəs] 生意
demand [dɪˈmɑ:nd] 需求
café [ˈkæfeɪ] 咖啡店
parking [ˈpɑ:kɪŋ] 停车
spaces [speɪsis] 位置
truck [trʌk] 卡车
van [væn] 面包车
hospital [ˈhɒspɪtl] 医院

动词

prepare [prɪˈpeə(r)] 准备
provide [prəˈvaɪd] 提供
park [pɑ:k] 停靠;停
locate [ləʊˈkeɪt] 坐落于;位于
ensure [ɪnˈʃʊə(r)] 确保;保障

形容词

local [ˈləʊkl] 当地的
convenient [kənˈvi:niənt] 方便的;便利的
second [ˈsekənd] 第二的
upper [ˈʌpə(r)] 上面的
prepared [prɪˈpeəd] 准备好的
opposite [ˈɒpəzɪt] 对面的;相反的
safe [seɪf] 安全的

副词

freshly [ˈfreʃlɪ] 新鲜地
nearby [ˌnɪəˈbaɪ] 在……附近

短语

post office 邮局
police station 警察局
high demand for 对……需求大
hundreds of 几百
far away from 远离……

Passage 14 配套单词填空练习

1. We are going to the beach tomorrow, have you p ________ your shorts and sunglasses?
2. White collars work in o _________ while blue collars work in workshops.
3. The car is too small to carry all the luggage, we need a v ________.
4. Drivers are not allowed to p ______ their car here.
5. It is not s ________ to look at your phone when you go across the road.
6. Is there any shops n _______? Yes, the nearest one is next to the library.

7. Although we live in urban area, we usually go to c _________ to enjoy fresh air and green food.

8. This product sells really well, so there is a high d _________ for it in the market.

9. Our school is l _______ in the south of the library.

10. The bookstore is o __________ the road, I think we should go across the road.

11. They caught the thief and took him to the p _________ station.

12. The school library has been refurbished, and there are two e __________ for students to enter it.

13. My brother is a doctor, so he works in that h __________.

14. There are shops and supermarkets near my house, it is c ____________ to live here.

15. If you want to join our school library you need p ________ your student card.

16. Before you hand in your test paper, you should check to e ________ you have written answers correctly.

17. The postman is collecting letters in the p ________ office.

18. Do you have p ______? Yes, I raise a cute and fluffy dog.

19. The company plans to advertise for its products so that the b _______ will be better.

20. Trees need water, air and s ___________ to grow.

21. The elevator doesn't work so I have to climb 23 f ________ to go back home.

22. I will wait for you at the c ________ around the corner, then we can have a cup of coffee there.

23. H ________ of students took part in that competition.

24. Our math teacher is not l _________; instead, she comes from other city.

25. The u _______ layer of the ocean is warm but the bottom layer is cold.

26. Let’s go to the g __________ to buy the things we need.

27. The lake is in the c __________ of the park.

28. Many people choose to live in t ______ because it is quiet and peaceful there.

29. He lost his credit card so he went to the b ________ to get a new card.

30. Mom doesn’t allow me to eat fast food, such as hamburgers and c _________.

Passage 15

Dining out

My family would dine at a restaurant when there is a special occasion. For example, when it is my grandpa's birthday. Our favorite restaurant is located in city and it is called "Lucky Spoon". It sells seafood and traditional dishes. When it's my grandpa's birthday, he will decide what we order from the menu. Once he makes the decision, we wave to the waiter to signal that we are ready to order. My grandpa likcs lamb chops, my parents prefer pork, and I like steak best. When the steak comes, I always give it a big bite—yummy. After we finish our dinner, my dad would pay for the bill.

Except such special occasions, we don't eat out often. Our school program provides healthy eating guide to us. We are told that eating fast food, like KFC, is bad for our health. I think fast food is quite tasty, but they contain a lot of oil and sugar. These are not nutritious, so they cannot provide nutrients for our body.

However, eating fast food becomes a trend among many families. Fast food is unhealthy, because it contains much of oil, sugar and salt. Eating too much of these three ingredients causes children to grow fat or obese. Obesity will then lead to serious disease like diabetes in their later life.

必备词汇：

名词

restaurant [ˈrestrɒnt] 餐厅
occasion [əˈkeɪʒn] 场合
grandpa [ˈgrænpɑ:] 爷爷或外公
seafood [ˈsi:fu:d] 海鲜
dish [dɪʃ] 菜肴
menu [ˈmenju:] 菜单
decision [dɪˈsɪʒn] 决定
waiter [ˈweɪtə(r)] 服务员
lamb [læm] 羊肉

pork [pɔ:k] 猪肉
steak [steɪk] 牛排
bill [bɪl] 账单
guide [gaɪd] 指南
oil [ɔɪl] 油
sugar [ˈʃʊgə(r)] 糖
nutrient [ˈnju:triənt] 营养成分
trend [trend] 趋势
salt [sɔ:lt] 盐
ingredient [ɪnˈgri:diənt] 配料
obesity [əʊˈbi:sətɪ] 肥胖症
diabetes [ˌdaɪəˈbi:ti:z] 糖尿病

动词

dine [daɪn] 用餐
decide [dɪˈsaɪd] 决定
order [ˈɔ:də(r)] 点餐;下单
wave [weɪv] 挥手
signal [ˈsɪgnəl] 示意
prefer [prɪˈfɜ:(r)] 更喜欢
contain [kənˈteɪn] 含有
cause [kɔ:z] 导致

形容词

special [ˈspeʃl] 特殊的
traditional [trəˈdɪʃənl] 传统的
yummy [ˈjʌmɪ] 好吃的
healthy [ˈhelθɪ] 健康的
tasty [ˈteɪstɪ] 可口的
nutritious [njuˈtrɪʃəs] 有营养的
unhealthy [ʌnˈhelθɪ] 不健康的
fat [fæt] 胖的
obese [əʊˈbi:s] 肥胖的

副词

once [wʌns] 一旦

介词

except [ɪkˈsept] 除了

短语

lamb chops 羊排
fast food 快餐
dine out 外出就餐
eat out 外出吃饭
make a decision 做决定
give sth a bite 咬一口
lead to 导致

Passage 15 配套单词填空练习

1. We usually eat at home and occasionally we will d _______ out.
2. Carbon dioxide emission l _______ to global warming.

3. Eating junk food frequently is really u __________. It's bad for people's health.

4. Most of the r ___________ menus show food calories to customers.

5. Which one do you prefer? Lamp, beef or p _________?

6. Smoking may cause asthma, o _________ and heart disease.

7. People who suffer from d __________ can't eat sweets or fruits.

8. I like seafood such as fish , crabs and prawns, I think they are y _________.

9. Lisa g ________ the apple a bite and threw it into the bin because it had gone bad.

10. Comparing with strawberries, I p _________ cherries.

11. You should eat some n __________ food instead of junk food.

12. The boy used to be f _________ but now he is thin.

13. He has no time to cook so he always eats f _______ food.

14. It was a common day, nothing s __________ happened.

15. My uncle is a cook who cooks delicious d __________.

16. Soft drinks c __________ lots of sugar.

17. I o _________ a meal online, but it hasn't been delivered yet.

18. It is a t ___________ custom to eat dumplings on new year's eve.

19. All of us arrived on time e _________ Sam; he was late for 20 minutes.

20. The majority of foreigners prefer to split the b _________ when they eat together.

21. The newly opened café offers d __________ desserts.

22. How many i __________ are there in the recipe?

23. W _________ have different roles in a restaurant, like waiting at the table and washing dishes.

24. O _________ he makes up his mind, he will never change his decision.

25. The police s __________ him to pull over.

26. My g __________ will cook and my grandma will chat with me on weekends.

27. O _______ people are likely to have high blood pressure than slim people.
28. It is not a formal o _________, so you can wear casual clothes.
29. The butcher sells lamp chops and s ________.
30. The coach g ________ the team members how to improve their skills.

Passage 16

A Day at the Seaside

During last summer holiday, my parents brought my sister and I to the Bondi Beach. It is not far away from Sydney. The distance is around eleven kilometers. Bondi Beach is famous for its surfing beach and walking track. Everyday, the light brown sand catches the rolling waves on the flat beach, and it never ends. It was hot during our last visit. The sun baked us over our heads, and the heat made us sweat heavily. We built sand castles, splashed in the water, and hunt for ocean animals such as shellfish on the beach.

"Ouch, my leg was bitten by something!" I cried.

My sister looked around my legs and declared "no big deal! It was just a jellyfish". My sister pulled the jellyfish out from my leg. Even if I still felt the pain, but I felt less worried. This incident nearly ruined my day.

Several hours passed when we played on the beach. Later, tide was coming, and waves became strong and wild. The waves rolled onto the beach and destroyed our castle quickly. Big kids went straight into the water, and started surfing along the rolling tides. I think they were really brave. There are dangerous animals like sharks in the ocean, so I think it is better to be careful. Unlike sharks, whales are giants in the sea, but they seem gentle.

When the evening came, we packed up our things to ensure we did not leave anything behind. We spent the night in a hotel and travelled home the next day. I hoped we could do more travelling in the future.

必备词汇：

<u>名词</u>

seaside [ˈsi:saɪd] 海边

holiday [ˈhɒlədeɪ] 假期

distance [ˈdɪstəns] 距离

kilometer [ˈkɪləʊˌmiːtə] 千米
surfing [ˈsɜːfɪŋ] 冲浪
track [træk] 小径
wave [weɪv] 波浪
heat [hiːt] 热浪；热
ocean [ˈəʊʃn] 海洋
shellfish [ˈʃelfɪʃ] 贝壳
jellyfish [ˈdʒelɪfɪʃ] 水母
pain [peɪn] 疼痛
incident [ˈɪnsɪdənt] 突发事件
hour [ˈaʊə(r)] 小时
tide [taɪd] 潮水
shark [ʃɑːk] 鲨鱼
whale [weɪl] 鲸
hotel [həʊˈtel] 酒店

动词

bring [brɪŋ] 带（brought）
catch [kætʃ] 接住；抓住
end [end] 结束
bake [beik] 炙烤
sweat [swet] 出汗
splash [splæʃ] 溅；泼水
hunt [hʌnt] 寻找
declare [dɪˈkleə(r)] 宣布
pull [pul] 拉
pass [paːs] 度过
ruin [ˈruːɪn] 毁掉
destroy [dɪˈstrɔɪ] 破坏
pack [pæk] 打包
ensure [ɪnˈʃʊə(r)] 确保
travel [ˈtrævl] 旅行

形容词

famous [ˈfeɪməs] 著名的；有名的
light [laɪt] 浅色的；轻微的
brown [braʊn] 棕色的
rolling [ˈrəʊlɪŋ] 滚滚的；滚动的
flat [flæt] 平坦的
worried [ˈwʌrɪd] 担忧的
strong [strɒŋ] 强力的；强壮的
straight [streɪt] 直的；直接的
brave [breɪv] 勇敢的
gentle [ˈdʒentl] 温和的；温柔的

介词

during [ˈdjʊərɪŋ] 在……期间
around [əˈraʊnd] 大约
over [ˈəʊvə(r)] 在……上面
unlike [ˌʌnˈlaɪk] 与……不同

短语

at the seaside 在海边
over one's head 在…头顶
no big deal 没什么大不了
go straight 直走
pack up 打好包
leave behind 落下；忘记

Passage 16 配套单词填空练习

1. To make us s ___________, we exercise in the gym four times a week.
2. When I am on holiday, I like walking along the s __________ and enjoy the beach.
3. The sun b ________ so hard that the flowers withered.
4. We saw beautiful fishes and j ________ in Melbourne aquarium.
5. This town has been r ________ by earthquake.
6. There are many f __________ historical sites to visit in my hometown.
7. It's breezy today, here comes a g _______ wind.
8. Go s _________ and turn left at the cross road, then you will see the gallery.
9. What did you do during summer h _________?
10. I like l ________ colors, such as white, sky blue and so on.
11. The b _________ student saved the little boy from drowning.
12. I saw lions h ________ for food in the documentary.
13. It is too heavy for one horse to pull the carriage.
14. The submarine can descend to 10 k _________ down in the sea.
15. Sleeping in a h _________ is not as comfortable as sleeping at home.
16. Time p ________ quickly, I will graduate next month.
17. It's not a big d _______ to fail, as long as you work hard, you will succeed sooner or later.
18. When will we finish the meeting? A _________ 4 pm.
19. If you plan to t ________ abroad, you should learn some basic foreign languages.
20. The postman is busy p ________ up packages in the post office.
21. The names of excellent students are r _________ on the screen.
22. U _________ his brother who is outgoing, little James is always silent.
23. S _________ hunt for food by their accurate sense of smell.
24. What is the d _________ between the two villages?
25. Jean went fishing with her family and they c _________ some crabs.

26. People like going s _________ in the ocean in a hot summer day.

27. Follow the t ________ on the map, you will come to the reptile park.

28. They sail around the island against the t _________.

29. Your p _________ will be reduced after you eat this medicine.

30. That road is f ________ and smooth.

Passage 17

Food and Cooking

My mother's interest is cooking; she always stays in the kitchen when she has free time. She is able to cook food of different regions. But she does not like curry. Anyway, my mum is a great chef in my heart. She often follows recipes to cook new food for us. She even hosts our birthday parties at home for us.

My mum loves shopping for different cookers such as frying pans and pots. She insists that these tools can help her make wonderful meals for us. But I think she has bought so many pieces of cookers that we don't have enough space to store them.

My parents have balanced diet, but actually I am a meat lover. This means I only love eating meat, and I'm not a big fan for vegetables. Vegetables are good for our health, but I just cannot bear its smell. Years ago, I already attempted to eat more veggie, but none of them attracted me. Recently, I read some articles about the bad things of not eating vegetable, so I forced myself to occasionally eat some. Bit by bit, vegetable becomes a part of my diet now.

必备词汇：

名词

cooking [ˈkʊkɪŋ] 烹饪
interest [ˈɪntrəst] 兴趣
region [ˈri:dʒən] 地区
curry [ˈkʌrɪ] 咖喱
chef [ʃef] 大厨
recipe [ˈresəpɪ] 食谱
cooker [ˈkʊkə(r)] 厨具
pan [pæn] 平底锅
pot [pɒt] 罐
tool [tu:l] 工具
meal [mi:l] 膳食
piece [pi:s] 一件
diet [ˈdaɪət] 饮食
fan [fæn] 爱好者
smell [smel] 气味

none [nʌn] 没有人;一个也没有
article [ˈɑ:tɪkl] 文章

动词
stay [steɪ] 待在
host [həʊst] 主办;主持
insist [ɪnˈsɪst] 坚持说
mean [mi:n] 意味着
bear [beə(r)] 忍受
attempt [əˈtempt] 尝试
force [fɔ:s] 强迫

形容词
wonderful [ˈwʌndəfl] 美妙的
enough [ɪˈnʌf] 足够的
balanced [ˈbælənst] 平衡的
attractive [əˈtræktɪv] 吸引人的

副词
anyway [ˈenɪweɪ] 无论如何
actually [ˈæktʃuəlɪ] 事实上
already [ɔ:lˈredɪ] 已经
recently [ˈri:sntlɪ] 最近
occasionally [əˈkeɪʒnəlɪ] 偶尔

短语
bit by bit 逐渐
a part of 一部分

Passage 17 配套单词填空练习

1. The weather becomes warm b _______ by bit.
2. Bob likes c _________ , he can make delicious dishes.
3. Where have you been? I haven't seen you r _________.
4. Parents should not f ________ their kids to do things; instead, they should stimulate kids' interest.
5. My mum decided to keep a d _________ in order to lose weight.
6. The a __________ of that writer is really popular online.
7. We are decorating the kitchen and we need buy new c _________.
8. They live in a remote r _________ where the transport is not convenient.
9. Normally, we all have three m _________ a day, breakfast, lunch and dinner.
10. Success m _________ you need work hard.
11. What a w ___________ trip it is ! Yes, we all enjoyed ourselves.
12. He is a c ___________ in a five star rating hotel.

13. That cartoon is a ___________ to children, they all want to watch it.

14. I'd like to go to the party but a _________ I have to finish my homework.

15. I prefer to s _______ at home rather than go outside on a hot summer day.

16. Have you bought the present for Ellen's birthday? Yes, I have bought it a _________.

17. We always go for a walk after dinner but o _________ we go to the cinema.

18. I can't b ________ the noise from next door, my neighbo(u)r is refurbishing their house.

19. Let's add one more ingredient to the r _________.

20. Some people like eating c _________, especially people from India.

21. The patient a __________ to stand up, but he failed.

22. There are e __________ food in the fridge so we don't need to go to the supermarket today.

23. People in modern society should keep life and work b __________.

24. My father is a f _________ of collecting.

25. If you have a dream, you should i _________ on it.

26. The little girl i ________ she didn't make a mistake.

27. Do you know who the h ________ of the program is? No idea.

28. Language is a t ________ of communication.

29. The dish s ________ great.

30. N ________ of the students were absent, they all presented at the school party.

Passage 18

Adventure in the Wild

During last school holiday, my parents took us to camping on a small island in the northern Sydney. It took us great labour to set up our tents. Sleeping in the wild was an exciting experience for me. When the night fell, the sky became dark. We could hear insects making low buzzing sounds in the grassland. I wanted to stay outside the tent to watch stars. But my brother thought I was mad, because he reckoned insects would sting me.

The next day, we went to explore the island with the guide of the island map. We found a cave in the mountain. My dad suggested that we made an adventure inside. He said perhaps we could find some treasures. The caves seemed centuries ago, and we pretended we were a pack of pirates. Standing at the edge of the cave, we could see the deep blue sea below us. It was totally dark inside the cave. We used a torch to light our way. The surface of the cave was rough. So we had to move slowly. The rocks over our head were sticking out sharply. We felt excited and we expected to find something valuable. Finally, we arrived at the bottom of the cave, and we could not go further. We did not discover anything, so we felt unhappy with this result. I wanted to leave some trace of my visit, so I carved my name on the wall with a rock. That's an absolutely cool mark!

On our way back, we noticed a kangaroo eating grass on a slope. There was a small river running across the mountain like a giant curling snake.

必备词汇：

名词

adventure [əd'ventʃə(r)] 探险

camping ['kæmpɪŋ] 野营

island ['aɪlənd] 岛屿

labour/labor [ˈleɪbə(r)] 劳动;体力
tent [tent] 帐篷
experience [ɪkˈspɪəriəns] 经历
night [naɪt] 夜晚
insect [ˈɪnsekt] 昆虫
sound [saʊnd] 声音
grassland [ˈgrɑ:slænd] 草地
star [stɑ:(r)] 星星
map [mæp] 地图
cave [keiv] 山洞
mountain [ˈmaʊntən] 山
treasure [ˈtreʒə(r)] 宝藏
century [ˈsentʃərɪ] 世纪
pirate [ˈpaɪrət] 海盗
edge [edʒ] 边缘;边
torch [tɔ:tʃ] 手电筒
surface [ˈsɜ:fɪs] 表面
bottom [ˈbɒtəm] 底部
result [rɪˈzʌlt] 结果
trace [treis] 痕迹
mark [ma:k] 标记
slope [sləʊp] 山坡
river [ˈrɪvə(r)] 河流
snake [sneik] 蛇

动词

take [tʊk] 花费(took)
fall [fɔ:l] 降临(fell)
reckon [ˈrekən] 猜想
sting [stɪŋ] 叮咬
explore [ɪkˈsplɔ:(r)] 探索
suggest [səˈdʒest] 建议;表明
pretend [prɪˈtend] 假装
stand [stænd] 站;站立
light [laɪt] 照明
expect [ɪkˈspekt] 期待;预测
discover [dɪˈskʌvə(r)] 发现
carve [kɑ:v] 刻下;刻画
notice [ˈnəʊtɪs] 注意到;留意到

形容词

northern [ˈnɔ:ðən] 北部的
exciting [ɪkˈsaɪtɪŋ] 激动人心的
dark [da:k] 黑暗的;深色的
low [ləʊ] 低的;低沉的
mad [mæd] 疯狂的
next[nekst] 下一个的
deep [di:p] 深的
blue [blu:] 蓝色的
valuable [ˈvæljuəbl] 值钱的
cool [ku:l] 酷炫的
giant [ˈdʒaɪənt] 巨大的
curling [ˈkɜ:lɪŋ] 卷曲的

副词

outside [ˌaʊtˈsaɪd] 在……外面
inside [ˌɪnˈsaɪd] 在……里面
perhaps [pəˈhæps] 可能
below [bɪˈləʊ] 在……下面
totally [ˈtəʊtəlɪ] 完全

slowly [ˈsləʊlɪ] 慢慢地
sharply [ˈʃɑ:plɪ] 尖尖地
finally [ˈfaɪnəlɪ] 最终
further [ˈfɜ:ðə(r)] 更远
absolutely [ˈæbsəlu:tlɪ] 绝对
across [əˈkrɒs] 跨过

短语
set up 搭起来
stick out 伸出来
arrive at 到达
run across 流过
a pack of 一群

Passage 18 配套单词填空练习

1. Cars move s __________ to give way to the pedestrians.
2. The interior of the gym is being refurbished, so we have to exercise o __________.
3. At the main entrance, there is a g __________ map to show different parts of the park.
4. Since smoggy weather is serious, the sky is not b __________.
5. There are many v __________ resources such as coal, petrol, water, and so forth.
6. He is an adventurous person, in other words, he likes a __________ very much.
7. What is the r __________ of your final exam?
8. Edison invented l __________ and many other inventions.
9. I bought colorful markers to m __________ my notes.
10. My teacher s __________ me practicing in this way, I think I should accept her suggestion.
11. We will learn the simple present tense this term and the present perfect tense n ________ term.
12. After the war, the solider can't s _________ up, he can only move in his wheelchair.
13. He dives in the d __________ ocean, 8 kilometers down.
14. The price of this book is l _________, it's really a bargain.

15. There are many s __________ around this area, so the wind is strong here.
16. We saw s _________ in the reptile park.
17. P _________ you can draw pictures to help you remember things, it may be effective.
18. My brother prefers d ________ color, like navy blue and black.
19. P __________ used to rob ships in this area.
20. Bees can s _________ once, then they will die.
21. Students are e ________ the trip next week. They are really looking forward to it.
22. Scientists d _________ fossils in that city.
23. Some animals are on the e __________ of extinction.
24. The southern part of the city is cloudy while the n ________ part of the city is sunny.
25. He p _________ to be asleep but actually he is awake.
26. The game is really e ___________. People are excited when they watch it.
27. In 21 c __________, people can take full advantage of new technology.
28. When you go a _________ the road, you should watch out.
29. We went camping last week and lived in a t __________ on grassland.
30. Bees and bugs are all i _________.

Passage 19

Which Language Is More Difficult: English or Chinese?

I think English is a hard language. But many native English speakers say Chinese is harder than English. Chinese is becoming a popular second language in Australian schools. I would laugh when I hear this remark, because Chinese seems extremely easy to me.

My classmates felt amazed when I told them I could speak both English and Chinese fluently. They said I'm a language champion, because I have managed one of the most difficult languages in the world.

But I think they can achieve the same outcome if they keep learning Chinese regularly. It's definitely hard at the beginning of learning to write Chinese characters. Gradually, when they build up a collection of 1,000 Chinese characters, they achieve a magnificent success in learning Chinese.

There is also an official Chinese characters writing competition in my country, any student can participate in it. Along the progress of the competition, there will be only 3 candidates for the final winner. The education Minister will issue the final winner a gold medal and a certificate of achievement.

必备词汇：

名词

language [ˈlæŋgwɪdʒ] 语言
remark [rɪˈmɑːk] 评论
champion [ˈtʃæmpiən] 冠军
outcome [ˈaʊtkʌm] 成果
character [ˈkærəktə(r)] 字
collection [kəˈlekʃn] 收集
success [səkˈses] 成功
competition [ˌkɒmpəˈtɪʃn] 比赛
progress [ˈprəʊgres] 进展；进步
candidate [ˈkændɪdət] 候选人
winner [ˈwɪnə(r)] 获胜者
minister [ˈmɪnɪstə(r)] 部长
certificate [səˈtɪfɪkət] 证书

achievement [ə'tʃi:vmənt] 成就；成绩

动词

laugh [lɑ:f] 发笑
amaze [ə'meɪz] 吃惊
manage ['mænɪdʒ] 成功对付；管理
achieve [ə'tʃi:v] 完成；达到
participate [pɑ:'tɪsɪpeɪt] 参加
issue ['ɪʃu:] 正式发给

形容词

native ['neɪtɪv] 本地的
popular ['pɒpjələ(r)] 受欢迎的
second ['sekənd] 第二的
extreme [ɪk'stri:m] 极度的
magnificent [mæg'nɪfɪsnt] 宏伟的
official [ə'fɪʃl] 官方的
final ['faɪnl] 最后的

副词

extremely [ɪk'stri:mlɪ] 极度地
fluently ['flu:əntlɪ] 流利地
regularly ['regjələlɪ] 定期地
definitely ['defɪnətlɪ] 肯定地
gradually ['grædʒuəlɪ] 逐渐地

短语

gold medal 金牌
build up 积累

Passage 19 配套单词填空练习

1. Canada's o __________ languages are English and French.
2. Most of the students p __________ in that competition last year.
3. The ancient buildings in Egypt are m __________.
4. After hearing the joke, he can't stop l __________.
5. We can use timer to m __________ our time.
6. Rookie is a n __________ American word which means a person who is new to something.
7. I can speak two l __________, which are Chinese and English.
8. The restaurant is p __________, so if we want to dine there, we need book in advance.
9. He is a c __________ of the company's manager.
10. USA is a short name for united s __________ of America.

11. After many years, the scientist finally a _________ his goal.

12. The champion has won a gold m __________ and a wreath.

13. We are all a _________ at the news.

14. After the f __________ exam, we can enjoy our holiday.

15. The performance of the band was a s _________, everyone enjoyed it last night.

16. People should have health check r _________ to know their health conditions better.

17. Jimmy is so clever that he can speak English f ________ after 2 months' learning.

18. Here are my stamp c __________; I love collecting stamps.

19. If you complete this task, you will have a sense of a ___________.

20. Our teacher praised students who have made great p __________ during last term.

21. My brother is a news analyst who likes to write r ________ and comments after he reads news.

22. In e ________ weather conditions, like the South Pole, people need more calories to keep warm.

23. W _________ of local contests will participate in the national math competition.

24. All of the scientists are satisfied with the experiment o ___________.

25. English is d _________ useful in our daily life.

26. I love Australia, e _________ in summer.

27. To join this trip, old people need to provide their health c _________ to prove they are healthy.

28. He bought a s __________ hand bicycle instead of a brand new one.

29. The foreign m __________ made a speech in the conference.

30. I g ___________ adapt to the new environment.

Passage 20

Taking Train to Get Around

Taking train to somewhere can be fun. But you should arrive at the train station early. If you are late, you will miss your train. The train is a type of public transport. The company called Metro operates the public transport in Melbourne.

You need to purchase tickets to travel by train. There are single tickets and return tickets. So make sure you choose the right type of tickets before you boarding the train. During your train journey, you can often hear announcement from the train radio. It will tell you the next station you will arrive. If you are doing a long trip, you even can take a rest on train.

I love taking train ride, because I may bump into interesting passengers. Once upon a time, I met an interesting old lady on the train. She looks like seventy years old. Her hair is all grey. Even though she is old, but her looks fit and strong. I saw her reading a huge book.

When I sat opposite to the old lady, she remained focusing on her book. Then she raised her head and said, "Are you wondering what I'm reading now?" I replied yes politely. Then the lady turned the cover of the book to me, which read: The Power of Magic. I just could not imagine why an old lady was attracted by magical stuffs. We had a short chat about the book, then we turned to our own business. Along the journey, we remained chat occasionally, and this made my trip not boring.

必备词汇：

名词

train [treɪn] 火车

station [ˈsteɪʃn] 站；站台

transport [ˈtræspɔ:t] 交通

company [ˈkʌmpənɪ] 公司
ticket [ˈtɪkɪt] 车票
journey [ˈdʒɜːnɪ] 行程
announcement [əˈnaʊnsmənt] 通知
radio [ˈreɪdiəʊ] 广播
trip [trɪp] 旅程
ride [raɪd] 乘坐；车程
passenger [ˈpæsɪndʒə(r)] 乘客
lady [ˈleɪdɪ] 女士
seventy [ˈsevntɪ] 七十
hair [heə(r)] 头发
magic [ˈmædʒɪk] 魔力；魔法
stuff [stʌf] 东西；材料
business [ˈbɪznəs]（个人）事务

动词

miss [mɪs] 错过
operate [ˈɒpəreɪt] 运营；经营
purchase [ˈpɜːtʃəs] 购买
choose [tʃuːz] 选择
board [bɔːd] 上车
bump [bʌmp] 碰撞；颠簸
remain [rɪˈmeɪn] 保持；仍然是
focus [ˈfəʊkəs] 集中
raise [reɪz] 抬起；升起
turn [tɜːn] 翻转；转动
imagine [ɪˈmædʒɪn] 想象
attract [əˈtrækt] 吸引

形容词

late [leɪt] 迟到
public [ˈpʌblɪk] 公共的
single [ˈsɪŋgl] 单一的
right [raɪt] 正确的
long [lɒŋ] 长途的；长的
grey [grei] 灰色的
fit [fɪt] 健康的
huge [hjuːdʒ] 巨大的
magical [ˈmædʒɪkl] 有魔力的

形容词

quiet [ˈkwaɪət] 安静的

副词

early [ˈɜːlɪ] 早
before [bɪˈfɔː(r)] 在……之前
once [wʌns] 一次
politely [pəˈlaɪtlɪ] 礼貌地

短语

public transport 公共交通
single ticket 单程票
return ticket 往返票
grey hair 银发
take train 搭火车
make sure 确保
take a rest 休息
bump into 遇见；不期而遇
once upon a time 有一次

look like 看起来像

even through 尽管

focus on 集中在 …… 上

one's own business 自己的事儿

Passage 20配套单词填空练习

1. We should switch off the light b _________ we leave the classroom.
2. I look l _________ my father, especially my eyes and eyebrows.
3. You have been working for six hours, so it's time to take a r _________.
4. Which book do you c _________, science fiction or that comic book?
5. I prefer to travel by t _________ rather than by plane, because I can enjoy the scenery on the way.
6. Even t _________ he tried his best, he failed.
7. We can take public t _________ like buses and trams to protect our environment.
8. The bus is crowded because there are many p _________ on it.
9. It is hard to i _________ how many cells are in our body.
10. Get up right now, or you will be l _________ for school.
11. My parents and I go to the cinema o _________ a week.
12. Young people's hair is black, while many old people have g _________ hair.
13. My grandpa listens to the r _________ broadcast everyday.
14. The little boy is a _________ by the performance.
15. You need prepare lots of s _________ like scissors, glue, marker and other things.
16. The c _________ sells products of excellent quality.
17. These answers are r _________ but the rest of them are wrong.
18. I b _________ into him on the way home.
19. How long is the r _________ to the zoo?
    20 minutes.
20. I think people should not smoke in p _________ places.

21. He p __________ a new house last year, which cost him a lot of money.
22. That matter has nothing to do with us; it's his own b ____________.
23. Did you receive our school a ___________ that our school library will be refurbished next term.
24. We see him off at the train s ___________.
25. They are too noisy that I can't f_________ on my homework.
26. Is it complicated to o _____________ the device? No, it's simple to use.
27. Although he got up e ____________, he was still late because of the traffic jam.
28. To keep f __________, we'd better eat more vegetables and exercise regularly.
29. I don't know the exact length of the river, but it's very l ___________.
30. It is a great opportunity, don't m _________ it.

Passage 21

Getting Lost

My cousin Tony has an annoyingly poor sense of direction, even though he is a grownup. This means he can get lost easily in a crowded place. Previously, he lost his direction when he went to a new country for travelling. Luckily, a kind woman offered help to him. If the woman had not helped him, Tony would have not been able to find his way back to his hotel.

Now my cousin grasped a new trick to avoid getting lost. Once, he demonstrated to me how his trick worked. When he was confused about his location, he took a photo of the icon building near him, then he uploaded it to the Internet and searched for his exact location, and then the Internet would show his location and provide him guide to find his way. However, unexpected things always happen. Yesterday, Tony went to the royal Melbourne show with his friends. They had loads of fun at first. Then they separated to play fancy facilities. Unfortunately, Tony could not locate his friends later in the show ground. He yelled names of his friends but no one answered.

So the frustrated Tony felt that he needed to go home by train. He got cross with himself because he did not know where the train station was. He exclaimed crazily, "Well, I will never come to such a crowded place again. "

When Tony was trying to figure out the way to the train station, his phone rang. It was his friend calling him. They were looking for him as well. At that moment, Tony felt relieved. A couple of minutes later, Tony saw his friends appeared in front of him. Then, they went home together.

必备词汇：

名词

cousin [ˈkʌzn] 堂 / 表兄弟（姐妹）
direction [dəˈrekʃn] 方向
grownup [ˈgrəʊnʌp] 成人
country [ˈkʌntrɪ] 国家
trick [trɪk] 把戏；诀窍
location [ləʊˈkeɪʃn] 位置
icon [ˈaɪkɒn] 象征；标志
yesterday [ˈjestədeɪ] 昨天
show [ʃəʊ] 表演
facility [fəˈsɪlətɪ] 设施
ground [graʊnd] 地面；场
moment [ˈməʊmənt] 时刻
second [ˈsekənd] 秒

动词

lose [lu:z] 迷失；丢失
offer [ˈɒfə(r)] 给予
grasp [grɑ:sp] 掌握
avoid [əˈvɔɪd] 避免
demonstrate [ˈdemənstreɪt] 示范
confuse [kənˈfju:z] 使迷惑
take [teɪk] 画（像）；摄（影）（took）
upload [ˌʌpˈləʊd] 上传
search [sɜ:tʃ] 搜索
happen [ˈhæpən] 发生
separate [ˈseprət] 分开
locate [ləʊˈkeɪt] 找出；找到
yell [jel] 大叫
relieve [rɪˈli:v] 减轻；松口气
appear [əˈpɪə(r)] 出现

形容词

annoying [əˈnɔɪɪŋ] 恼人的；讨厌的
crowded [ˈkraʊdɪd] 拥挤的
previous [ˈpri:viəs] 以前的
exact [ɪgˈzækt] 确切的
unexpected [ˌʌnɪkˈspektɪd] 意想不到的
royal [ˈrɔɪəl] 皇家的
fancy [ˈfænsi] 引人注目的；华丽的
frustrated [frʌˈstreɪtɪd] 沮丧的

副词

annoyingly [əˈnɔɪɪŋlɪ] 恼人地
previously [ˈpri:vɪəslɪ] 以前
later [ˈleɪtə(r)] 后来

短语

get lost 走失
loads of 很多
at first 首先
by train 乘坐火车
get cross with sb. 生……的气
figure out 弄明白
as well 也

feel relieved 感到松口气

in front of 在……前面

Passage 21 配套单词填空练习

1. I don't have brothers or sisters but I have two c __________.
2. Sports can help us r __________ our stress.
3. There's something wrong with the internet; I can u __________ my files.
4. I achieved my goal, my brother did it as w __________.
5. Can you help me with this question? I can't f __________ it out.
6. Tommy failed the exam and felt f __________, let's go and cheer him up.
7. In western c __________, people like to hug and kiss each other when they say goodbye.
8. It's impolite to y __________ at others.
9. After hearing the news, she feels r __________.
10. L __________ of people have phoned you, I think you should call them back.
11. Parents will not g __________ cross with their children seriously.
12. My p __________ address is Unit 12 Preston, but now I live in port of Melbourne.
13. You are a g __________ instead of a child, you should be responsible for your own behavior.
14. The hiking team got l __________ in the forest. They couldn't find a way out.
15. If you g __________ this skill, it is beneficial to your future career.
16. Can you tell me the l __________ of your school? I don't know its exact address.
17. What recreational f __________ are available in your neighbo(u)rhood?
18. The bus is c __________ at peak time.
19. We can s __________ information through Internet.
20. The result is really u __________, we all feel astonished when we heard it.

21. An accident h ___________ last night.
22. The noise is a ___________; it makes me not able to focus on my work.
23. There are 60 s ___________ in one minute.
24. The bookshop o ___________ students free bookmarks.
25. They are e ___________ for help.
26. We visited f ___________ palace last week.
27. Compass shows the crew d ___________.
28. It's difficult to s ___________ legend from truth.
29. We should not play t ___________ on our classmates.
30. This word usually a ___________ in our textbook.

Passage 22

When I Feel Sick

I often have cold and cough in winter. When I feel sick, my mum would take me to our family doctor. When I was young, I felt scared to see doctors. Now, I'm a big boy now, so seeing doctors becomes a normal part of my life. When my illness is serious, the doctor would give me some medicine. I always recover after I take the medicines for several days.

Doctors are experts in looking after our health. There are many types of doctors. Some doctors are specialists; some doctors take care of the health of our body; some doctors look after the health of our mind, and they are called mental health doctor. The Australian government has made very strict rules to regulate doctors, because their jobs relate to people's health even life. The Health Minister will review these rules annually to ensure if they are updated.

I think being a doctor is a demanding job. They need to learn all types of diseases. Doctors have to work for a long time. Doctors also need to calm down their patients when their patients have serious diseases. My ideal job is to become a doctor when I grow up. I think doctor is a job of great value, especially, emergency doctors can rescue dying people.

必备词汇：

名词

cold [kəʊld] 感冒
cough [kɒf] 咳嗽
doctor [ˈdɒktə(r)] 医生
part [pɑ:t] 部分
illness [ˈɪlnəs] 病
medicine [ˈmedsn] 药
expert [ˈekspɜ:t] 专家
health [helθ] 健康
type [taɪp] 种类
specialist [ˈspeʃəlɪst] 专科医生
mind [maɪnd] 精神

government [ˈgʌvənmənt] 政府
rule [ru:l] 规定
minister [ˈmɪnɪstə(r)] 部长
job [dʒɒb] 工作
disease [dɪˈzi:z] 疾病
patient [ˈpeɪʃnt] 病人
value [ˈvælju:] 价值
emergency [iˈmɜ:dʒənsi] 急诊

动词

recover [rɪˈkʌvə(r)] 恢复
review [rɪˈvju:] 回顾；复习
ensure [ɪnˈʃʊə(r)] 确保
rescue [ˈreskju:] 营救

形容词

sick [sɪk] 病的；不舒服的
scared [skeəd] 害怕的
normal [ˈnɔ:ml] 正常的
serious [ˈsɪərɪəs] 严重的
mental [ˈmentl] 精神的
strict [strɪkt] 严格的
updated [ʌpˈdeɪtɪd] 更新的
demanding [dɪˈmɑ:ndɪŋ] 吃力的；要求多的
calm [kɑ:m] 冷静的
ideal [aɪˈdi:əl] 完美的；理想的
dying [ˈdaɪɪŋ] 奄奄一息的

副词

annually [ˈænjuəlɪ] 每年
especially [ɪˈspeʃəlɪ] 尤其

短语

mental health 精神健康
relate to 与……有关
look after 照顾
take care of 照顾
calm sb. down 使……冷静下来
be of great value 有很大的价值

Passage 22 配套单词填空练习

1. I love this place, e ____________ in summer.
2. The patient r ___________ well, he can walk now.
3. Smoking leads to many d ___________ such as asthma and lung cancer.
4. When you feel angry, you should c ____________ yourself down.
5. He is a s ___________ in this field, he has done a great many experiment about this illness.
6. This is my i ___________ job, it's perfect!

7. Most of my friends are s ____________ of snakes.

8. Our school celebrates this event a ____________.

9. This m ____________ can help you relieve your pain, remember to take it three times a day.

10. Students should obey r ____________ and disciplines of their school.

11. Jimmy has caught a c ____________ so that he was absent from school yesterday.

12. After graduation from university, he got a good j ____________.

13. It is important for us to r ____________ what we learned, or we will easily forget them.

14. The damage of this house is s ____________ because of the earthquake.

15. The little bird is d ____________; let's send it to a veterinarian.

16. The learning materials in our school are u ____________. Librarians upgrade them frequently.

17. Parents ought to be s ____________ with their kids, or the kids will be spoiled.

18. Although she is s ____________ she still sticks to finishing her work.

19. He is a great d ____________ who has cured loads of patients.

20. This exhibition in the museum is of great v ____________.

21. The financial m ____________ says that the employment rate is rising.

22. We should pay attention to physical and m ____________ health.

23. If there is an e ____________ please call 000.

24. Dad just can't stop c ____________, I think he has smoked too much.

25. To improve our memorization, we'd better r ____________ our lessons in time.

26. Mom will help me to take c ____________ of my pet when I go abroad.

27. This department store sells various t ____________ of products.

28. White pollution is s ____________, you can see plastic bags everywhere.

29. Put on your warm coat, or you will catch a c ____________ because of the bad weather.

30. His father is a lifesaver who r ____________ people in danger.

B 游洋 aeas7—9

词汇宝典

Passage 1

An Amazing Trip to the Zoo

Our school planned to take us to the zoo at the end of this term. When Monday comes, the weather seems sunny. Our parents have prepared us tasty picnics. As usual, we set out to the zoo by bus. Upon arrival, we get in through the children's entrance. We see naughty monkeys and fearsome lions. I feel fearful for them. A hungry monkey spoils my lunch, because it snapped at my sandwich unexpectedly. I forget that monkeys have a bad name for their naughty acts. Their behaviors disappoint me.

But things get better for me when my friend Luke shares his garlic bread with me. When we are about to go indoor to see butterflies, I spot a short slow animal within the fence. I find it is a baby kangaroo. It looks very curious about everything. I think it is having an adventure around her home. After wave bye-bye to the kangaroo, we enter into the butterfly house. The butterfly house offers us magical view. I am more interested in the butterfly exhibit. As the exhibit is available everyday, so you can go there any day.

It does not take too long for us to complete visiting all the animals. Then, we take seat in the rest area and refresh ourselves with some yummy snacks. Similar to the morning, we return to school by bus. The bus is full of our noisy chats about the amazing trip. We really enjoy it and I cannot wait to share it with my family.

必备词汇：

名词

act [ækt] 行为

behaviour [bɪˈheɪvjə] 行为

adventure [ədˈventʃə] 冒险

area [ˈeərɪə] 区域

arrival [əˈraɪv(ə)l] 达到

butterfly [ˈbʌtəflaɪ] 蝴蝶
entrance [ˈentr(ə)ns] 入口
exhibit [ɪgˈzɪbɪt] 展览
fence [fens] 围栏;篱笆
monkey [ˈmʌŋkɪ] 猴子
parent [ˈpeər(ə)nt] 父母
picnic [ˈpiknik] 野餐
sandwich [ˈsænwɪtʃ] 三明治
trip [trɪp] 行程;旅程
term [tɜ:m] 学期
view [vju:] 视野;景观

动词

complete [kəmˈpli:t] 完成
disappoint [dɪsəˈpɒɪnt] 令人失望
offer [ˈɒfə] 提供
plan [plæn] 计划
return [rɪˈtɜ:n] 返回
refresh [rɪˈfreʃ] 恢复精神
seem [si:m] 看起来
spoil [spɒɪl] 破坏

形容词

amazing [əˈmezɪŋ] 令人赞叹的
available [əˈveɪləb(ə)l] 可得到的;有空的
curious [ˈkjʊərɪəs] 好奇的
hungry [ˈhʌŋgrɪ] 饥饿的
fearsome [ˈfɪəs(ə)m] 令人害怕的
fearful [ˈfɪəfʊl] 感到害怕的
indoor [ˈɪndɔ:] 室内的
magical [ˈmædʒɪk(ə)l] 神奇的
naughty [ˈnɔ:tɪ] 淘气的
noisy [ˈnɒɪzɪ] 吵闹的
scary [ˈskeərɪ] 吓人的
tasty [ˈteɪstɪ] 美味的;好吃的
short [ʃɔ:t] 矮小的
slow [sləʊ] 慢的

副词

unexpectedly [ˌʌnɪkˈspektɪdlɪ] 意料之外地

短语

rest area 休息区
interest in 对……感兴趣
set out 出发
take seat 坐下
as usual 像往常一样
get better 变好了
take too long 花太长时间
full of 充满
similar to 类似的
snap at 大咬一口

Passage 1 配套单词填空练习

1. You ought to be ashamed of your foolish b__________.

2. The lawyer is not a______________ now because he has something important to do.

3. Irene spent hours doing research in her science project, so she might be really i__________ in science.

4. The volunteering work he took in Africa can be considered as an excited a____________.

5. She was c______________ to know what had happened.

6. A huge snowdrift is blocking the e_________________ to the driveway.

7. The paintings which are e___________ in the national museum are ordered in chronological sequence.

8. Our conversation was cut short by the a____________ of the teacher.

9. I was d_____________ by the food and the inattentive service.

10. Consequently, when most people think of f_________ sea creatures, sharks come immediately to mind.

11. I went to University of Melbourne in order to c___________ my master degree.

12. I used to believe my mother had m_____________ powers.

13. It can be s____________ to get out of our comfort zone and try something new.

14. This approach is r___________ because it breaks down barriers.

15. She dismayed me by refusing my o_______________.

16. Mom s_____________ the soup with too much salt.

17. The tourist g__________ took us to see the impressive view of the mountains.

18. The cake looks t____________. Do you think I can try one piece?

19. We have to r___________ the books to the library on time.

20. A f___________ divides off the western side of the garden.

21. A n__________ motorway has ruined village life.

22. We just sat there giggling like n___________ schoolchildren.

23. Your problem is s______ to mine.

24. The new school t_______ will begin in September.

25. It's evident that the p__________ is impracticable.

26. You've been depressed for weeks. It's time you s___________ out of it.

27. That s_____________ to be a sensible idea.

28. Reading the Bible, we enter into an a__________ new world of thoughts.

29. They s_________ out late that afternoon.

30. So at this point, you may be wondering if I think my father was a good p_________.

Passage 2

School Rules Against Online Bullying

My school adopts strict school rules against online bullying. My school principal acknowledges that there are many positive opportunities on the Internet, but there are also risks of doing things wrong on the Internet.

At the beginning of every new term, my school always holds a talk about online safety, so that new students have access to information about the school rules. The core of the talk is to help students get familiar with the category of behaviors that is regarded as bullying. Students are not allowed to engage in these behaviors; otherwise, they may face dismal consequences, such as behavior report, or being expelled from school in serious cases.

Recently, posting selfies online becomes very trendy. However, posting improper photos of other students is strictly prohibited, because posting these photos may be regarded as a kind of online bullying. If you post such photos, you may be warned and asked to delete or remove them. If you are not aware that the photo is not improper, then the school administrators may give you a short session of online safety talk. It is designed to help you understand the boundaries of right and wrong behaviors online.

Since the unwise users of the Internet will be banned from using the Internet at school, so our principal cautions us to behave properly when using the Internet.

必备词汇：

<u>名词</u>

risk [rɪsk] 危险

access [ˈækses] 入口

information [ɪnfəˈmeɪʃn] 信息

core [kɔ:] 核心

category [ˈkætəgəri] 类别

behaviour [bɪˈheɪvjə] 行为

consequence [ˈkɔnsɪkwəns] 结果

administrator [əd'mɪnɪstreɪtə] 管理者
session ['seʃ(ə)n] 课时
boundary ['baʊnd(ə)rɪ] 分界线
safety ['seftɪ] 安全

动词

adopt [ə'dɒpt] 采用
bully ['bʊlɪ] 恐吓
acknowledge [ək'nɒlɪdʒ] 承认
hold [həuld] 召开;拿着
regard [rɪ'gɑ:d] 把……看作
allow [ə'laʊ] 允许
engage [ɪn'geɪdʒ] 从事
expel [ɪk'spɛl] 开除
caution ['kɔʃən] 警告
prohibit [prə(ʊ)'hɪbɪt] 阻止
post [pəust] 张贴;发布
warn [wɔ:n] 警告
delete [dɪ'li:t] 删除
remove [rɪ'mu:v] 去除;移除
ban [bæn] 禁止

形容词

strict [strɪkt] 严格的
positive ['pɑzətɪv] 积极的
familiar [fə'mɪlɪə(r)] 熟悉的
dismal ['dɪzməl] 沮丧的
serious ['sɪərɪəs] 严重的;严肃的
strict [strɪkt] 严格的;完全的
trendy ['trendɪ] 时髦的
improper [ɪm'prɒpə] 不恰当的
wise [waɪz] 聪明的;明智的
unwise [ˌʌn'waɪz] 不明智的

副词

otherwise ['ʌðəwaɪz] 要不然
strictly ['strɪktlɪ] 完全地
properly ['prɒpəlɪ] 恰当地
against [ə'genst] 反对

短语

be aware that 意识到
be designed to 旨在;目的在于……
at the beginning of 在……开端;伊始

Passage 2 配套单词填空练习

1. They a__________ our methods after we show them why our methods are better.
2. They fear that local students would look down upon and b__________ their children, because they are new here.

3. I enjoyed being able to go out and buy t__________ clothes.

4. The river marks the b__________ between the two regions.

5. Managers can concentrate on their c________ activities.

6. He was accused of i_________ behaviour in his business dealings.

7. Stop and listen to the universal language of music and bring that p_________ energy with you everywhere you go.

8. I a____________ the truth of his statement.

9. Smoking is p____________ in public buildings or in the crowded bus.

10. This question will come forward at the next s_____________.

11. There's no right or wrong answer with r____________ to "What's a good cup of coffee?"

12. On balance, we must move forward and a_______ these new technologies.

13. I must also warn you that if you do anything like this again, I will have no choice but to e_________ you.

14. Sickness or bad luck often makes a person feel d_________.

15. I c_________ him against the danger.

16. We all take r_________. We all want innovation.

17. Regardless of where we are and what we are doing, we want a__________ to our data.

18. I bet there are more teachers, and maybe even a___________ involved.

19. Nobody can envisage the c____________ of total nuclear war.

20. They must know and obey the s_______ rules.

21. You'd better rub him down with a dry towel. O_______ he'll catch cold.

22. If you e__________ someone in conversation, you have a conversation with them.

23. Riding scooter is b________ at our school.

24. Are you a________that there will be no camping this year?

25. When your parents apply a new school for you, they need to tick the c_________ of their occupations, namely, types of their jobs.

26. It would be w________ for surfers to check if there are sharks before they dive into the water.

27. Students with i__________ behaviours will receive warning from the school.

28. Are you for or a_________ the new school rule of not allowing students to use mobile phones at school?

29. Double check the content before you p_______ it online.

30. Students should be educated about the negative effects of b_______ behaviours.

Passage 3

To Stay Safe Online

The ability to distinguish acceptable and unacceptable online behaviors is absolutely important for young people. Because unacceptable behaviors may be an abuse of other people, while those who engage in such behaviors are often accused of online bullying.

For young people who are active online, they need to be careful with activities they involve in. In addition, they need to be cautious about strangers they bump into online. So administration of using computer in schools becomes an important issue to be addressed by schools. Some schools adopt very strict rules against using the Internet improperly, while some schools admit that their soft or benign rules should be adjusted to adapt to the increasingly complex online virtual world.

Although adults are free to take advantage of the advanced technology, many experts give advice to young people about online safety. People leave behind footprint with any action they do online, and negative online footprints can affect people's job prospect in the future. So young people should think ahead before diving into the online world.

Here are some online safety tips for young people:

Alter your privacy setting from public to private, so that your personal data will not be disclosed without permission.

Check the background information before making friends online.

Do not disclose your personal information to unfamiliar people.

Separate the online world from the real world—this is one of the key tips!

必备词汇：

名词

ability [ə'bɪlətɪ] 能力
abuse [ə'bju:s] 滥用；伤害
activity [æk'tɪvɪtɪ] 活动
stranger ['streɪn(d)ʒə] 陌生人
issue ['isju:] 议题；问题
technology [tek'nɒlədʒɪ] 科技
expert ['ɛkspɜ:t] 专家
advice [əd'vaɪs] 建议
tip [tɪp] 小建议
footprint ['fʊtprɪnt] 脚印
prospect ['prɒspekt] 前景
privacy ['prɪvəsɪ] 隐私
permission [pə'mɪc(ə)n] 许可
alternation [ˌɔ:ltə'neiʃn] 更改
disclosure [dis'kləuʒə(r)] 公开

动词

distinguish [dɪ'stɪŋgwɪʃ] 区别
accuse [ə'kjuz] 指责 (of)
abuse [ə'bjus] 滥用；侮辱
bump [bʌmp] 颠簸而行；撞
address [ə'drɛs] 处理
adopt [ə'dɒpt] 采用；采取
adjust [ə'dʒʌst] 调整
affect [ə'fɛkt] 影响
alter ['ɔltə] 改变
disclose [dɪ'sklʊz] 公开
separate ['seprət] 使分离

形容词

active ['æktɪv] 活跃的
unacceptable [ʌnək'septəb(ə)l] 不能接受的
careful ['keəfʊl] 仔细的
cautious ['kɔ:ʃəs] 谨慎的
soft [sɒft] 软弱无力的
benign [bɪ'naɪn] 温和的
complex ['kɒmpleks] 复杂的
virtual ['vətʃuəl] 虚拟的
advanced [æd'vɑ:nst] 高级的
negative ['negətɪv] 消极的
key [ki:] 关键的

副词

absolutely ['æbsəlu:tlɪ] 完全地
increasingly [in'kri:siŋlɪ] 不断地

短词

involve in 参与
in addition (to) 另外
take advantage of 利用
bump into sb. 偶遇……

Passage 3 配套单词填空练习

1. In doing translation, one should not a__________ the meaning of the original to suit one's own taste.

2. Farrakhan says black leaders must a__________ moral issues to make progress in the days ahead.

3. So many children who commit violent crimes have themselves been brutalized by years of a__________ and neglect.

4. What are the characteristics that d___________ the Chinese from the Japanese?

5. She also says the study does not prove that n___________ emotions or distrust lead to bad health effects and shorter life.

6. I tried to avoid her, but it was just my luck to b____________ into her.

7. How dare he use my office without my p____________?

8. The journalist refused to d___________ the source of her information.

9. To attract investors, Panama has a__________ its tax and labour laws.

10. If you are c___________, you give serious attention to what you are doing, in order to avoid harm, damage, or mistakes.

11. Her assistant was a_____________ of theft and fraud by the police.

12. Telling a complete s____________ about your life is difficult.

13. All the young men are e________ drivers. They are good at driving.

14. V_________ every country on earth uses Celsius to measure temperature.

15. We must achieve modernization of science and t__________, otherwise we will lag behind other nations.

16. That is u___________, but it is not irreversible. We can retake the lead.

17. He left f____________ behind him on the sand.

18. He is a_____________ beyond suspicion.

19. Those are things that a__________ me, that I find from time to time.

20. I hope to see your boundless p___________.

21. In a___________ to these arrangements, extra ambulances will be on duty

B aeas 7 | 9

until midnight.

22. Being a student representative requires strong communication a_________, because the role involves lots of talking and public speaking.

23. The public transport is faced with a serious i________ of frequent delays.

24. The cancer is b____________, so the patient can recover soon after the operation.

25. Better to be c__________ when you go out alone.

26. No one shall enter the building without a p__________.

27. My mum made some a_________ to my uniform, as it is a bit bigger for me.

28. The d_________ of the previous Parliament's decision raised huge reaction among the public.

29. Oil and water in the bottle will s_________ from each other after you shaking them.

30. The k_________ to eating well is to eat various foods from different food groups.

Passage 4

Music Band and Music Agents

It is a typical practice for a musical band to use agency service or hire an agent to promote their music. Once the agent or agency sign an agreement with the musical band, they are bound to push sale of their albums or tickets for live performance. This usually yields better results than the music band doing promotion alone.

The competition in the music industry is really fierce, so many music bands start to use their music to reflect this competitive reality. This is an innovative angle to extend the art of music.

For bands who have tour across Australia, they need a local agent to arrange accommodations and rent premises and hire security staff.

Apparently, when preparing the launch of the performance, agents also assist in deciding makeup appearance and costume of performers. They need to decide on the ultimate appearance that would turn out to be most appealing on stage.

必备词汇：

名词

agency [ˈeɪdʒənsɪ] 代理
agreement [əˈgriːm(ə)nt] 协议
band [bænd] 乐团
sale [seɪl] 销售；促销
album [ˈælbəm] 相簿
performance [pəˈfɔːm(ə)ns] 演出
competition [ˌkɔmpəˈtɪʃn] 竞争
industry [ˈɪndəstrɪ] 产业
reality [rɪˈælətɪ] 现实
tour [tʊə(r)] 巡回
accommodation [əˌkɒməˈdeɪʃn] 住宿
premise [ˈpremɪs] 前提
costume [ˈkɔstjuːm] 服装

动词

hire [ˈhaɪə] 雇用

promote [prəˈməʊt] 推广；促进

sign [saɪn] 签字；签名

bind [baɪnd]（bound）约束

push [pʊʃ] 推动

yield [ji:ld] 出产

reflect [rɪˈflɛkt] 反射

extend [ɪkˈstɛnd] 延伸

rent [rent] 租用

形容词

typical [ˈtɪpɪkəl] 典型的

live [laɪv] 现场的

fierce [fɪrs] 猛烈的

innovative [ˈinəvətiv] 革新的

local [ləʊkl] 当地的

ultimate [ˈʌltəmət] 最终的

appealing [əˈpilɪŋ] 有魅力的

短语

tour across Australia 跨澳大利亚巡回

turn out to be 最终成为……

security staff 保安

Passage 4 配套单词填空练习

1.You need to h____________ some skilled labours.

2. Inside the theatre, they were giving a p__________ of Bizet's *Carmen*.

3. I even tried to be i___________ in my preaching.

4. The coal i_____________ is running down as coal is gradually replaced by oil.

5. The a____________ will be effective from November.

6. Really focused pronunciation practice can y__________ great results.

7. The a____________ contains many memorable songs.

8. A f__________ animal or person is very aggressive or angry.

9. When people b_________ with each other, they form a relationship based on love or shared beliefs and experiences.

10. The sun r__________ off the snow-covered mountains.

11. We want two good musicians for our rock b__________.

12. Cheney is everyone's image of a t______________ cop: a big white guy,

six feet, 220 pounds.

13. If that p______________ is true then that conclusion is false.

14. The main stem will e____________ to around 12 feet, if left to develop naturally.

15. There was a sense of humour to what he did that I found very a______________.

16. Most Australian schools are now made up of l________ and international students.

17. I want to watch a l_________ talk show.

18. It is the r________ that only those who have high marks can go to university.

19. Tourists need to sort out their a_____________ before they set off; otherwise, they will need to pay more on hotels if they book it on spot.

20. Large companies spend a huge amount of money on p_________ their products.

Passage 5

Writer's Festival

Melbourne hosts a writer's festival annually. At the festival, the most popular authors will receive awards, while average writers can get more exposure to readers. Sometimes, readers are just not aware of these writers. Writers, film script writers and readers can attend the festival.

In addition to enjoying speeches from renowned writers, readers also can get a bargain for books at the festival, which means they can buy books at discounted prices. Further, fantastic writers share their path of success in writing. Some stories are very inspiring, while others are very encouraging. It is a delight to be surrounded with talents from around Australia and the world.

"No opportunity awaits you!"—I learned this quote from last writer's festival. I love writing, so I tried to put my writing together to see if I can write a book. My dream job is to become a writer when I grow up. But when things did not unfold as I wished, I forgot my initial dream. That quote reminded me of my ambition. I repeated that quote in my mind for many times when I tended to give up.

必备词汇：

名词

festival [ˈfestəvl] 节日
author [ˈɔ:θə] 作者
award [əˈwɔ:d] 奖
exposure [ɪkˈspəʊʒə] 显露
script [skrɪpt] 脚本
speech [spi:tʃ] 演讲
bargain [ˈbɑ:gɪn] 便宜货
discount [ˈdɪskaʊnt] 折扣
path [pæθ] 道路
delight [dɪˈlaɪt] 高兴
quote [kwot] 引用
ambition [æmˈbɪʃn] 雄心；抱负

动词

host [host] 主持

receive [rɪˈsi:v] 收到

attend [əˈtend] 出席

await [əˈwet] 等待

unfold [ʌnˈfold] 呈现

tend [tend] 倾向

bargain [ˈbɑrgən] 讨价还价

surround [səˈraʊnd] 围绕；包围

remind [rɪˈmaɪnd] 提醒

repeat [rɪˈpi:t] 重复

形容词

annual [ˈænjuəl] 每年的

popular [ˈpɒpjələr] 受欢迎的

average [ˈævərɪdʒ] 普通的；平均的

renowned [rɪˈnaʊnd] 出名的

fantastic [fænˈtæstɪk] 极出色的

inspiring [ɪnˈspaɪərɪŋ] 启发的；发人深省的

encouraging [eŋˈkʌrɪdʒɪŋ] 鼓励的

initial [ɪˈnɪʃəl] 开始的；最初的

副词

annually [ˈænjʊəlɪ] 每年

短语

tend to 倾向于

give up 放弃

in mind 在脑海里

Passage 5 配套单词填空练习

1. I gave the letter to the local press and they q__________ from it.
2. She was a very strong, impressive character and one of the most i___________ people I've ever met.
3. They give 10% d___________ for cash payment.
4. We refuse to b_________ over the price.
5. When you r__________ a visitor or a guest, you greet them.
6. A p_________ is a long strip of ground that people walk along to get from one place to another.
7. He was suffering from e____________ and shock but his condition was said to be stable.
8. How f_____________ the dragon boat teams were!
9. So we're e___________ everyone to come and join us.

10. He picked up Ron's letter and u______________ it.

11. Tonight she h____________ a ball for 300 guests.

12. We are anxiously a_____________ the outcome of their discussion.

13. We all t____________ to like those similar to us.

14. The s______________ was delivered to the director ahead of schedule.

15. It was of course a d______________ for them to meet again after such a long separation.

16. I___________ here to acknowledge you received it.

17. The whole town was immersed in a f___________ atmosphere.

18. The site has one million visitors a_____________.

19. The a____________ delineated many characters in his story.

20. The old lady loves to be s___________ by small kids, so she goes to the local library very often.

21. You can easily remember that long word if you r_________ it for several times.

22. That picture has r___________ me of my last trip in USA.

23. Who a____________ last night's meeting?

24. Never g__________ ___________ before you try your best.

25. Henry is a boy full of a___________; he wants to become a millionaire when he grows up.

Passage 6

Movie Reviews about *The Great Gatsby*

Though some movies are awful, while some movies are so touchy that I cannot help giving positive comments on them.

The movie *The Great Gatsby* is based on the American classic novel "*The Great Gatsby*" published in 1925; alternatively speaking, the movie is adapted from the novel. The original novel was widely acclaimed for its elegant language and style. So the director of the movie faced enormous challenges to make his movie shine under the shadow of its printed counterpart.

When the movie was released for public view, it triggered extreme comments. People who loved it thought it was a great success. People, who loved the original book more, thought the movie was a disaster. In my opinion, this view seems a baseless bias.

Some critics made positive and inspiring comments:

"The movie has successfully balanced the beautiful language in the book and the restricted length faced by all movies. The specific angles in the movie created astonishing visual effects. The movie brought life to the battle that the billionaire Gatsby tried to win back Daisy, and it was intriguingly presented in the movie."

Some picky critics wrote like this:

This new adaptation could not beat the preceding ones out. The director failed to present the depth of Gatsby's mind described in the book. The performance of the casting crews was just beyond average. There was no mystery plotted in the movie, but a simple blast of gunshots. It did not spark viewer's imagination, as viewers could easily solve the crime behind the gunshots.

However, I think movie is a kind of media that filmmakers adopt to reflect people's life experience. So, different people can form different interpretations of the same movie. Life is made up with bitter and sweet experiences. When we have similar experiences, we may easily find empathy with those who have alike gone through the same encounters. I believe that each movie has something deep behind the plot, something that entice us to think about our own life.

必备词汇:

名词

review [rɪˈvju:] 反馈;评价
comment [ˈkɒment] 评论
director [daɪˈrektər] 导演
shadow [ˈʃædəu] 阴影
counterpart [ˈkaʊntəpɑ:t] 对应物
disaster [dɪˈzɑ:stə] 灾难
bias [ˈbaɪəs] 偏见 (against sth.)
critic [ˈkrɪtɪk] 评论家
battle [ˈbætl] 战斗
adaptation [ˌædəpˈteɪʃən](电影)改编
mind [maɪnd] 头脑;聪明人
casting [ˈkæstɪŋ] 角色的分派
billionaire [ˌbɪljəˈnɛr] 亿万富翁
crew [kru:] 全体人员
mystery [ˈmɪstrɪ] 神秘
blast [blæst] 爆炸
gunshot [ˈgʌnʃɑt] 枪炮声
media [ˈmi:diə] 媒介;方法
film [fɪlm] 电影
filmmaker [ˈfɪlmˌmeikə] 电影制作人
interpretation [ɪnˌtɜ:prəˈteɪʃən] 解释;理解
empathy [ˈempəθɪ] 共鸣;同感
encounter [inˈkauntə(r)] 遭遇;际遇

动词

acclaim [əˈklem] 称誉;赞赏
publish [ˈpʌblɪʃ] 出版
base [bes] 以……作基础
adapt [əˈdæpt](电影)改编
release [rɪˈli:s] 释放;公布
trigger [ˈtrɪgɚ] 触发
seem [si:m] 似乎
balance [ˈbæləns] 使……平衡
restrict [rɪˈstrɪkt] 限制
beat...out 战胜;打败
present [ˈprezənt] 展现
plot [plɔt] 密谋
spark [spɑ:k] 触发;引起
adopt [əˈdɒpt] 采用
reflect [rɪˈflekt] 反映
form [fɔ:m] 形成

interpret [ɪnˈtɜːprɪt] 理解;解释
entice [ɪnˈtaɪs] 诱使
encounter [ɪnˈkaʊntə] 遭遇;遇到

形容词

awful [ˈɔ:fəl] 糟糕的
touchy [ˈtʌtʃɪ] 易生气的
positive [ˈpɒzətɪv] 积极的;正面的
classic [ˈklæsɪk] 经典的
original [əˈrɪdʒənəl] 原先的;最初的
elegant [ˈɛləgənt] 优美的
enormous [ɪˈnɔrməs] 巨大的
extreme [ɪkˈstrim] 极端的
specific [spəˈsɪfɪk] 特有的;特定的
intriguing [ɪnˈtri:gɪŋ] 引人入胜的
picky [ˈpɪkɪ] 挑剔的
astonishing [əsˈtɒnɪʃɪŋ] 使人吃惊的
intriguing [ɪnˈtri:gɪŋ] 引起好奇心的
preceding [ˈprisidɪŋ] 在先的
bitter [ˈbɪtər] 苦涩的;令人痛苦的
alternative [ɔ:lˈtɜ:nətɪv] 另外的

副词

alternatively [ɔ:lˈtɜ:nətɪvlɪ] 或者
alike [ə:laɪk] 相似地;相同地

短语

can't help doing sth. 忍不住
beyond average 中等以上
go through 经历;经过

Passage 6 配套单词填空练习

1. What I need is a list of specific unknown problems we will e___________.
2. A b___________ is a big explosion, especially one caused by a bomb.
3. A c___________ is a group of people with special technical skills who work together on a task or project, such as people work on airplanes.
4. The source of the gunshots still remains a m___________.
5. Patricia looked beautiful and e___________ as always.
6. You shouldn't be wearing blue eye s___________.
7. If you describe someone as t___________, you mean that they are easily upset, offended, or irritated.
8. Here was a bike path running along this side of the wall, right at

its b__________.

9. She has fought a constant b_________ with her weight.

10. If there is a c___________ of another thing, they are similar in some ways.

11. The restaurant has been widely a___________ for its excellent French cuisine.

12. He called for the immediate r____________ of all political prisoners.

13. I suggested he should a___________ himself to his new conditions.

14. If you r______________ something, you put a limit on it in order to reduce it or prevent it from becoming too great.

15. How are you going to i___________ the new school rule against bringing mobile phones to school?

16. His new book will be p____________ in February.

17. If people p_________ to do something or plot something that is illegal or wrong, they plan secretly to do it.

18. The b___________ refuse to contribute to the refugees.

19. They had died of g___________ wounds.

20. The war cost an e__________ sum of money.

21. He had a_____________ blue eyes, like pale sapphires.

22. This isn't a miracle. This is a d___________.

23. Many parents have b___________ against popular music.

24. This i_____________ book is both thoughtful and informative.

25. This e___________ view hasn't captured popular opinion.

26. She informed us that eighteen members of the staff had left during the p_____________ year, so these people wouldn't be here any longer.

27. Didn't you disapprove of his c_____________?

28. I'm the news d__________ at Radio Beijing.

29. Good children's books can e__________ children to imagine.

30. My little brother is a very p________ eater, as he rarely eats veggies.

Passage 7

Australia's Mining Industry

The mining industry is booming in Australia. Minerals mined out are sold across the border to foreign countries such as China. Australia contains many gigantic mines in the world, they have huge commercial values for Australia. During the financial crisis, many countries were faced with tough challenges, because their finance industry collapsed. That caused recession in many countries. Many related industries were severely injured by the crisis, and many businesses even closed down.

In the middle of the gloomy prospect, the resilient mining industry emerged to be the most stable income source to maintain the stability of the Australian society. Australian residents enjoyed tax benefits contributed by mining companies. Mining was gradually climbing up to be the number one industry in Australia. Mining used to be an important income source on the government's annual budget. It was estimated that Australia earned billions of dollars from exporting minerals.

Australia has established its reputation as a country rich in natural resources, but many countries are exploring their vast lands to maximize their economic potential. So Australia exports minerals to other countries, but imports manufactured products from other countries, like USA.

必备词汇：

名词

mine [maɪn] 矿

mining [ˈmaɪnɪŋ] 矿业

crisis [ˈkraɪsɪs] 危机

recession [rɪˈsɛʃən] 经济衰退

prospect [ˈprɑspɛkt] 前景

business [ˈbɪznɪs] 生意；公司

income [ˈɪnkʌm] 收入

source [sɔ:s] 来源;源头
stability [stəˈbɪləti] 稳定;稳固
society [səˈsaɪətɪ] 社会
resident [ˈrezɪdənt] 居民
budget [ˈbʌdʒɪt] 财政预算
reputation [repjʊˈteɪʃ(ə)n] 名气
resource [riˈsɔ:s] 资源
manufacture [mænjʊˈfæktʃə] 制造品
potential [pəˈtenʃəl] 潜力

动词

boom [bu:m] 迅速发展
mine [maɪn] 开采
contain [kənˈten] 包含
collapse [kəˈlæps] 倒塌
injure [ˈɪndʒə] 伤害;损害
estimate [ˈestɪmeɪt] 估计
emerge [ɪˈmɜ:dʒ] 出现;(从困境中)存活下来
export [ɪkˈspɔrt] 出口
establish [əˈstæblɪʃ] 建立
maintain [meɪnˈteɪn] 保持
contribute [kənˈtrɪbju:t] 贡献(to)
earn [ɜ:n] 挣钱;赚得
maximize [ˈmæksəˌmaɪz] 增至最大限度
manufacture [mænjʊˈfæktʃə] 制造
import [ɪmˈpɔ:t] 进口

形容词

booming [ˈbu:mɪŋ] 繁荣的
gigantic [ˌdʒaɪˈgæntɪk] 巨大的
commercial [kəˈmɜ:ʃ(ə)l] 商业的
financial [faɪˈnænʃəl] 金融的
tough [tʌf] 严酷的;坚韧的
related [rɪˈleɪtɪd] 相关的
resilient [rɪˈzɪljənt] 有弹性的;适应性强的
stable [ˈsteɪbəl] 稳定的
gloomy [ˈglu:mɪ] 黑暗的
foreign [ˈfɔrən] 外国的
vast [væst] 巨大的

副词

severely [səˈvɪrlɪ] 严格地
gradually [ˈgrædʒuəlɪ] 逐渐地

短语

be faced with 面对
close down 倒闭
in the middle of 在……之中
used to 过去……

Passage 7 配套单词填空练习

1. When she was eight years old, her father took her inside a factory to watch the m__________ of printing presses.

2. If a place is g___________, it is almost dark so that you cannot see very well.

3. The c____________ bank is willing to lend money to these customers.

4. Business is b___________ since I expanded the shop.

5. The company was aiming to m____________ profits.

6. We e___________ the cost to be five thousand dollars.

7. They are supposed to use the box to c___________ books.

8. As soon as the girl saw blood she c__________.

9. A good encyclopedia is a m_________ of information.

10. Some families don't have the r___________ to feed themselves adequately.

11. She was on her first f_____________ holiday in a new country without her parents.

12. A t_________ person is strong and determined, and can tolerate difficulty or suffering.

13. One of the products that the company e___________ is clothing.

14. A great many bank clerks were laid off due to the r____________.

15. I am waiting for something with better pay and more career p_____________.

16. Many families on low i_____________ will be unable to afford to buy their own home.

17. This college has a good academic r________________.

18. The v___________ majority of the population was German.

19. He was s____________ punished for his carelessness.

20. China keeps i_________ quality food from other countries, such as beef and baby formula.

21. The building cast a g_________ shadow over the river as the sun sets.

22. Some retail shops have to c________ ________ due to the booming online shops.

23. To live in a s________ family is a humble dream for many poor children.

24. Students with r____________ personality can walk out of failure quickly.

25. Iron ore can be explored from iron m_______.

26. My father is the person who e________ a living for us.

27. As the sunset shadows the quiet street, I saw a man e________ from the corner of the bleak house.

28. The economy will be i_________ if the government increases tax.

29. My parents always prepare a b_________ at the beginning of each year, so they know how much they can earn and how much they can spend.

30. The ship g__________ disappeared on the horizon.

Passage 8

Life Work Balance

Modern lifestyle is super busy, so modern people need to find a way to keep life work balance. Some parents are so occupied with their jobs, they miss many opportunities to accompany their kids in their childhood. Nowadays, many people struggle between work and family; they have to split their time and attention among several responsibilities. Mums are traditionally responsible for raising children, so they are particularly under pressure to balance their domestic responsibility and career pursuit.

Previously, most mums stayed at home to care their children, while dads earned income to provide a comfortable living for their family. For mums committed their time to offer comfort to their kids when these little young souls felt insecure. Without doubt, mum usually ensures happy life of kids.

Many mums dream their kids to be excellent in their entire life. Despite that many modern mums are busy with work, they try to organize things neatly so that they can manage to accomplish these tasks. Many mums can handle multi-tasks.

Mums are role models for their children too. Their practice of achieving a balanced life will influence their children's attitude towards work and personal life at their later stage of life. Mum's commitment is regarded as indispensable contribution to kids' happy and healthy growth.

必备词汇：

名词

lifestyle [ˈlaɪfstaɪl] 生活方式

balance [ˈbæl(ə)ns] 平衡

opportunity [ˌɒpəˈtjuːnətɪ] 机会

childhood [ˈtʃaɪldhʊd] 童年

attention [əˈtenʃən] 注意力；考虑

responsibility [rɪˌspɒnsəˈbɪlətɪ] 责任

career [kəˈrɪər] 事业

pursuit [pəˈsjuːt] 追求

comfort [ˈkʌmfət] 安慰;舒适

soul [səul] 小孩;灵魂

attitude [ˈætɪtʊd] 态度

contribution [kɒntrɪˈbjuːʃ(ə)n] 贡献

practice [ˈpræktɪs] 实践

commitment [kəˈmɪtmənt] 奉献;投入

动词

occupy [ˈɒkjəpaɪ] 占据;占用

accompany [əˈkʌmpənɪ] 陪伴

struggle [ˈstrʌgl] 挣扎

split [splɪt] 劈开;分开

raise [rez] 抚养

commit [kəˈmɪt] 奉献; 犯罪

offer [ˈɒfər] 给予

ensure [ɪnˈʃʊr] 确保

organize [ˈɔːgənaɪz] 组织;安排

manage [ˈmænɪdʒ] 成功做到;管理

handle [ˈhændl] 处理

achieve [əˈtʃiːv] 取得

influence [ˈɪnfluəns] 影响

形容词

modern [ˈmadən] 现代的

occupied [ˈɔkjupaɪd] 已占用的

traditional [trəˈdiʃənəl] 传统的

responsible [rɪˈspɒnsɪb(ə)l] 负有责任的

domestic [dəˈmestɪk] 家庭的;国内的

previous [ˈpriːviəs] 以前的

comfortable [ˈkʌmfətəbəl] 舒适的

insecure [ˌɪnsɪˈkjʊər] 缺乏信心的

excellent [ˈeksələnt] 优秀的

entire [ɪnˈtaɪər] 整个的;全部的

personal [ˈpɜːsənəl] 个人的

indispensable [ˌɪndɪˈspensəbəl] 必需的

副词

super [ˈsuːpər] 尤其;非常

traditionally [trəˈdiʃənəlɪ] 传统上

particularly [pəˈtɪkjələlɪ] 尤其

neatly [ˈniːtlɪ] 整齐地;简单而聪明地

previously [ˈpriːviəslɪ] 以前

短语

under pressure 处于压力之下

without doubt 毫无疑问

despite that 尽管

role model 模范

Passage 8 配套单词填空练习

1. He was o___________ in translating an English novel.
2. He r__________ himself into a sitting position.
3. He took up a compromising a___________ towards the question.
4. If the chicken is fairly small, you may simply s______ it in half for cooking.
5. American economists have made important c_____________ to the field of financial and corporate economics.
6. They weren't legally r_____________ for their death but were they in some larger sense morally r_______________?
7. I have never c_____________ any crime.
8. Can you figure out a way to e____________ that you all escape?
9. Life became a s_______________ for survival.
10. I needed to change my l_____________ and become more active.
11. Eat a b_____________ diet to stay healthy.
12. Your s__________ is the part of you that consists of your mind, character, thoughts, and feelings. Many people believe that your s____________ continues existing after your body is dead.
13. To tell the truth, I don't know if I can h__________ the job.
14. He was not able to a____________ inner calm.
15. There is no d_______________ that man has had an impact on the Earth's climate.
16. In Japan, people t_______________ bow as a form of greeting.
17. With a couple of nights' cramming, Jim m_________ to pass his final exam.
18. Can you find out how the author o__________ the story?
19. Video games have i_____________ behaviour among many young children.
20. A happy c_____________ ensures children's healthy growth and development.

21. What is your final p________? To be a doctor or an artist?

22. The i____________ kid rushed to her mum with tears in her eyes.

23. The environment is an e__________ system, so any change in the nature can affect the rest part.

24. The government may seek some p__________ information from you when you apply for visa.

25. Hard working is i___________ in your study if you want to achieve good results.

26. The after-school activities offer many o_________________ to children to learn various skills.

27. Professor Lewis has made huge c______________ to the education of poor children in Africa.

28. I guess from his p___________ behaviours that he would not make much effort in our group project.

29. Many dishwashers are designed for d___________ use only, so they are not suitable for use in restaurant.

30. My mum has an unusual c_________ path, because she has started a new career in her 30s.

Passage 9

Travelling Broadens Our Vision

It gradually becomes a fashion to travel abroad, as domestic travelling isn't regarded as entertaining as oversea travelling.

After finish their high school, many students in Australia choose to take a gap year to travel around the world. After they spend months in a foreign country, they soon settle down well in their new environment.

Those school finishers need to bear in mind several things before they set off. They need to book flight tickets, buy travel insurance before departing from their home country. They should ensure their suitcases do not exceed the maximum weight limit; otherwise, they will be charged extra fees or penalty.

Keeping in contact with family is important when they going abroad. If a radical event happens in the destination country, travelers can seek assistance from their families. Travelers should stay alert all the time, even a civilized city like Rome has many thieves; travelers need to watch their valuables closely; if they make a slip in any way, they may lose their property for ever. If such a tragedy occurs, they may need to obtain replacement bank account cards in order to withdraw money.

Therefore, travelers need to be cautious of both personal safety and property security when going abroad.

必备词汇：

名词

vision [ˈvɪʒən] 远见；眼界
fashion [ˈfæʃən] 潮流
insurance [ɪnˈʃʊər(ə)ns] 保险
suitcase [ˈsutˌkes] 手提箱
limit [ˈlɪmɪt] 限度
charge [tʃɑrdʒ] 费用
penalty [ˈpenəltɪ] 罚款

destination [ˌdestɪˈneɪʃən] 目的地
assistance [əˈsɪstəns] 帮助;协助
thief [θif] (thieves) 小偷
valuables [ˈvæljuəblz] 贵重物品
slip [slɪp] 疏忽;小错
tragedy [ˈtrædʒədɪ] 悲剧
replacement [rɪˈpleɪsm(ə)nt] 代替

动词

broaden [ˈbrɔ:dən] 拓宽;开阔
settle [ˈsetl] 安定
entertain [entəˈteɪn] 使……开心;娱乐
choose [tʃu:z] 选择
book [bʊk] 预订
depart [dɪˈpɑ:t] 出发;动身
exceed [ɪkˈsid] 超越
charge [tʃɑrdʒ] 收取费用
seek [sɪ:k] 寻求
occur [əˈkɜ:r] 发生
obtain [əbˈten] 获得
withdraw [wɪðˈdrɔ:] 撤回;取回

形容词

domestic [dəˈmestɪk] 本国的
oversea [əuvəˈsi:] 海外的;国外的
entertaining [entəˈteɪnɪŋ] 娱乐的
extra [ˈekstrə] 额外的
civilized [ˈsɪvəˌlaɪzd] 文明的
radical [ˈrædɪkl] 极端的
alert [əˈlɜ:t] 机警的

副词

abroad [əˈbrɔ:d] 到国外
closely [ˈkləʊslɪ] 密切地
therefore [ˈðeəfɔ:(r)] 因此

短语

set off 出发
home country 故国;故乡
gap year 空档年;一年假期
settle down 安定下来
bear in mind 铭记在心
stay alert 保持警觉
all the time 一直

B aeas 7 | 9

Passage 9 配套单词填空练习

1. Out of all visitors, 70% were d______________ visitors and 30% were from overseas, the report said.
2. My house was insured with a local i________________ company.
3. As Jack is ill, we have to get a r_______________ for him.
4. There is no l________________ to how much fresh fruit you can eat in a day.

5. He is now the clown of the group, e_____________ the others and initiating play.

6. What's the service c_____________ for a deposit?

7. How much does the car parking company c_________ for casual parking?

8. The population on the Earth will e____________ six billion in the next ten years.

9. The t_____________ was caught by the police.

10. I believed that in c_____________ countries, torture had ended long ago.

11. If you s___________, you accidentally slide and lose your balance.

12. The country needs a period of calm without more surges of r_____________ change.

13. They have suffered an enormous personal t______________.

14. They can also o__________ government subsidies for funerals and weddings.

15. Many Jews deported to the camp hid their v____________ fearful of being robbed by the Nazi.

16. If you want to catch that train, we'd better s_________ off for the station immediately.

17. After high school, students should take at least one year off to work or travel before beginning college, this is what we called a g__________ year.

18. Better to b________ tickets earlier to secure your seat!

19. More accidents o_________ on roads during Christmas than other time.

20. You'd better check the weather of your d___________ before you set off.

21. There are various ways to b___________ your horizon, one is reading extensively.

22. Parents can w_______ their previous permission if they change their mind.

23. A f_______ of using smart Google glasses emerges quickly.

24. Drivers who park cars in an unpermitted area may be charged a p________.

25. A person's v__________ depends on how much he/she knows the world.

26. The young mother made a s________ by forgetting to take the baby out of the car.

27. It is a real t_________ that babies who are died from being left in car in summer days.

28. Can you get me a r_______________ key? I lost the original one.

29. Customers need to pay e_________ fees if they request additional packaging.

30. Students should b______ ____ ________ that cheating during exams is not permitted.

Passage 10

Safety Instructions in Cooking Class

Many students have selected cooking as an elective subject in their junior school. But cooking can be dangerous. Students can burn or even scald themselves, cut their fingers or fall on the slippery floor. To minimize risks of injury, students are required to abide by the following procedures:

Students should put on safety equipment or clothes before initiate any cooking activity. Students cannot be barefoot when enter the kitchen.

Do not bring any chemical goods to the kitchen.

Please only take what you need in your cooking, even though we have a large collection of cookers in the storage.

You can find basic tools like brush or cleaning sponge on the kitchen bench.

Make sure to place butter, cheese or other perishable food back to the fridge after use.

Please constantly check if everything is in order, and conduct yourself properly in the kitchen.

There is a first-aid case in the cabinet of the public kitchen, you can get a bandage for cut wounds.

If there is a fire, please fetch the fire extinguisher at the back of the kitchen. Please stay calm and get out of the kitchen orderly.

I have faith that you can cope with the pressure of learning to cook, so believe in yourself and enjoy the flavours you are going to create.

必备词汇：

名词

safety [ˈseɪftɪ] 安全

instruction [ɪnˈstrʌkʃən] 指示

risk [rɪsk] 风险

injury [ˈɪndʒəri] 伤
procedure [prəˈsi:dʒə] 程序
equipment [ɪˈkwɪpm(ə)nt] 设备
kitchen [ˈkɪtʃɪn] 厨房
goods [gʊdz] 物品
collection [kəˈlekʃ(ə)n] 收藏品
cooker [ˈkʊkə(r)] 炊具
storage [ˈstɔrɪdʒ] 仓库
tool [tu:l] 工具
sponge [spʌn(d)ʒ] 海绵
bench [bentʃ] 工作台；长凳
first-aid case 急救箱
bandage [ˈbændɪdʒ] 绷带
wound [wund] 伤口
extinguisher [ɪkˈstɪŋgwɪʃə] 熄火器
faith [feθ] 信任

动词

select [sɪˈlekt] 挑选
burn [bɜ:n] 烫伤；燃烧
scald [skɔ:ld] 烫伤
cut [kʌt] 割伤
fall [fɔ:l] 跌倒；摔倒
minimize [ˈmɪnɪmaɪz] 把……降到最低限度
require [rɪˈkwaɪr] 要求
initiate [ɪˈnɪʃieɪt] 开始
check [tʃek] 检查
fetch [fɛtʃ] 取来
cope [kop] 对付
wound [wund] 使受伤

形容词

selected [sɪˈlektɪd] 精选的
slippery [ˈslɪpərɪ] 滑的；狡猾的
barefoot [ˈbɛrˈfʊt] 赤脚的
chemical [ˈkɛmɪkl] 化学的
basic [ˈbeɪsɪk] 基本的
perishable [ˈperɪʃəb(ə)l] 易腐烂的

副词

constantly [ˈkɔnstəntlɪ] 不断地
properly [ˈprɔpəlɪ] 恰当地
orderly [ˈɔ:dəlɪ] 有序地

短语

in order 按顺序
put on 穿上
place sth. back 把……放回
first-aid 急救
abide by 遵守
conduct oneself 举止；表现

B aeas 7 | 9

Passage 10 配套单词填空练习

1. If you have f____________ in someone or something, you feel confident

about their ability or goodness.

2. Fires were b_____________ out of control in the centre of the city.

3. Jane adapted quickly to the new p____________.

4. This fact is too evident to r___________ proof.

5. Please feel assured that we'll a__________ by our promise.

6. All video e_____________ is on sale today and tomorrow.

7. You don't take frozen foods because they are p____________ on a road trip.

8. I keep a box of tools and a fire e____________ in my car for use in an emergency.

9. A bomb exploded in a hotel, killing six people and w____________ another five.

10. If you refer to the s____________ of something, you mean that it is kept in a special place until it is needed.

11. He is a s___________ customer, and should be carefully treated.

12. That old man is a s_________ person, and he always takes advantage of others.

13. Someone who is b___________ is not wearing anything on their feet.

14. Sylvia just f__________ a towel from the bathroom after she had bath.

15. It was amazing how my mother c___________ with bringing up three children on less than thirty dollars a week.

16. Language is c__________ and gradually evolving.

17. S___________ is a very light soft substance with lots of little holes in it, which can be either artificial or natural. It is used to clean things or as a soft layer.

18. Apply a dressing to the wound and b____________ it.

19. He has a large c____________ of stamps.

20. Tomorrow is the auction day; everything in the room should be placed in o_______.

21. The whole food chain is affected by the overuse of c_____________ in agricul-

ture.

22. Children need b_________ stuffs such as food and shelter to grow healthily.

23. My father just renovated our kitchen, so we have an island b_________ in the middle of the kitchen.

24. When you travel by air, you are not permitted to take illegal g_______ with you.

25. Students should follow their teacher's i___________ in class.

26. Children should be taught to c___________ themselves properly in public.

27. The Green party just i_____________ an environment protection campaign.

28. I s__________ my arm when I took the roasted chicken out of the oven.

29. Drivers should abide b______ traffic rules when driving.

30. My brother can assemble his model cars without using t__________.

Passage 11

Mysterious Pirate Life

There are many stories about pirates. By definition, pirates are essentially a bunch of criminals, even though stories often portrait pirates in a romantic way. I bet that's because romantic yet mysterious pirates appeal more to readers. No one knows why some people ended up with becoming pirates. I guess some were forced to be pirates because they had no other choice. Historically, some criminals were cast away; consequently, they would join other pirates to survive.

Generally speaking, pirates can be violent when they commit crime of robbing other ships. Sailors often felt frightened if they chanced upon pirates in the middle of sea. Captain pirates often commanded their ship to chase civilian ships until the ship cease to fight back. Then pirates board the ship, and take control of the ship; pirates gather and steal all valuable property from the ship. With their pockets filled with valuable things, they abandon the ship eventually, often leaving the crews of the ship unscathed and drifting on the wide sea.

Piracy still exists in the modern society. In the past decades, piracy is growing in spite of the increased security measures on cargo ships. Some countries declared that it lost billions of dollars to pirates annually.

必备词汇：

名词

pirate [ˈpaɪrət] 海盗

piracy [ˈpaɪrəsɪ] 海盗抢劫

definition [defɪˈnɪʃ(ə)n] 定义

choice [tʃɔɪs] 选择

crime [kraɪm] 罪

sailor [ˈselɚ] 水手

property [ˈprɒpəti] 财产

pocket [ˈpɑkɪt] 口袋

decade [ˈdekeɪd] 十年

measure [ˈmeʒər] 方法;措施
cargo [ˈkɑrgo] 货物

动词

portrait [ˈpɔːrtrət] 描绘
bet [bet] 敢肯定; 打赌
appeal [əˈpiːl] 吸引
survive [səˈvaɪv] 幸存
rob [rɑb] 抢劫
frighten [ˈfraɪtən] 使害怕
command [kəˈmɑːnd] 指挥
chase [tʃeɪs] 追赶
cease [siːs] 停止
board [bɔːd] 登上
gather [ˈgæðə] 收集
steal [stiːl] 偷窃
abandon [əˈbænd(ə)n] 放弃
drift [drɪft] 漂流
exist [ɪgˈzɪst] 存在
declare [dɪˈklɛr] 宣布

形容词

criminal [ˈkrɪmɪnl] 犯罪的
romantic [rə(ʊ)ˈmæntɪk] 浪漫的
mysterious [mɪˈstɪərɪəs] 神秘的
violent [ˈvaɪələnt] 暴力的
frightened [ˈfraɪtnd] 害怕的
unscathed [ʌnˈskeɪðd] 毫发无损的

副词

essentially [ɪˈsɛnʃəlɪ] 本质上
historically [hɪˈstɒrɪklɪ] 历史上

短语

a bunch of 串,群
make a living 过活
in spite of 尽管
even though 尽管
end up with 以……告终
be forced to 被迫……
be cast away 流放 ;漂流
commit crime 犯罪
chance upon sb. 偶遇
fight back 反击
take control of 掌控
chance sth. 冒险

B aeas 7 | 9

Passage 11 配套单词填空练习

1. Hunger goaded him to s___________ a loaf of bread from the bakery.
2. I suggest we g______________ enough firewood to last the night.
3. P__________ are sailors who attack other ships and steal property from

them.

4. If you d____________ that something is true, you say that it is true in a firm, deliberate way.

5. A group of gunmen attacked a prison and set free nine c______________.

6. When we're together, all he talks about is business. I wish he were more r__________.

7. A s___________ fell overboard and was rescued.

8. It is an a______________ performance, which attracts thousands of viewers.

9. We were a pretty inexperienced b__________ of people really.

10. She was f____________ of making a mistake.

11. In the past, many old people beg food to s______________the cold bleak winters.

12. He took his flashlight from his jacket p____________ and switched it on.

13. The boat calls at the main port to load its regular c____________ of bananas.

14. Mrs. Yacoub was r _______________ of her designer watch at her Westchester home.

15. She is an e____________ selfish person.

16. In s______________ of these insults, I managed not to get angry.

17. Within a d___________, the technology will make a leap.

18. It is a c__________ to take other's property away without permission.

19. The government took several m___________ to lighten traffic jam.

20. *Harry Potter* portrayed a m____________ world of magic.

21. The passing speedy truck left me no c__________ to brake, so my car just hit the truck.

22. Many young people don't know what they will e______ _____ _______.

23. The car accident left two passengers u__________, so they didn't need any medical treatment.

24. Students find d___________ of words is hard to memorize.

25. P__________ means the act of pirates.

26. Miss Jane is p__________ as a gentle beautiful lady of Victorian times.

27. I b_______ Thomas will be late again. because he is always late for any appointment.

28. Passengers need to go through security check before they b________ the airplane.

29. Some animals do not e_________ any longer, such as dinosaurs.

30. Those books are p________ of the library.

Passage 12

The Structure of Australian Governments

As Australia became a federation in 1901, so the Australian governments are composed of three levels of governments—the federal, the state and the local governments.

Australia is a democratic country, which is demonstrated by its citizens' voting right. Every adult Australian has a right to choose their political representative. Australia is a country of freedom. People can believe in different religions freely. They can be conservative or liberal in their political life. Voters can choose several candidates in a general election of these governments. Candidates come from different walks of life, like medical or legal professions. The latest federal election occurred in 2016, and the next one will commence in 2019.

There are two major national parties in Australia. One needs to defeat the other to become the governing party of the nation. Upon declaring the ruling party of Australia, the other party automatically becomes the opposing party. Politicians in both parties promise to make policies that please the majority of voters before election. They often debate about the effectiveness of their policies.

At the local level, city councils manage the running of basic facilities in the city, such as museum, gallery and stadiums. So common citizens have more dealing with the local government than with the State or Federal government.

必备词汇：

名词

federation [ˈfedəreɪʃən] 联邦

voting [ˈvəʊtɪŋ] 选举

adult [ˈædʌlt] 成年人

effectiveness [əˈfektɪvnɪs] 有效

representative [ˌreprɪˈzentətɪv] 代

表人

freedom [ˈfriːdəm] 自由

religion [rɪˈlɪdʒən] 宗教信仰

conservative [kənˈsɜːvətɪv] 保守的

liberal [ˈlɪbərəl] 自由主义者

state [stet] 国家

candidate [ˈkændɪdeɪt] 候选人

profession [prəˈfeʃ(ə)n] 职业

policy [ˈpɒləsɪ] 政策

running [ˈrʌnɪŋ] 运营

facility [fəˈsɪlətɪ] 设施

gallery [ˈgælərɪ] 画廊

stadium [ˈstedɪəm] 体育场

dealing [diːlɪŋ] 打交道

动词

demonstrate [ˈdemənstreɪt] 展示

occur [əˈkɝ] 发生

commence [kəˈmɛns] 开始

defeat [dɪˈfiːt] 击败

please [pliːz] 使……高兴

debate [dɪˈbeɪt] 辩论

manage [ˈmænɪdʒ] 管理

形容词

federal [ˈfedərəl] 联邦的

democratic [deməˈkrætɪk] 民主的

political [pəˈlɪtɪkl] 政治的

conservative [kənˈsəːvətɪv] 保守的人

liberal [ˈlɪbərəl] 自由主义的

several [ˈsɛvrəl] 几个的

national [ˈnæʃənəl] 国家的；全国的

governing [ˈgʌvənɪŋ] 统治的

ruling [ˈruːlɪŋ] 掌权的

automatic [ˌɔːtəˈmætɪk] 自动的

opposing [əˈpozɪŋ] 反对的

副词

freely [ˈfriːlɪ] 自由地

automatically [ɔːtəˈmætɪklɪ] 自动地

短语

general election 大选

different walks of life 各行各业

voting right 选举权

city council 市政府

B aeas 7—9

Passage 12 配套单词填空练习

1. All other p____________ parties there have been completely banned.

2. For s__________ years, he had no home.

3. The book he most wanted to write was the one which nearly d__________ him.

4. The small countries joined together into a f_________.

5. He is a c__________ for the office of Governor.

6. Let us move forward, then, into a new era of openness, e__________ and accountability.

7. The little girl c__________ to cry when she saw the snake.

8. The s_________ is being used for a match.

9. I admire those who are honest, l____________, and considerate.

10. The attitude of the medical p________ is very much more liberal now.

11. The performances will c___________ in a minute.

12. There are many r___________ in the world.

13. He only applied for a job as a branch manager with Hertz to p___________ his mother.

14. I have a friend who has the o______________ view and felt that the war was immoral.

15. A d______________ country, government, or political system is governed by representatives who are elected by the people.

16. The government alternated between the Labour and C__________ parties.

17. Should Catalonia be a s________? And should that s________ be independent?

18. My policy just says their r________________ will help you.

19. Humans should cherish the f_________ of education for everyone.

20. That is a n___________ contest, and the best players from every part of the country will compete in the contest.

21. Mr. Johnson is a c______________, so he always prefers not to make changes in his life.

22. The r___________ party makes policies to govern the country.

23. Birds fly f_________ in the sky.

24. Tom just bought an a_____________car, and he said it was easier to handle than the manual one.

25. The v__________ for student representatives will commence next week.

26. A________ users can download the apps without a prior permission from parents.

27. The park is equipped with new play f____________ for children.

28. My math teacher just d___________ that hard question for us yesterday, but I forgot the most important part.

29. The USA is also a f_________ country.

30. The ticket for the modern art g_________ is 30 dollars.

Passage 13

Unexpected Assembly

Today, we got an urgent notice from the notice board. It required all students to assemble in the hall at noon. Upon the clock turning 12 in the afternoon, the hall was packed with curious students. The principal rushed onto the stage and indicated all students to be quiet.

The principal puffed and announced loudly, "An incident just happened in this morning's surfing class. A student nearly drowned, but it's lucky that he was rescued in time." All students then became silent and a terribly sick feeling arose in my stomach.

The Principal sweep all of us with his cold eyes, and went on, "the student is currently in hospital and will be discharged tomorrow. The teachers on scene will soon review the safety procedures and produce a report shortly. However, we have to cancel the original plan for your surfing class tomorrow. We are investigating the drowning causes. So far, no one complained anything about the surfing class, but apparently, you are not allowed to do any water sports until our student's safety procedure has been reviewed."

The principal paused for a second and then continued, "I hope you be mindful that the weather conditions at the seaside can be complex. Weather can change dramatically even without you noticing it, so when you are in the water, please keep constant alert to the change of weather condition. Today's incident is considerably distressing to both parents and school executive officers. But I hope it will not distract you from your normal life."

Then the principal dismissed the assembly. We felt so disappointed by the unexpected news. With a deep sigh, we gradually walked out of the hall and returned to the classroom.

必备词汇：

名词

assembly [əˈsembli] 集会；集合
hall [hɔ:l] 大厅
stage [steɪdʒ] 舞台；讲台
incident [ˈɪnsɪdənt] 突发事件
executive [ɪgˈzekjʊtɪv] 执行官
officer [ˈɔfɪsə(r)] 官员
principal [prɪnsɪpəl] 校长
sigh [saɪ] 叹气
cause [kɔ:z] 起因

动词

announce [əˈnaʊns] 宣布
assemble [əˈsɛmbl] 集合
indicate [ˈɪndɪkeɪt] 指示
puff [pʌf] 喘气
drown [draʊn] 溺水
rescue [ˈrɛskju:] 营救
arise [əˈraɪz] 出现 (arose, arisen)
sweep [swi:p] 扫除
pause [pɔ:z] 暂停
continue [kəntɪnju:] 继续
discharge [dɪsˈtʃɑ:dʒ] 出院
review [riˈvju:] 复查；检验
produce [prəˈdju:s] 出具；生产
cancel [ˈkænsəl] 取消
investigate [ɪnˈvestɪgeɪt] 调查
complain [kəmˈpleɪn] 投诉；抱怨
distract [dɪˈstrækt] 分心
dismiss [dɪsˈmɪs] 解散
disappoint [ˌdɪsəˈpɔɪnt] 使……失望
pack [pæk] 包装；塞满
rush [rʌʃ] 冲；奔

形容词

unexpected [ʌnɪkˈspektɪd] 意外的
urgent [ɜ:ˈdʒənt] 紧急的
mindful [ˈmaindfl] 深切注意的；切记的
considerable [kənˈsɪd(ə)rəb(ə)l] 相当大(或多)的
constant [kɒnstənt] 持续不断的
original [əˈrɪdʒənəl] 原本的
apparent [əˈpærənt] 明显的
dramatic [drəˈmætɪk] 戏剧性的；激动人心的
distressing [dɪˈstrɛsɪŋ] 使人痛苦的
normal [ˈnɔ:məl] 正常的
complex [ˈkɒmpleks] 复杂的

副词

shortly [ˈʃɔ:tlɪ] 很快
dramatically [drəˈmætɪkəlɪ] 剧烈地

apparently [əˈpærəntlɪ] 显然地

considerably [kənˈsɪdərəblɪ] 很；非常

短语

at noon 中午

be packed with 挤满了……

in time 及时

on scene 在现场的

rush onto 冲上……

notice board 告示板

Passage 13 配套单词填空练习

1. It a__________ out of very particular circumstances in the development of the Internet.
2. He made a brief, u__________ appearance at the office.
3. The owner of the shop was s__________ his floor when I walked in.
4. An e__________ is someone who is employed by a business at a senior level. Executives decide what the business should do, and ensure that it is done.
5. Peter a__________ that he had no intention of wasting his time at any university.
6. He was given a conditional d__________ and ordered to pay Miss Smith $500 compensation.
7. It took r__________ 90 minutes to reach the trapped men.
8. All the people a__________ at Mary's house.
9. If someone, especially an official, i__________ an event or a claim, they try to find out what happened or what is the truth.
10. Doing it properly makes c__________ demands on our time.
11. Tom admits that playing video games sometimes d__________ him from his homework.
12. In consequence he was d__________ from his post.
13. It is very d__________ to see your baby attached to tubes and monitors.

14. Today we drill to a___________ in a clear square near the building as if there is an emergency of fire.

15. Henry p_______ when he runs, because he is a bit fat.

16. It is easy to d________ near the water, if you don't know how to swim.

17. The flight to Sydney is c____________ due to the stormy weather.

18. Our o_________ plan is to visit Gold Coast in January, but we have to put it off as my husband became ill recently.

19. There is a_____________ sadness on her face.

20. Being stuck in the traffic can be d_________ when you are rushing to catch a flight.

21. The business runs according to n_______ office hours.

22. The bus is p________ ________ eager swimmers who are longing to get to the beach.

23. Some customers have c_______________ about the poor battery of the phones.

24. Students can easily be d___________ by noise when they are in class.

25. The police officer i_________ the driver to pull over at the road.

26. without p________ for a second, the speaker continues on and on for two hours.

27. You don't need to r________, as the bus will not come in ten minutes.

28. The police officers o______________ commenced the preliminary investigation.

29. Their help just came i______ _________.

30. That incident is quite c___________, so I guess it will take long time to investigate.

Passage 14

Brief Guidelines on Reading Classic Novels

Year 8 students are asked to read English classic novels, and to write a text response essay accordingly. There are many authors with great fame, so students have many options. Once you gain knowledge of elements of a successful novel, you can appreciate the novels deeply.

Some authors like Charles Dickens constructed novels in a clever way, so readers can easily follow the actions or conversations of the characters in the novel. Novels are a special way to reflect conflict in reality. For example, fighting with enemy is reflected as a physical or verbal conflict, while struggling in a difficult situation is reflected as environmental conflict.

When you understand the types of conflicts, you can confidently interpret the actions and minds of characters in the novel. Authors usually adopt creative ways to express their understanding of the society. It can be the crash between poor people and the officials. It can be collision between the innovative minds with the traditional culture.

Authors unwrap their opinions on the society through their characters and plots of the story. That's why some people comment that novel is a subtle description of the real life. When you are equipped with this general knowledge, I believe many students will enjoy classic novels more.

必备词汇：

名词

guideline [ˈgaɪdlaɪn] 指南
novel [ˈnɑvl] 小说
essay [ˈeseɪ] 议论文
author [ˈɔθɚ] 作者
fame [fem] 名声
option [ˈɒpʃən] 选项
knowledge [ˈnɒlɪdʒ] 知识
element [ˈelɪmənt] 元素
conversation [kɒnvəˈseɪʃ(ə)n] 交谈

character [ˈkærəktər] 角色；个性
conflict [ˈkɑnflɪkt] 冲突
reality [rɪˈælətɪ] 现实
type [taɪp] 类型
collision [kəˈlɪʒən] 碰撞
crash [kræʃ] 碰撞

动词

gain [geɪn] 获得
appreciate [əˈpriːʃieɪt] 欣赏
interpret [ɪnˈtɝprɪt] 理解；解释
construct [kənˈstrʌkt] 建立
follow [ˈfɔləu] 跟随；遵守
express [ɪkˈspres] 表达
unwrap [ʌnˈræp] 打开
comment [ˈkɔment] 评论

形容词

brief [briːf] 简要的
classic [ˈklæsɪk] 经典的
physical [ˈfɪzɪkəl] 身体的；物理的
verbal [ˈvɜːbəl] 言语的
environmental [ɪnˌvaɪərənˈmentl] 环境
innovative [ˈinəuveitɪv] 创新的
subtle [ˈsʌtl] 微妙的
classical [ˈklæsɪkl] 经典的

副词

accordingly [əˈkɔrdɪŋlɪ] 相应地
confidently [ˈkɔnfədəntlɪ] 确信地

短语

be equipped with 具备

Passage 14 配套单词填空练习

1. I'd a____________ any information you could give me.
2. If you i____________ something in a particular way, you decide that this is its meaning or significance.
3. We must try to minimize e____________ degradation.
4. That was really i____________, from a stylistic point of view.
5. The plane was completely burnt out after the c____________.
6. A n____________ is a long written story about imaginary people and events.
7. We have a different background, a different history. A____________, we have the right to different futures.
8. Something that is s____________ is not immediately obvious or noticeable.

9. I can c______________ say that my Chinese and English are pretty good.

10. If you have a c____________ with someone, you talk with them, usually in an informal situation.

11. Haruki Murakami is Japan's best-selling a___________.

12. Did you enjoy c_______________ music even when you were very young?

13. The novel is c________________ from a series of on-the-spot reports.

14. If you achieve f______________, you become very well-known.

15. They have come into c____________, sometimes violently.

16. They were on their way to the airport when their van was involved in a c_____________ with a car.

17. Our club is very welcoming, so everyone can e________ their ideas freely.

18. Students will be tested on their k_____________ base and skills along their secondary education.

19. The plots of the thriller story are u__________ in a very clever way.

20. There is always dilemma between the r__________ and the dream.

21. With a b___________ self-introduction, our new English teacher started her first lesson.

22. The scenic site provides free camping g__________ to non-local tourists.

23. I've got an e______ to finish by this weekend.

24. Students can g____ practical knowledge through observing adults doing things.

25. What would you c__________ on the new movie *The Grinch*?

26. *Harry Potter* has become c_________ novels in 20 years.

27. What other o__________ do we have but accepting the election result?

28. These two guys had v_________ disputes a couple of minutes ago.

29. The c______________ called Scrooge in the book *A Christmas Carol* is very famous as the book was written by Charles Dickens.

30. Citizens should f_______ the law and rule of their own countries.

Passage 15

Career Path

Year 10 students often receive handy advice on career path at school, because Year 11 is a critical point in their life to determine which path they will take in the following years. Although our society advocates diversity of careers, but we also understand it is not an easy decision to make.

Some students want to go to college and learn skills, while some students endeavor to go to university to pursue higher education. Although the number of students wishing to go to college has doubled, university goers still dominate the total number of students in most high schools.

Students who want to receive formal training of skills will be streamed to colleges or training institutes, while other students need to sit university entrance exams to get into university. Our school will guide students to prepare the entrance exams.

Meanwhile, our school will hold information night regularly for TAFE courses. Those who want to better sharpen practical skills are welcomed to join the night.

必备词汇：

名词

advice [əd'vaɪs] 建议
career [kə'rɪr] 职业
path [pɑ:θ] 道路
diversity [daɪ'vɜ:sətɪ] 多样性
college ['kɒlɪdʒ] 大专学院
institute ['ɪnstɪtut] 学院
endeavor [ɛn'dɛvɚ] 努力
training ['trenɪŋ] 训练
course [kɔ:s] 课程

动词

receive [rɪ'si:v] 收到
determine [dɪ'tɝmɪn] 决定
advocate ['ædvəkeɪt] 倡导

endeavour [enˈdevər] 努力尝试

pursue [pəˈsjuː] 追求

double [ˈdʌbəl] 翻倍

dominate [ˈdɒmɪneɪt] 支配

stream [striːm] 分流；导向

guide [gaɪd] 指导

hold [həuld] 举行 (held)

sharpen [ˈʃɑːpən] 打磨

形容词

handy [ˈhændɪ] 现成的；方便的

critical [ˈkrɪtɪkl] 关键的

following [ˈtrenɪŋ] 接着的

formal [ˈfɔːməl] 正式的

副词

meanwhile [ˈmiːnwaɪl] 同时

regularly [ˈregjələlɪ] 定期地

短语

higher education 高等教育

sit an exam 参加考试

Passage 15 配套单词填空练习

1. The incident happened at a c____________ point in the campaign.
2. Actually, my coaching c____________ has been much more rewarding than my running c_________, he stated.
3. An i____________ is an organization set up to do a particular type of work, especially research or teaching.
4. They will post the ticket to me as soon as they r______________ my cheque.
5. I enrolled for a t______________ session for therapists as my professional development course.
6. They not only make it possible for us to do this but make it a great e__________ due to their support.
7. The investigation will d________________ what has really happened.
8. The book is expected to d______________ the best-seller lists, which means it will be the bester seller for a really long time.
9. The Education Department endeavours to s___________ young people to appropriate career paths that match their talents.
10. He called for much higher spending on education and t_____________.

11. Some environmentalists a__________ not to use plastic products in our daily life.

12. When we are young, we should e_____________ to make positive contribution to our society.

13. If you truly p_______ your dream, you should not give up easily.

14. The number of Chinese tourists has d__________ till the end of this year, namely, twice of last year's number.

15. Tomorrow's conference is a f________ occasion, so attendees are required to dress according to the business attire.

16. College students are required to s_______ final exams during November.

17. My neighbo(u)r, Mr. Tod, often offers me h_______ tips on how to excel on surfing.

18. Students need to s________ their writing skills when they start persuasive writing.

19. The international technology conference will be h________ in Shanghai.

20. Do you need any one to g________ through your visit of the museum?

21. Ms. Thornell attends a local public speaking club r________.

22. There will be flood if a river r________ too much water.

23. Trinity c________ is a famous school in Melbourne.

24. Those who will s_______ the scholarship exam will receive notice shortly.

25. There is more than one p________ to success. You just need to try your best.

26. Cultural d_________ is highly appreciated in Australia, that is, different cultures are valued highly.

Passage 16

Exam Tips

As the academic officer of the school, I'm more than happy to give you some useful tips when you are cracking exams as the term approaches the end. I know that you are under much pressure at the time of reviewing your notes. Please don't feel upset if you have a pile of notes to go through in the limited period of time. Here are my tips to help you prioritize your study load.

First, create your study environment. No matter if you prefer to study alone or in a group, find a comfortable place with sufficient light.

Second, draw up an exam timetable, and set aside a specific time each day for study, and divide that time into several time slots, for example half hour or one-hour slot; but your time slot should not be too chunky, like two hours for each slot.

Third, make your study interesting. You can keep some variety in your schedule. For example, you can study a difficult subject one day, then move forward to an easier one the next day.

Fourth, ask for help if you get stuck for complicated questions. You can ask your parents, classmates, even online study specialists. You can have a discussion with your teacher too.

Fifth, take regular break. For every half hour of study and concentration, give your brain a short rest. You can stretch your body or stare out the window to get relaxed.

Sixth, reward yourself with a treat after you finish each study session. You can play a game, watch some funny video or chat with friends.

I hope you will find these tips handy and useful. And I wish you success in your final exams.

必备词汇：

名词

tip [tɪp] 小建议；小费

note [nəut] 笔记

period [ˈpɪərɪəd] 时期

load [ləʊd] 负担

slot [slɑt] 时间段

variety [vəˈraɪətɪ] 多样；种类

schedule [ˈʃedju:l] 时间表

concentration [kɒns(ə)nˈtreɪʃ(ə)n] 专心

timetable [ˈtaɪmteɪb(ə)l] 时间表

treat [tri:t] 款待

动词

crack [kræk] 攻克；裂开

approach [əˈprəʊtʃ] 接近

review [rɪˈvju:] 复习

prioritize [praɪˈɔrɪtaɪz] 把……区分优先次序

prefer [prɪˈfɜ:r] 更喜欢

divide [dɪˈvaɪd] 分开

stretch [strɛtʃ] 伸展

stare [stɛr] 凝视

reward [rɪˈwɔrd] 报酬

vary [ˈveərɪ] 改变；变化

形容词

academic [ˌækəˈdemɪk] 学术的

useful [ˈju:sfəl] 有用的

upset [ʌpˈset] 心烦的；苦恼的

limited [ˈlɪmɪtɪd] 有限的

stuck [stʌk] 被卡住的

sufficient [səˈfɪʃnt] 足够的

chunky [ˈtʃʌŋkɪ] 大块的

complicated [ˈkɒmplɪkeɪtɪd] 结构复杂的

handy [ˈhændɪ] 便利的

various [ˈveəriəs] 各种各样的

副词

alone [əˈləun] 独自

短语

a pile of 大量

go through 检查；浏览

study load 学习负担

draw up 制定

set aside 留出

Passage 16 配套单词填空练习

1. Don't pour hot water into the glass or it will c__________.

2. If you p____________ the tasks that you have to do, you decide which are the most important and do them first.

3. Neal kept interrupting, breaking my c______________.

4. You see I feel I don't have s______________ background information.

5. How do you r______________ if he's testing your general knowledge?

6. I don't mind fitting my t_____________ round yours.

7. If you t_____________ someone or something in a particular way, you behave toward them or deal with them in that way.

8. If you say that something is c_____________, you mean it has so many parts or aspects that it is difficult to understand or deal with.

9. A______________ is used to describe things that relate to schools, colleges, and universities.

10. Try s_______________ your legs and pulling your toes upwards.

11. The book gives h________________ hints on looking after indoor plants.

12. Tamara s________________ at him in disbelief, shaking her head.

13. I wanted to r_____________ them with a treat.

14. I s___________ a stamp on the letter.

15. The boat was s____________ fast in the mud.

16. Visitors can book a time s_________________ a week or more in advance.

17. A p_____________ of things is a mass of them that is high in the middle and has sloping sides.

18. As spring a____________, the snow on the mountain cap begins melting.

19. Young children can learn to speak a foreign language just in a short p_________ of time.

20. You'd better d_______ _______ a plan before you set off for exploration in Africa.

21. Instead of surfing, I p_________ to watch movie in the cinema.

Passage 17

Food Shortage and Food Security

We seem to live in affluent society. But do you know that many people still face food shortage. The food harvested from farms is not always adequate to feed all people in the world.

Although humans have invented advanced technology, many crops still fail due to extreme weather, such as drought or flood. In modern agriculture, many technologies are used in agriculture to promote crop productivity and farming methods are largely innovated. But humans still cannot handle the impact of climate or extreme weathers on crops. For example, humans cannot control when flood will happen, or where a hurricane will make a landfall.

In spite of all the development of technology, farming is still mostly affected by the nature. Therefore, some agricultural countries like USA and China invest a large amount of money on inventing new breeds of crops that can resist extreme weathers. They believe they can derive seeds capable of resisting drought through numerous experiments. They hope to introduce these innovated seeds to the market soon.

必备词汇：

<u>名词</u>

shortage [ˈʃɔrtɪdʒ] 不足

security [sɪˈkjʊərətɪ] 安全

crop [krɑp] 农作物

drought [drɑut] 干旱

flood [flʌd] 洪水

agriculture [ˈægrɪkʌltʃər] 农业

productivity [ˌprɒdʌkˈtɪvətɪ] 生产力

hurricane [ˈhʌrɪkən] 飓风

climate [ˈklaɪmət] 气候

landfall [ˈlændfɔ:l]（风暴）登陆

technology [tekˈnɒlədʒɪ] 科技

development [dɪˈveləpm(ə)nt] 发展

breed [bri:d] 品种
seed [si:d] 种子
experiment [ɪkˈsperɪmənt] 实验
farming [ˈfa:mɪŋ] 农耕

动词

harvest [ˈhɑ:vɪst] 收获
feed [fi:d] 喂养
promote [prəˈməʊt] 提升
invent [ɪnˈvɛnt] 发明
resist [rɪˈzɪst] 抵抗
derive [dɪˈraɪv] 得到
introduce [ˌɪntrəˈdju:s] 引进

形容词

advanced [ədˈvɑ:nst] 高级的
affluent [ˈæfluənt] 富裕的
adequate [ˈædəkwət] 充足的
extreme [ɪkˈstri:m] 极端的
agricultural [ˌægrɪˈkʌltʃərəl] 农业的
capable [ˈkepəbl] 能胜任的
numerous [ˈnju:mərəs] 许多

副词

largely [ˈla:dʒlɪ] 大部分;主要地
mostly [ˈməustlɪ] 大部分

短语

a large amount of 大量的
impact on 冲击力;影响力

Passage 17 配套单词填空练习

1. The kitchen is c___________ of catering for several hundred people.
2. They're also fairly wealthy and a_____________ and all these other sorts of things.
3. A_____________ is also the oldest industry in the world.
4. If you r____________ something such as a change, you refuse to accept it and try to prevent it.
5. She was p___________ into some kind of managerial job.
6. Scientific inventions such as these have raised labour p____________ by a big margin.
7. He questions meant to plant s___________of doubts in the minds of jurors.
8. They should be allowed to wait for cheaper t______________ to be

developed.

9. Edison i__________ the light bulb.

10. Most of us d__________ pleasure from treating ourselves nicely.

11. Block d____________ around doors and windows.

12. Such schemes mean little unless they i_____________ on people.

13. Vietnam is suffering from food s_____________.

14. D_____________ is the growth of something such as a business or an industry.

15. More than 70 people were killed in the f_____________, caused when a dam burst.

16. The c___________ was ready to be reaped and garnered.

17. Samsung has i__________ a new model of mobile phone to the market recently.

18. That new b_______ of peach is not sour but purely sweet.

19. Without a_________ food and water, we cannot survive for long.

20. People with e__________ behaviours can be very dangerous.

21. There are n__________ stars in the sky, so I think it will be a sunny day tomorrow.

22. A large a___________ of money was spent on improving living condition of refugees.

23. Cherry is usually h_________ in summer.

24. The hurricane made l__________ near Japan.

25. Scientist can obtain data from numerous e___________.

26. The election result l__________ depends on the NSW voters.

27. Currently, scientists and environmentalists are concerned with the issue of c_________ change.

Passage 18

Games That Are Good for Our Brain

There are countless games that claim to beneficial for the brain. One typical example is a game app called Lumosity. It is comprised of several areas that users can choose to practice, for example, memory consolidation, speed reading and problem solving. Playing such games can boost people's mental health, which means their brains can work better. It is found by researchers that people's short memory can be enhanced with daily memory exercise.

Besides, playing games also help reduce considerable stress that is accumulated along a hectic day. Too much stress is harmful to people's mental health, so they should relieve themselves from it. Several researches have examined the players of brain games, and found that their tension level is lower than average people, especially, those who play the games daily.

Doctors often recommend such brain games to elderly, who are threatened by the risk of memory loss. Memory loss is the fuel of function loss of the brain. So it is critical to slow down the process of memory loss. One possible way is to exercise people's brains, just like they exercising their bodies. So no matter what your age is, you can play some brain games to enhance your brain function.

必备词汇：

名词

area [ˈeəriə] 区域;领域

consolidation[kənˌsɒlɪˈdeɪʃən] 巩固

brain [brein] 大脑

researcher [rɪˈsɜːtʃər] 研究者

exercise [ˈeksəsaɪz] 练习

stress [stres] 压力

tension [ˈtɛnʃən] 紧张

fuel [ˈfjuəl] 燃料

function [ˈfʌŋkʃən] 功能
researcher [rɪˈsətʃə] 调查者
loss [lɒs] 丧失;损失

动词

claim [kleɪm] 声称
comprise [kəmˈpraɪz] 包含
practice [ˈpræktɪs] 练习
boost [bʊst] 促进
enhance [ɪnˈhæns] 提高
reduce [rɪˈdju:s] 减少
accumulate [əˈkju:mjʊleɪt] 堆积
relieve [rɪˈlɪv] 解除
examine [ɪgˈzæmɪn] 调查
recommend [rekəˈmend] 推荐
threaten [ˈθrɛtn] 威胁
lose [lu:z] 丧失(lost)

形容词

countless [ˈkaʊntləs] 多得数不清的
beneficial [ˌbenɪˈfɪʃəl] 有益的
typical [ˈtɪpɪkəl] 典型的
mental [ˈmɛntl] 精神的
daily [ˈdeɪlɪ] 每天的
considerable [kənˈsɪd(ə)rəb(ə)l] 相当大
hectic [ˈhektɪk] 忙乱的
harmful [ˈhɑ:mfəl] 有害的
elderly [ˈeldəlɪ] 老年的
possible [ˈpɒsəbəl] 可能的

副词

besides [bɪˈsaidz] 另外

短语

be comprised of 由……组成
slow down 放慢;减缓
short memory 短期记忆
memory loss 记忆丧失

Passage 18 配套单词填空练习

1. An e______________ patient was sitting in her wheelchair; she looks like in her 70s.
2. The company is b______________ a new product.
3. The t______________ between the two countries is likely to remain.
4. To e______________ something means to improve its value, quality, or attractiveness.
5. M____________ means relating to the process of thinking.

6. Twelve departments c______________ this university.

7. So she chooses to be a r____________ at a lab and is very happy with her work.

8. You use e_____________ as a polite way of saying that someone is old.

9. F___________ is a substance such as coal, oil, or petrol that is burned to provide heat or power.

10. But unlike China, he will spend money too liberally to a_____________ much wealth.

11. I just spent a holiday there and would r______________ it to anyone.

12. There was a c______________ lapse of time between the two events.

13. He said army officers had t______________to destroy the town.

14. The medicine manufacturers c_______ that they have found a cure for some cancers.

15. Driving less can r_________ air pollution.

16. The new study aims to e___________ the causal relationship between smoking and lung cancer.

17. What's your d______ routine?

18. One b_____________ effect of laughing is that it lifts our mood.

19. What is p_________ worst result that you can expect?

20. Most modern people are living a h______ lifestyle.

21. Which a_______ in science are you interested in, chemistry or physics?

22. The function of memory may be l_________ when people aging.

23. Smoking is h_________ for health. That's why the government taxes the sale of tabaco.

24. C____________ of knowledge takes long time.

25. A landscape of red desert is a t___________ landscape of the outback of Australia.

26. Memory loss can be s________ _______ if we exercise our brains every day.

Passage 19

Popularity of Social Media

As a widespread social media, Wechat is often compared with Facebook. Individuals treat social media as a powerful channel to promote their personal brands, while companies see social media as an effective platform for publishing their advertisement.

Most individuals prefer online social media to print media such as newspapers, because they think social media can reach more potential customers or clients. Individuals mainly compete for followers. The more followers they attract, the wider their posts will be spread.

Similar to individuals, companies take all efforts to attract followers. Advertising via social media reforms the traditional advertising ways. Companies rely on advertising to expand their businesses.

Some people distribute false information on social media to draw attention, but that attention will not sustain for long time.

Ordinary users should be careful to make sensible comments on social media. If not, improper words may cause disputes. Disputes can damage a person's image. That's the drawback of using social media as an advertising tool.

必备词汇:

名词

popularity [ˌpɒpjəˈlærətɪ] 流行
individual [ˌɪndɪˈvɪdʒuəl] 个人
channel [ˈtʃænl] 渠道;海峡
brand [brænd] 品牌
reach [riːtʃ] 范围;可及的范围
platform [ˈplætfɔːm] 月台
advertisement [ədˈvɜːtɪzm(ə)nt] 广告
customer [ˈkʌstəmər] 顾客
client [ˈklaɪənt] 客户
follower [ˈfɒləuə] 追随者

drawback [ˈdrɔbæk] 缺点
dispute [dɪˈspju:t] 争议
image [ˈɪmɪdʒ] 形象

动词
compare [kəmˈpeər] 比较
publish [ˈpʌblɪʃ] 发布；出版
reach [ri:tʃ] 达到
expand [ɪkˈspænd] 扩张
compete [kəmˈpi:t] 竞争
sustain [səˈsten] 维持
distribute [dɪˈstrɪbju:t] 散布
draw [drɔ:] 吸引
damage [ˈdæmɪdʒ] 损害

形容词
widespread [ˈwaɪdspred] 广泛流行的
powerful [ˈpaʊəfʊl] 强大的
effective [ɪˈfektɪv] 有效的
potential [pə(ʊ)ˈtenʃ(ə)l] 潜在的
false [fɒls] 虚假的
ordinary [ˈɔ:dənərɪ] 普通的
sensible [ˈsensɪb(ə)l] 明智的
comparison [kəmˈpærɪsn] 比较

副词
via [ˈvaɪə] 通过

短语
take effort to 努力
social media 社交媒体
draw attention 吸引注意

Passage 19 配套单词填空练习

1. But how do you create and p__________ an e-book?
2. If you say that an example of something is an a______________ for that thing in general, you mean that it shows how good that thing is.
3. The Americans recognize that the U.N. can be the c________________ for greater diplomatic activity.
4. The train at P_________ 2 goes to the city.
5. A d_____________ is an aspect of something or someone that makes them less acceptable than they would otherwise be.
6. If someone is b_______________ as something bad, people think they are that thing.

7. The society e______________ into a worldwide organization.

8. He s______________ your objection to our questioning.

9. The company has identified 60 p_____________ customers.

10. She was a s_______________ girl and did not panic.

11. We wanted to know how w________________ this problem was.

12. The Internet is p__________ tool for learning, because you can find all kinds of knowledge there.

13. Some wise men said our world is full of o__________ people.

14. You can easily find f__________ news on the Internet, so you need to distinguish truth from falsity.

15. The local people are regular c__________ to the restaurant.

16. The emergency team has t________ all e________ to save the life of the injured man.

17. Internet users all have online i__________, which can be positive or negative.

18. That kind of wealth is out of most people's r_________.

19. These four teams need to c___________ against each other to win a place in the semi-final.

20. My reading task is to c_________ two poetries and list their similarities.

21. Most pop stars have millions of f_________.

22. When there is a d_________ , it is better to seek a third-party assistance in resolving the dispute.

23. The Pokemon has gained p____________ quickly among young players.

24. Both i_____________ and companies are bound by cyber law when using the Internet.

25. That medicine is e_________ for treating hair loss.

26. You can renew the book v_________ online library service.

Passage 20

Same Festival, Different Celebrations

The New Year Day is celebrated in the whole world in different ways. In China, The New Year Day is celebrated according to the lunar year. Contrarily, Japan and western countries celebrate it on the first of January of calendar year.

All of the celebrations are wrapped in tradition. It is a tradition for Chinese to exchange gifts between friends. Chinese people believe this is a blissful way to maintain friendship.

The other Chinese tradition is to host a wonderful gathering dinner with family on the New Year Eve. The family member with greater social status usually takes charge of the gathering, because the annual dinner has a significant meaning to Chinese people. Another Chinese tradition is dragon parade on the street. Dragon is a symbol of energy and fortune in the Chinese culture.

In the first half month of the new year, Chinese spend time with their family and look forward to the beginning of a new year. New year festival is an ideal time to make new year resolutions to encourage themselves. When the New Year arrives, they laugh a lot to bring good luck. Then they enjoy traditional food and drinks.

However, Japanese people have different forms of celebration. It usually begins with the ringing of bells for 108 times. Japanese also like hanging paper lobsters, as lobsters represent happy, long life in Japanese culture. People also play fireworks to wish a bright future.

No matter how people celebrate the New Year, I love this festival.

必备词汇：

名词

calendar [ˈkæləndər] 日历

celebration [ˌseliˈbreiʃn] 庆祝活动

tradition [trəˈdɪʃən] 传统

gathering [ˈgæðərɪŋ] 团聚

status [ˈstetəs] 地位;状况

meaning [ˈminɪŋ] 意义

lobster [ˈlɑbstə] 龙虾

fireworks [ˈfaɪrˌwə:ks] 烟火

parade [pəˈred] 游行

symbol [ˈsɪmbəl] 象征

fortune [ˈfɔrtʃən] 运气

resolution [ˌrezəˈlu:ʃən] 决心

form [fɔ:m] 形式

time [taim] 次(可数名词)

firework [ˈfaiəwɜ:k] 烟花

动词

wrap [ræp] 包

celebrate [ˈselɪbreɪt] 庆祝

exchange [ɪksˈtʃeɪndʒ] 交换

maintain [meɪnˈteɪn] 保持

encourage [ɪnˈkʌrɪdʒ] 鼓励

host [host] 当主人招待

arrive [əˈraɪv] 到达

resolve [rɪˈzɒlv] 下决心;解决

form [fɔ:m] 形成

形容词

lunar [ˈlu:nə] 月的

blissful [ˈblɪsfəl] 极快乐的;有福的

significant [sɪgˈnɪfɪk(ə)nt] 重要的

ideal [aɪˈdɪəl] 理想的

bright [braɪt] 光亮的

significance [sɪgˈnɪfɪk(ə)ns] 重要的

副词

contrarily [ˈkɔntrərili] 相反地

短语

according to 根据

take charge of 主持

look forward to 期待

lunar year 农历年

calendar year 公历年

gathering dinner 团年饭

dragon parade 舞狮

Passage 20 配套单词填空练习

1. While the Swedish birds also died after a f__________ event, he said, mass

B aeas 7 | 9

die-offs are more likely connected to disease or weather.

2. When things aren't going well, he e______________ me, telling me not to give up.

3. A l__________ is a sea creature that has a hard shell, two large claws, and eight legs.

4. They are celebrating the end of their school days with a p__________.

5. The c_____________ of Christmas is a custom.

6. It is also called the Spring Festival or the L__________ New Year.

7. Investors are starting to wonder how long their good f_____________ can last.

8. If you say that someone m____________ that something is true, you mean that they have stated their opinion strongly but not everyone agrees with them or believes them.

9. The m_____________ of the passage is obscure.

10. Keep your r______________, but go easy on yourself.

11. Most 11-year-olds are not encouraged to develop reading skills; a small but s____________ number are illiterate.

12. If someone h___________ a party, dinner, or other function, they have invited the guests and provide the food, drink, or entertainment.

13. Nurses are undervalued, and they never enjoy the same s______________ as doctors.

14. The b___________ headlights were highlighting the way, and I found her favourite CD.

15. Make sure you w___________ up in the cold wind.

16. C_____________, thinking space may be as small and narrow as the Greek philosophers thought it was.

17. As soon as the airplane a_______at the airport, passengers finally relieved from worry.

18. People often make r_____________ at the New Year, but few of them can

really realize them.

19. It is b________ that Jimmy made a new friend on his first day to school.

20. The supposed condition is i________, and it is rare to happen in the real life.

21.Can you double check the date with a c___________?

22. We can e_________ gifts at the coming Christmas party.

23. A________ _____ the newsletter to parents, students will be free from school on next Wednesday.

24. When shall we have a g________? We haven't seen each other for ages.

25. Countries with long history usually have many t_________.

26. The statue is a s__________ for freedom.

27. Our manager will t__________ _________ ___ the annual meeting this time.

28. We are l______ _______ ___ seeing you soon.

Passage 21

Diary about Field Trip

Last week, our class participated a field trip in the gold mining site. It was organized by our school with the local mining museum. The mission assigned to us is to learn the history and life of past miners.

In the morning, we signed up our presence at the supervising teacher, then we took a long bus ride to the site in Bendigo. Our first stop was to examine beautiful rocks exposed along the old mining slope in Bendigo. The old mining site is successfully transformed to a sightseeing spot. Then we walked along the trail leading to the mountain top, as no motor vehicles were allowed to drive up the trail.

At noon, we returned to the town square and had our lunch. After lunch, we visited the miner's museum. It revealed to us how miner's life was like. A museum officer, namely the curator, guided us through the display of stuffs and items commonly used among miners in 1860s in Victoria. Most miners had a dream to make a fortune in the gold rush. They worked diligently in the dark holes underground. Obviously, the living conditions of past miner's life was quite harsh. I could hardly identify faces of miners in the old photos, because their faces were covered with black ash from mining. However, after scanning the brief history of successful miners, I began to understand the pride of past poor miners who discovered a big gold mine at that time. Poor or rich, I thought all miners should be respected for having dreams in harsh situation.

Later, we took the same route to return to school. The long bus journey was boring. I had a brief discussion with my friends about this trip, and I intended to write an article for my school magazine.

必备词汇:

名词

diary [ˈdaɪərɪ] 日记

field [fi:ld] 田野

trip [trɪp] 行程;旅程

site [saɪt] 地点;现场

mission [ˈmɪʃən] 任务

miner [ˈmaɪnər] 矿工

presence [ˈprezəns] 到场

ride [raɪd] 一程;乘坐

stop [stɔp] 停靠站;站

sight [saɪt] 景物;视线

sightseeing [ˈsaɪtˌsi:ɪŋ] 观光

spot [spɒt] 地点;场所

underground [ˌʌndəˈgraʊnd] 地下

condition [kənˈdɪʃən] 条件;状况

mining [ˈmaɪnɪŋ] 矿业

trail [treɪl] 小径;痕迹

display [dɪˈsple] 展览

slope [sləʊp] 斜坡

motor [ˈməʊtər] 电机

vehicle [ˈvɪəkəl] 车辆

square [skweər] 广场

curator [kjʊˈreɪtər](展览馆)向导

display [dɪˈspleɪ] 展示

stuff [stʌf] 东西

item [ˈaɪtəm] 物品

ash [æʃ] 灰

pride [praɪd] 自豪感

route [ru:t] 路线

journey [ˈdʒɜ:nɪ] 旅程

discussion [dɪˈskʌʃn] 讨论

article [ˈɑ:tɪkəl] 文章

magazine [ˌmægəˈzi:n] 杂志

动词

participate [pɑ:ˈtɪsɪpeɪt] 参加

assign [əˈsaɪn] 指派;分配

supervise [ˈsu:pəvaɪz] 监督

expose [ɪkˈspəʊz] 暴露

reveal [rɪˈvi:l] 显示

transform [trænsˈfɔ:m] 改变

allow [əˈlaʊ] 允许

cover [ˈkʌvə] 覆盖

identify [aɪˈdentɪfaɪ] 识别

scan [skæn] 扫描;浏览

respec t[rɪˈspɛkt] 尊重

intend [ɪnˈtɛnd] 打算

discover [dɪˈskʌvər] 发现

discuss [dɪˈskʌs] 讨论

ride [raid] 骑(马/车)

形容词

local [ˈləukl] 当地的;本地的

past [pa:st] 过去的

sightseeing [ˈsaɪtsi:ɪŋ] 游览的

harsh [hɑrʃ] 严酷的;刺耳的;粗糙的

diligent ['dɪlɪdʒənt] 努力的；勤奋的

副词

commonly ['kɑmənlɪ] 一般地

namely ['neɪmlɪ] 也就是说

短语

make a fortune 发财

leading to 通向

field trip 实地考察旅行

exposure to 接触；暴露

living condition 生活条件

gold rush 黄金潮

sign up 签到

Passage 21 配套单词填空练习

1. Citizens have the right to know and to s________ the government through their political representatives.
2. The car could hardly get along on the s____________.
3. The pretty girl's ugly secret was r_____________.
4. If you go s__________ or do some s____________, you travel around visiting the interesting places that tourists usually visit.
5. I was though disappointed, but I r_____________ your decision.
6. Industrialization t________________ the world in a significant way.
7. He said many h______________ and unkind things about his opponents.
8. Department stores d________________ their goods in the windows.
9. His novel is a vivid portrayal of life in a m_____________ community.
10. I cannot i______________ the signature.
11. The underside of the rock was c____________ with seaweed.
12. This money is i______________ for the development of the tourist industry.
13. He was following a t_____________ through the woods.
14. When you r___________ a horse, you sit on it and control its movements.
15. A Task c_____________ requires more than one person to complete all of the work involved.

16. Year 10 students will go to a f______ _____ next week.

17. The m________ of the organisation is to help the elderly widows.

18. The p________ of new Major made audience excited.

19. The longer-term e________ to books can foster amazing reading habit among young children.

20. After a d________ with his group mates, Lucas began to draw up a plan for their group project.

21. D_________ students will be rewarded good results.

22. The living c_________ of English peasants were really terrible.

23. There are always legends about dwarfs living u_________, that is, below the surface of the Earth.

24. It is exactly his p_______ experience that led to his success today.

25. It is a good habit to keep a d_________.

26. A kind of eyeless fish was d____________ in Australia recently.

27. Visitors are advised to keep an eye on their valuable i____________.

28. The p_______ of being a veteran can be seen in the eyes of the old man.

29. Matthew Flinders conducted a j________ around the Australian coast to draw a map.

Passage 22

Getting Involved in Charity

Most charities do not run a business for profit. Instead, they have a special cause to promote social justice and equality. Charities often advocate the public to donate money to help people who are facing great strain in life; some of them was sacked from former employment, while others could not work due to chronic diseases or disability. We can't deny the fact that children in such families will suffer as well.

I once worked as a volunteer in a charity called Salvo. My job is to help tidy and sort out clothes donated by others. Many people will reject clothes out of fashion, though these clothes are still in good condition. Salvo collects rejected clothes and re-sell them at a cheap price. The money raised from the sale will be streamed to poor families to help them purchase daily essentials.

My experience enabled me to appreciate the hardship of some people, I also tasted the joy of being useful and helpful at a young age.

必备词汇：

名词

charity [ˈtʃærətɪ] 慈善

cause [kɔ:z] 事业

justice [ˈdʒʌstɪs] 正义

equality [ɪˈkwɒlətɪ] 平等

strain [stren] 压力

employment [ɪmˈplɔɪmənt] 职业；雇佣

disease [dɪˈzi:z] 疾病

hardship [ˈhɑrdʃɪp] 艰难

disability [dɪsəˈbɪlɪtɪ] 无能力

profit [ˈprɑfɪt] 利润

essentials [ɪˈsɛnʃlz] 必需品

volunteer [ˌvɑlənˈtɪr] 志愿者

动词

involve [ɪnˈvɒlv] 涉及；参与

donate [ˈdə(u)neɪt] 捐赠

sack [sæk] 解雇

deny [dɪˈnaɪ] 否认;否定
suffer [ˈsʌfər] 受苦
reject [rɪˈdʒɛkt] 拒绝;扔掉
purchase [ˈpɜːtʃəs] 购买
enable [ɪnˈeɪb(ə)l] 使能够
advocate [ˈædvəkət] 提倡
employ [ɪmˈplɔɪ] 雇佣
tidy [ˈtaɪdɪ] 收拾整齐
raise [reɪz] 筹集
taste [teɪst] 品尝

形容词

former [ˈfɔːmə(r)] 以前的;前任的
chronic [ˈkrɑnɪk] 慢性的
rejected [ˈriːdʒektɪd] 扔掉的

副词

instead [inˈsted] 相反;反之
once [wʌns] 曾经

短语

get involved in 参与;参加
as well 也;同样
out of fashion 过时
sort out 分类

Passage 22 配套单词填空练习

1. Apparently, she's been ill for long time, it's a sort of c____________ condition.
2. Many people are suffering economic h_____________.
3. Do the v____________ help the old people too?
4. They used to d___________ large sum of money to the Red Cross every year.
5. The union s_____________ their manager due to poor performance.
6. Disability can make extra demands on financial resources because the d_________ need extra care.
7. H______________ is a situation in which your life is difficult or unpleasant, often because you do not have enough money.
8. You can improve your p_________ by sensible planning of your business.
9. The s___________ on the rope made it broken.
10. This week he is to visit China to discuss the p____________ of military

supplies.

11. After being a famous pop star, the actress began her humble c_______ of bringing education to African children.

12. It is often said that j__________ is done if the criminal serves their punishment.

13. Many families are under the cold s________ of finance because of the bad economy.

14. The e______________ rate kept sliding down as companies are forced to close due to the financial crisis.

15. Writing letters seems o______ __ __________.

16. I was lucky enough to see the ballet dance of Swan Lake o________ in my life.

17. Did you t_______ the bitterness in that melon?

18. My mum asked me to t_______ my bedroom before I pop out to play.

19. We need to s______ _____ recyclable stuffs before we throw our rubbish away.

20. The f________ principal of our school gave us a speech yesterday.

21. I___________ of ignoring the little boy's request, his mum explained patiently why they could not buy that toy.

22. There is a second-hand shop that sells all kinds of r______ items.

23. Students should g________ ________ ________ all sorts of activities that help them understand this world.

24. Kids always s________ if their parents do not take care of them heartedly.

25. Sandy got very tricky rash on her skin; Sandy's little brother got similar things a_______ w______.

26. It is e_____________ for children to learn to distinguish right and wrong.

27. No one can d_______ that everyone is somehow responsible for the environmental problem.

Passage 23

Child Writers

There are many children with great talent for writing. Some even publish their books at a young age; this usually shocks the ordinary people. Many of these books not sell for a large volume of copies, but they definitely build confidence inside those young writers to unleash their infinite potentials.

I still remember that once our teacher introduced us a book written by a refugee girl. She fled from war threat in her own country. She finally landed in Australia after months drifting on the vast sea. The writer vividly recounts how the girl endures and overcome life-threatening storms, hunger and hopelessness.

Recently, the government initiated a children's writing competition in junior and senior schools. It called enthusiastic young writer to give it a go. The government also set great reward for winners—a scholarship worth $3,000.

必备词汇：

名词

talent [ˈtælənt] 天赋；才华
volume [ˈvɒljuːm] 册；音量
copy [ˈcɒpɪ] 一本
refugee [ˌrefjʊˈdʒiː] 难民
confidence [ˈkɒnfɪd(ə)ns] 信心
threat [θret] 威胁
hunger [ˈhʌŋgə] 饥饿
hopelessness [ˈhəʊpləsnəs] 无助
scholarship [ˈskɑləʃɪp] 奖学金
competition [kɒmpɪˈtɪʃ(ə)n] 比赛

动词

publish [ˈpʌblɪʃ] 出版；发表
shock [ʃɑk] 使吃惊
unleash [ʌnˈliːʃ] 释放
introduce [ˌintrəˈdus] 介绍
flee [fliː] 逃跑
land [lænd] 登陆
initiate [ɪˈnɪʃɪet] 开始
recount [rɪˈkaʊnt] 详述
endure [ɪnˈdjuə] 忍耐
overcome [ˌəʊvəˈkʌm] 克服

形容词

ordinary [ˈɔrdnɛrɪ] 普通的

vast [vɑ:st] 广袤无垠的

junior [ˈdʒu:nɪər] 初级的

senior [ˈsi:nɪə] 高级的

vivid [ˈvɪvɪd] 鲜明的

drifting [ˈdrɪftɪŋ] 漂流的

enthusiastic [ɪnˌθju:zɪˈæstɪk] 满腔热情的

definite [ˈdefɪnɪt] 确定的；肯定的

infinite [ˈɪnfɪnət] 无穷的；无限的

hopeless [ˈhəʊpləs] 无助的

enthusiastic [ɪnˌθju:ziˈæstɪk] 热情的

副词

definitely [ˈdefɪnɪtlɪ] 肯定

vividly [ˈvɪvɪdlɪ] 生动地

短语

give it a go 试一试

Passage 23 配套单词填空练习

1. His mother was s____________ at the news.
2. The r____________ want to be resettled in London.
3. He was in c______________ with 10 others for the job.
4. On his first day as the newcomer, he breezed through the office to i__________ himself.
5. I cannot e______________ her rudeness any longer.
6. His hope and his c_______________ had never gone.
7. He was described by his s_____________ as a model officer.
8. Three hundred people in this town are dying of h___________ every day.
9. The enemy f______________ in disorder.
10. In many societies, young people are formally i_____________ into their adult roles.
11. The girl who won the s_______________ was quite outstanding.
12. His speech won round after round of e______________ applause.
13. The book paints a v_____________ picture of life in the city.
14. The piece of wood was d______________ down the river.

B aeas 7-9

15. The h__________ look in his eyes make me feel sorry for that boy in the movie.

16. I got a c________ of *The King of Ring* as my birthday gift.

17. Scientists believe we can find d_________ answers to most issues we are now facing.

18. Young children seem to have i____________ energy; they never feel tired.

19. Henry is an e_________________ fan for Michael Jackson, so he has collected Jackson's all albums.

20. Lying on the grass, the v____________ blue sky covered me like a giant blanket.

Passage 24

Parents and Teenage Years

When children grow into teenage years, it's easy for them to have argument with their parents. That's why parents call this period as trouble years.

It is normal for teenagers to push boundaries and experiment with extreme behaviors. Sometimes, they tip over into great trouble. Teenagers go through lots of physical, emotional and mental changes at this period, so it's normal for them to be uncertain of what is happening and get confused about what they should do.

When seeing teen children struggling, parents need to offer affection and support to their kids and assure them they will stay behind their kids no matter what happens. It is important for parents to shift more responsibility to children instead of controlling them. Being bossy, parents can easily cause rebelling behaviors in teenagers.

Parents need to stay connected with their teen kids, so that their kids can feel the love and attention. If parents find that their teen kids withdraw from family and stay alone, parents need to seek professional advice. Because this is a warning sign that their kids are in trouble. If parents take actions early, they can help their kids get back on track. To help teenagers to sail through these trouble years, parents need to be open-minded and creative in the way of handling teen problems.

必备词汇：

名词

argument [ˈɑ:gjʊm(ə)nt] 论证

behavior [bɪˈhevjə] 举止

boundary [ˈbaʊnd(ə)rɪ] 分界线

experiment [ikˈsperimənt] 实验

responsibility [rɪˌspɒnsɪˈbɪlɪtɪ] 责

任

rebel [rɪˈbɛl] 反抗

affection [əˈfekʃn] 爱

teenager [ˈtiːneɪdʒə] 青少年

动词

tip [tɪp] 倾倒

warn [wɔrn] 警告

handle [ˈhænd(ə)l] 处理

assure [əˈʃʊr] 保证

withdraw [wɪðˈdrɔ] 取回

connect [kəˈnɛkt] 连接

struggle [ˈstrʌgl] 挣扎;斗争

rebel [rɪˈbɛl] 反抗

形容词

teenage [ˈtiːneɪdʒ] 青少年的

physical [ˈfɪzɪkl] 身体的

emotional [ɪˈməʊʃ(ə)n(ə)l] 情绪的

bossy [ˈbɔsi] 专横的

open-minded [ˈəupənˈmaindid] 心胸宽的

uncertain [ʌnˈsɜːt(ə)n] 不确定的

extreme [ɪkˈstrim] 极端的

短语

tip over 行差踏错

go through 经历

stay behind sb. 支持

shift from…to… 从……转向……

get back on track 重返正轨

sail through 顺利渡过

Passage 24 配套单词填空练习

1. You may be p____________ and mentally exhausted after a long flight.
2. I want to w____________ a statement I made earlier.
3. If you accept r____________ for something that has happened, you agree that you were to blame for it or you caused it.
4. She was given promotion and more r____________.
5. When I had my first baby, friends w____________ me that raising a baby can cost a fortune.
6. You guys don't c____________ with each other.
7. She is completely fearless, imaginative and a little bit b____________.
8. His performance yesterday morning a____________ him of a record

eighth medal.

9. There's a strong a______________ for lowering the price.

10. The students perceived that his b______________ had changed.

11. Voters r_______________ against high property taxes.

12. If you say that someone can h_____________ a problem or situation, you mean that they have the ability to deal with it successfully.

13 .He was anxious and u_____________, wondering what he would hear.

14. If you t_____________ something somewhere, you pour it there.

15. It is hard to imagine Jesse capable of anything so e_______________.

16. Those two old men did not speak to each other since they had an argument last year.

17. The dumping trucks lined up like a snake, waiting to t_______ over their loads.

18. It is widely claimed that t________ years are trouble years for both youth and parents.

19. The young girl with a b______ look signalled another girl to get closer to her.

20. The condition of the patient is u________ until the specialist gives him another.

21. The fence between the Hills and the Johnsons is a firm b________ between these unfriendly neighbo(u)rs.

22. My parents are o_____________ persons, as they are willing to accept new ideas.

23. A sense of r______________ is very important for people who work as doctors or lawyers.

24. People can be hurt p________ or e_________, which means not only our bodies but also our heart can be hurt.

25. When children turn to their puberty age, they may incline to r________ against their parents to do things that usually are not allowed.

C 游洋 aeas 10－12

词汇宝典

Passage 1

School Announcement about Absence from School

Dear students,

Absence from school absolutely affects your academic results. Ever worse, frequent absence is unacceptable and you may be disciplined for that kind of behavior, for example, being expelled from school.

However, there are some acceptable reasons for being absent from school. You may apply for leave from school if you are involved in an accident or extreme family disruption, for example divorce of parents.

When you submit your application, you need to demonstrate adequate reasons for supporting your application. Simply alleging occurrence of family disaster without details is insufficient. All students are encouraged to attend school everyday, which can benefit students for boosting their study and maintaining their friendship. In one aspect, students can engage in study intensively; in the other aspect, students can enhance their interaction with friends at school. Extensive exposure to peer activities helps students build self-confidence and deal with emotional reactions. At the age of adolescence, being outspoken of one's feeling towards peers can better prepare adolescents to handle fierce emotions later in life.

Specifically to International Students:

For international students, your accommodation arrangements will be reviewed shortly. We acknowledge that there is a shortage of boarding places for the expanding size of international students; we appreciate that the waiting list is incredibly long. Accordingly, we will advise new applicants to make an alternative plan. We advise that new international students seek appropriate accommodation such as homestay to reside during your study. However, you need to obtain approval for your accommodation from the school before you can commence study in our school.

Student Wellbeing:

We advocate the notion of healthy mind and happy soul. This means we care a lot about our students' mood such as anxiety, exhaustion, nervousness or depression before exams. We have appointed a mental health expert as the wellbeing officer. He will soon present valuable, meaningful activities to extend our students' capacity for handling tough circumstances and boost their resilience from frustrating encounters.

必备词汇：

名词

absence [ˈæbs(ə)ns] 缺席

accommodation [əkɒməˈdeɪʃ(ə)n] 住处

accident [ˈæksɪdənt] 事故

allegation [ælɪˈgeɪʃ(ə)n] 主张，断言

announcement [əˈnaʊnsm(ə)nt] 公告；宣告

anxiety [æŋˈzaɪətɪ] 焦虑；渴望

application [ˌæplɪˈkeɪʃ(ə)n] 应用；申请

approval [əˈpruːv(ə)l] 批准；认可

arrangement [əˈreɪn(d)ʒm(ə)nt] 布置；安排

capacity [kəˈpæsɪtɪ] 能力；容量

circumstance [ˈsɜːkəmstəns] 环境

depression [dɪˈpreʃ(ə)n] 沮丧

discipline [ˈdɪsɪplɪn] 学科；纪律

divorce [dɪˈvɔːs] 离婚

exhaustion [ɪgˈzɔːstʃ(ə)n;eg-] 精疲力竭

emotion [ɪˈməʊʃ(ə)n] 情感；情绪

exposure [ɪkˈspəʊʒə; ek-] 暴露；曝光

resilience [rɪˈzɪlɪəns] 恢复力；弹力

动词

acknowledge [əkˈnɒlɪdʒ] 承认；答谢

advise [ədˈvaɪz] 建议

allege [əˈledʒ] 宣称

appreciate [əˈpriːʃɪeɪt; -sɪ-] 欣赏；感激

commence [kəˈmens] 开始

encounter [ɪnˈkaʊntə; en-] 遭遇，邂逅

enhance [ɪnˈhɑːns] 提高；加强

expand [ɪk'spænd] 扩张
extend [ɪk'stend] 延展;拓展
expose [ɪk'spəʊz; ek-] 揭露,揭发
frustrate [frʌ'streɪt] 挫败

形容词
absolute ['æbsəlu:t] 绝对的
academic [ækə'demɪk] 学术的
acceptable [ək'septəb(ə)l] 可接受的
adequate ['ædɪkwət] 充足的
anxious ['æŋ(k)ʃəs] 焦虑的
appropriate [ə'prəʊprɪət] 适当的
emotional [ɪ'məʊʃ(ə)n(ə)l] 情绪的
extensive [ɪk'stensɪv; ek-] 广泛的
extreme [ɪk'stri:m; ek-] 极端的
tough [tʌf] 艰苦的

Passage 1 配套单词填空练习

1. A new manager was appointed during her a__________.
2. The school is concerned of students' a_________ performance.
3. We a___________ indigenous people as traditional owner of our land.
4. Will future oil supplies be a__________ to meet world demands?
5. These a__________ have seriously hurt her reputation.
6. The president made an unexpected a____________ this morning.
7. Children normally feel a lot of a_________ about their first day at school.
8. Any advice that you can give me would be greatly a____________.
9. Is this an a__________ occasion to wear sneakers?
10. Alan is someone who always needs the a__________ of other people.
11. A____________ would be made to move the prisoners to another jail.
12. The stadium has a seating c__________ of 50,000.
13. Racism is wholly unacceptable under any c_____________.
14. The academic year c__________ at the beginning of October.
15. Mr. Thomas was suffering from d____________.
16. Order and d_________ have been placed in the hands of governing bodies.
17. Numerous marriages now end in d_________.
18. E___________ is the state of being so tired that you have no energy left.

19. It is extremely hard for people who have depression to control their e_________.

20. Every day we e__________ major and minor stresses of one kind or another.

21. Young people work hard to e_________ the quality of life.

22. They e__________ their retail operations during the 1980s.

23. The review e_________ widespread corruption (腐败) in the police force.

24. You should always limit your e__________ to the sun.

25. Her knowledge of music is e_________.

26. Several major roads are closed due to e_________ weather conditions.

27. It f__________ me that I'm not able to put any of my ideas into practise.

28. The plant fibre has incredible strength and r__________.

29. I would strongly a_________ against making a sudden decision.

30. The drought has made farmers a________ about the harvest.

Passage 2

Social Involvement

For all students of year 10 and above, it is crucial to engage in some social involvements to broaden their vision and consolidate the sense of social justice and responsibility. Students can consciously participate in volunteer work or charity, or unconsciously uphold right social values by just not doing wrong things.

School agenda for recruiting student volunteers:

For a school to raise moral students, we submitted an agenda for recruiting student volunteers to help out local communities. Currently, the coverage of the agenda extends to the following aspects: student consultants for high school subject consulting, amateur football coaches for coaching poor kids, and subject ambassadors who introduce subjects to other junior students.

Our mission is to help our students to extend outside the campus and motivate them to contribute their efforts to the growth of our community. We believe that the establishment of this student volunteer program is a valuable contribution to the personal growth of our thriving students.

To accumulate intangible experience alongside acquiring theories or theoretical knowledge, our students definitely will turn out to be responsible and sensible persons in the society.

Additionally, students may also find their ambition in upholding social justice. People at the bottom of the society often experience social injustice such as abuse or wrong accusations. Recently, the issue of injustice also arises along with arrival of refugees in Australia. For those students, the volunteer job as assistants in legal aid centres or refugee associations may sound very attractive.

If we just overlook the pains and sufferings of other people, our conscience will be questioned by ourselves. Showing sympathy towards vulnerable people is an inherent ability of humans.

Therefore, we will collaborate with our community, our students and parents to launch a collective student volunteer program soon.

必备词汇：

名词

amateur [ˈæmətə(r)] 爱好者

ambassador [æmˈbæsədə] 大使

ambition [æmˈbɪʃ(ə)n] 野心

arrival [əˈraɪv(ə)l] 到来

assistance [əˈsɪst(ə)ns] 辅助

belief [bɪˈliːf] 信仰

charity [ˈtʃærɪtɪ] 慈善

conscience [ˈkɒnʃ(ə)ns] 道德心，良心

consciousness [ˈkɒnʃəsnɪs] 意识；知觉

consultant [kənˈsʌlt(ə)nt] 顾问

definition [defɪˈnɪʃ(ə)n] 定义

establishment [ɪˈstæblɪʃm(ə)nt] 确立，制定

mission [ˈmɪʃ(ə)n] 使命，任务

sympathy [ˈsɪmpəθɪ] 同情

vision [ˈvɪʒ(ə)n] 视力；眼力

动词

arise [əˈraɪz] 出现；上升

consult [kənˈsʌlt] 请教；当顾问

contribute [kənˈtrɪbjuːt] 贡献

engage [ɪnˈgeɪdʒ; en-] 吸引，占用

motivate [ˈməʊtɪveɪt] 刺激；使有动机

uphold [ʌpˈhəʊld] 支撑；鼓励

accumulate [əˈkjuːmjʊleɪt] 累积；积聚

形容词

collective [kəˈlektɪv] 集体的

conscious [ˈkɒnʃəs] 意识到的

moral [ˈmɒr(ə)l] 道德的；精神上的

painful [ˈpeɪnfʊl; -f(ə)l] 痛苦的；疼痛的

vulnerable [ˈvʌlnərəbl] 易受攻击的

intangible [ɪnˈtæn(d)ʒɪb(ə)l] 无形的

inherent [ɪnˈhɪər(ə)nt; -ˈher(ə)nt] 固有的；内在的

crucial [ˈkruːʃ(ə)l] 重要的

副词

alongside [əlɒŋˈsaɪd] 在旁边

definitely [ˈdefɪnɪtlɪ] 清楚地，当然

Passage 2 配套单词填空练习

1. An a____________ is an official who lives in foreign country and represents his own country's interests there.
2. They had the a___________ to dominate this small country.
3. However, the differences a_________ in how to achieve that objective.
4. Linda phoned me on a________ so that I know she was safe.
5. Any a_________ you could give the police will be greatly appreciated.
6. We should respect different religious b_______.
7. He made substantial donations to c_______.
8. He should not sacrifice c_________ benefit to satisfy his own interests.
9. You didn't do anything wrong, you should have a clear c_________.
10. He is still c__________ but he is very badly injured.
11. He lost c___________ after that accident and never recovered.
12. If the symptoms get worse, c_________ the doctor.
13. A c__________ is a person who gives expert advice.
14. The company agreed to c_________ some money to charity.
15. There is no general agreement on a standard d________ of intelligence.
16. The debate about food safety has e________ the whole nation.
17. The e__________ of the regional government in 1980 did not end terrorism.
18. It is her m______ obligation to tell the police what she knows.
19. Teaching is all about m____________ people to learn.
20. The old photograph brought back p________ memories.
21. We expressed our s___________ for her loss.
22. Travelling around the world could broaden your v__________.
23. Old people are particularly v_____________ members of our society.
24. She has that i__________ quality which you might call charisma (领袖气质).
25. We will endeavour to u________ the high educational standards.

26. There are dangers i________ in almost every sport.

27. Her work has been c______ to the project's success.

28. As people a___________ more wealth, they tend to spend a greater proportion of their incomes.

29. A car pulled up a__________ (us).

30. He was an a_________ singer until the age of 40, when he turned professional.

Passage 3

Safety measures

Wandering around in the late night can be dangerous, particularly, for young kids or female students. International students should get familiar with the ways to seek assistance in case of emergency or urgent matters.

Generally speaking, Australia is a safe society, but there can be criminals who we cannot identify just by their looks or appearances. The survey shows that thefts in crowded places like train stations have increased, and the number of crimes has been climbing up these years. Accordingly, students should keep an eye on their own property when going out.

Before set off for some place, students should check if the place to go is generally safe or not. If it's in a remote area, students should ask parents or friends to accompany them. It is always better to tell someone where you go, so that they will know where to find you in case of an emergency.

Students are advised to be more cautious when hanging out at night. These safety measures are proved to be useful: ensure your handbags or backpacks are securely zipped; constantly check your surroundings and raise sense of caution against any suspicious person around you; to avoid dark streets or lanes if you are alone, instead, you'd better seek an alternative route with sufficient lighting; ultimately, to be alert to potential risk or danger is always the best precaution against becoming the victim of convicts.

必备词汇：

名词

safety [ˈseɪftɪ] 安全

emergency [iˈmɜ:dʒənsi] 紧急情况

female [ˈfi:meɪl] 女性；雌性

criminal [ˈkrɪmɪnl] 罪犯

look [luk] 样貌

appearance [əˈpɪərəns] 外貌;样貌
survey [ˈsɜ:veɪ] 问卷;调查
theft [θeft] 偷窃
crime [kraɪm] 罪行;犯罪行为
lighting [ˈlaitiŋ] 照明
convict [kənˈvɪkt] 罪犯
conviction [kənˈvɪkʃ(ə)n] 定罪
surroundings [səˈraʊndɪŋz] 环境;周围的事物
potential [pəˈtenʃl] 潜能
precaution [prɪˈkɔ:ʃ(ə)n] 预防,警惕
victim [ˈvɪktɪm] 受害者
measure [ˈmeʒə(r)] 措施;办法

动词

accompany [əˈkʌmpənɪ] 陪伴
wander [ˈwɒndə] 闲逛;漫步
identify [aɪˈdentɪfaɪ] 辨认;确定
zip [zip] 拉拉链; 闭上嘴巴
advise [ədˈvaɪz] 建议
prove [pru:v] 证明
alert [əˈlɜ:t] 警告
alter [ˈɔ:ltə;ˈɒl-] 改变
ensure [ɪnˈʃɔ:;-ˈʃʊə;en-] 保证,确保

形容词

crowded [ˈkraudid] 拥挤的
remote [rɪˈməʊt] 遥远的;偏僻的
cautious [ˈkɔ:ʃəs] 谨慎的
ultimate [ˈʌltɪmət] 最终的
constant [ˈkɒnst(ə)nt] 不变的;恒定的
suspicious [səˈspɪʃəs] 可疑的
alternative [ɔ:lˈtɜ:nətɪv; ɒl-] 供选择的
sufficient [səˈfɪʃ(ə)nt] 足够的;充分的

副词

particularly [pəˈtɪkjʊləlɪ] 尤其;特别是
securely [sɪˈkjʊəlɪ] 牢固地;安全地
constantly [ˈkɔnstəntlɪ] 不断地;持续地
ultimately [ˈʌltɪmətlɪ] 最终

短语

generally speaking 总体而言
climb up 上升
hang out 闲逛
set off 出发
in case of 倘若

C aeas 10 | 12

Passage 3 配套单词填空练习

1. A warning serves to make you more a______ to danger.
2. Drugs can a_______ your perception of reality.
3. A c________ action is careful, well considered, and sometimes slow or uncertain.
4. He has twice been c_________ of robbery.
5. He has a long record of previous c___________ for similar offences.
6. It is not possible to predict the u__________ outcome.
7. We must e__________ that all patients have access to high quality care.
8. The direction of the wind is c___________ changing.
9. The chameleon's (变色龙) skin replicates the pattern of its s________________.
10. Two officers became s___________ of two men in a car.
11. There were a____________ methods of travel available.
12. Will there be s___________ stocks to meet our demand?
13. We are aware of the p___________ problems and have taken every precaution.
14. Residents should take p____________ against burglary.
15. Road s_________of pedestrians becomes a concern, as more people has been hit by motor vehicles.
16. It is dangerous to w________ outside alone at night.
17. To find a place with sufficient l_________ is essential for your study.
18. When economy was down, you could expect t________ cases would go up.
19. The last year saw the c_________ up of school leavers, who didn't finish year 12.
20. The accident was caused by the driver not s____________ fastening his tool box to his truck.
21. Even children can become v________ of bullying, if schools don't take this issue seriously.

22. Judging people by their a______________ is not good.

23. As Christmas approaches, shopping centres become ever c___________ with busy shoppers.

24. Wellbeing counsellors are support to a__________ students who have well-being issues.

25. The s__________ showed that students would prefer more challenging out-door activities.

26. It is the school who u_____________ makes enrolment decisions.

27. If you c____________ review what you have learned, you would be less stressed when exam period comes.

28. I hope the passenger next to me would z________ up his mouth; he was talking since he boarded.

29. To h________ out with peers can increase teenager's social skills.

30. Some hypotheses put forwarded in the past are now finally p_______ to be correct.

Passage 4

Thoughts on Global Warming

Amid the heated ongoing discussion about impact of global warming, many countries put forward comprehensive schemes or resolutions to combat the issue of global warming. Scientists and governments have reached consensus that effects of global warming will be devastating, but the feasible solutions remain controversial.

The current discussion concentrates on the reduction of the greenhouse effect, which is regarded as the major contributor to the phenomenon of global warming. There is concrete evidence to show that greenhouse gases like carbon dioxide absorb heat from sun and prevent the sun's radiation from leaving our atmosphere. For example, it has been shown that there is a link between the increased use of fossil fuels and rising global temperatures. Accordingly, some scientists conclude that reducing greenhouse gases definitely will alleviate global warming.

Based on this assumption, many governments have conceded that they need to impose stricter rules on factories and manufacturers that generate greenhouse gases. Australia government made genuine effort in curtailing its carbon emission because it voluntarily took action years ago to enforce carbon tax as an incentive to reduce emission.

Some environmental protection organizations also took this initiative to advocate the reduction of carbon emission by individual household. These organizations emphasize that collective efforts by everyone can be powerful. For example, if people abandon driving to work, exhaust from vehicles will decrease remarkably; purchasing locally manufactured products can substantially reduce emission arising from international transport.

However, these efforts are not consistent, because some countries betrayed/deserted their initial pledge on cooperatively tackling global warming.

必备词汇：

名词

assumption [ə'sʌm(p)ʃ(ə)n] 假定
atmosphere ['ætməsfɪə] 气氛；大气
carbon ['kɑ:b(ə)n][化学] 碳
combat ['kɒmbæt] 战斗
emission [ɪ'mɪʃ(ə)n] 排放
pledge [pledʒ] 保证，誓言
volunteer [ˌvɒlən'tɪə] 志愿者
resolution [rezə'lu:ʃ(ə)n] 决议；解决
consensus [kən'sensəs] 一致
phenomenon [fɪ'nɒmɪnən] 现象
radiation [reɪdɪ'eɪʃ(ə)n] 辐射
incentive [ɪn'sentɪv] 动机；刺激
initiative [ɪ'nɪʃɪətɪv;-ʃə-] 主动权

动词

abandon [ə'bænd(ə)n] 遗弃；放弃
advocate ['ædvəkeɪt;-ət] 提倡
concede [kən'si:d] 承认；退让
concentrate ['kɒns(ə)ntreɪt] 集中
conclude [kən'klu:d] 推断；决定；作结论
emphasise ['emfəsaɪz] 强调
generate ['dʒenəreɪt] 使形成
tackle ['tæk(ə)l] 处理；对付
curtail [kɜ:'teɪl] 缩减；剪短；剥夺……特权
betray [bɪ'treɪ] 背叛；出卖

形容词

comprehensive [kɒmprɪ'hensɪv] 综合的
concrete ['kɒŋkri:t] 实际的；混凝土的
consistent [kən'sɪst(ə)nt] 一致的；坚持的
controversial [kɒntrə'vɜ:ʃ(ə)l] 有争议的
genuine ['dʒenjʊɪn] 真实的
substantial [səb'stænʃ(ə)l] 大量的；实质的
remarkable [rɪ'mɑ:kəb(ə)l] 卓越的；非凡的
voluntary ['vɒlənt(ə)rɪ] 自愿的
cooperative [kəʊ'ɒpərətɪv] 合作的
devastating ['devəsteitiŋ] 毁灭性的
feasible ['fi:zɪb(ə)l] 可行的

Passage 4 配套单词填空练习

1. He claimed that his parents had a____________ him.
2. She a___________ taking a more long-term view.
3. These calculations are based on the a_______________ that prices will continue to rise.
4. These factories are releasing toxic gases into the a________________.
5. New legislation aims to reduce c_________ emissions.
6. The film explores the c_________ between good and evil.
7. We offer you a c______________ training in all aspects of the business.
8. The government has c____________ that the new policy has been a failure.
9. The company is c_____________ on developing new products.
10. She c___________ the speech by reminding us of our responsibility.
11. The bomb shelter has c_________ walls that are three meters thick.
12. Her work is sometimes good, but the problem is she's not c______________.
13. They hold widely divergent opinions on c____________ issues.
14. I would like to e____________ how important it is for people to learn foreign languages.
15. Environmental groups want a substantial reduction in the e_________ of greenhouse gases.
16. Her latest film has g_____________ a lot of interest and excitement.
17. The boom of counterfeit products would hurt g____________ products.
18. The couple will exchange rings as a p________ of their love for one another.
19. The findings show a s_________ difference between the opinions of men and women.
20. The 20th century was r__________ for its inventions.
21. She does v___________ work for the Red Cross two days a week.
22. I made a r____________ to give up chocolate.

23. Could we reach a c____________ on this matter?

24. I asked them to turn down their music, but they're not being very c___________.

25. There are many ways of t___________ this problem.

26. There's evidence to suggest that child abuse is not just a recent p_____________.

27. The drought has had d_______________ consequences.

28. Many servicemen suffered r__________ sickness after the early atomic tests(原子弹试爆).

29. Bonus payments provide an i__________ to work harder.

30. It may be f__________ to clone（克隆）human beings, but is it ethical?

Passage 5

Election for Student Representative in the Student Union

Many students do not find interest in politics, but being involved in student representative election can be a rewarding experience and it also showcases the common framework of election procedure in our society.

Structure of a student union:

Normally, a student union consists of a president, two vice presidents and several members. The exact number of members depends on the size of the school. They also compose the union committee that has power to decide the day-to-day running of the union. The scope of their power is defined in and governed by the union constitution.

Election procedure:

First, candidates for positions in the union will be published on the election charter, and voters can view it online or in print. Candidates essentially campaign themselves in the hope to win. When the election day arrives, voters need to cast their ballot paper anonymously. The ballot paper will be counted and the final results is usually announced a couple of days after the election.

Governance of the union:

According to the constitution of a student union, the presidents are given most of power to manage the union, but they can delegate their power to other members to enable smooth operation of the union. Transparency of decision-making is compulsory, so the union needs to disclose any decision, which has been made by the presidents, to the students in a timely manner.

必备词汇：

名词

election [ɪˈlekʃn] 选举
interest [ˈɪntrəst] 兴趣
politics [ˈpɒlətɪks] 政治
union [ˈjuːniən] 联合；联盟
governance [ˈɡʌvənəns] 治理；管理
reward [rɪˈwɔːd] 奖赏；报酬
framework [ˈfreɪmwɜːk] 框架；体系
ballot [ˈbælət] 投票
scope [skʊup] 范围
constitution [kɒnstɪˈtjuːʃ(ə)n] 宪法
delegation [delɪˈɡeɪʃ(ə)n] 授权；代表（团）
representative [reprɪˈzentətɪv] 代表
procedure [prəˈsiːdʒə] 程序，手续；步骤
candidate [ˈkændɪdeɪt; -dət] 候选人，应试者
position [pəˈzɪʃn] 职位；位置
voter [ˈvəʊtə] 投票人
campaign [kæmˈpeɪn] 做竞选活动运动；活动；战役
transparency [trænˈspær(ə)nsɪ; trɑːn-; -ˈspeə-] n. 透明，透明度
operation [ˌɒpəˈreɪʃn] 运行；经营；手术

动词

elect [ɪˈlekt] 选举；选择
showcase [ˈʃəʊkeɪs] 展示；显示
compose [kəmˈpəʊz] 组成；作曲
cast [kɑːst] 投票
delegate [ˈdɛlɪˌɡeɪt] 委派……为代表
disclose [dɪsˈkləʊz] 公开；揭露
enable [ɪnˈeɪb(ə)l; en-] 使能够
manage [ˈmænɪdʒ] 管理
campaign [kæmˈpeɪn] 做竞选活动

形容词

essential [ɪˈsenʃ(ə)l] 必要的；本质的
rewarding [rɪˈwɔːdɪŋ] 有益的；值得的
compulsory [kəmˈpʌlsərɪ] 义务的；必修的
smooth [smuːð] 光滑的；平稳的；流畅的
timely [ˈtaɪmlɪ] 及时的

副词

afterwards [ˈɑːftəwədz] 然后
exactly [ɪɡˈzæk(t)lɪ] 正是；精确地

短语

in print 印刷的

be involved in 参与

consist of 由……组成

Passage 5 配套单词填空练习

1. Representatives were elected by b_________.
2. Britain has no written c_____________, which is unlike US.
3. Each union elects several p____________ to the annual conference.
4. The d___________ from Spain has arrived for a month.
5. The police have d__________ that two officers are under internal investigation.
6. Computerization has e_________ us to do away with a lot of paperwork.
7. Witnesses need to describe to the court e_________ what they saw.
8. The firm has d______________ in every major city.
9. The company has a new p_____________ for dealing with complaints.
10. There are three c____________ standing in the election.
11. Support from the Government will be e___________ if the project is to succeed.
12. This is the latest act of terrorism in a long-standing c__________ of violence.
13. The old-fashioned type of plastic lacked t_____________.
14. The law made wearing seat belts in cars c_____________; if you don't wear it, you will be given a fine.
15. Students are encouraged to be i___________ in more political activities.
16. The university campus c__________ of several ancient buildings.
17. People who are employed to m_________ business can earn high salaries.
18. The exhibition in the modern art museum s_________ the prime time of early Australian artists.
19. Australian citizens will need to e_________ their Prime Minister in 2019.
20. Doing volunteer work is quite r___________ for young people.

21. My parents hope I will have a s__________ transition to my new school next year.

22. The new version of Australian History is available online or in p________.

23. Business owners are responsible for smooth o__________ of their businesses.

24. The p_________ of CEO requires at least 10 years management experience.

25. The police widened the s_________ of their investigation, because they got new evidence.

26. Primary students are taught the f__________ of Australian government.

27. With no i_________ in music, Jim left the music school after his first year there.

28. Workers' U_________ is an important organization for workers to fight for their rights.

29. School committees are responsible for the g_________ of the schools.

30. Working as a volunteer means that you are not given r_______ for what you do.

Passage 6

My Personal Reflection on the Relationship between Music and Mood

From my perspective, playing a musical instrument is a way to lift daily mood in an effortless way. I only play one musical instrument, which is trumpet. I chose trumpet 5 years ago because it seemed easy. When I started learning trumpet, my parents did not expect I would continue. That's because I constantly gave them an impression of never finishing anything. But my routine of giving up in the mid of learning something came to a halt on the day I picked up trumpet.

I still can recall that day. I was a big fan for jazz music, so I was particularly attracted by melody that trumpet can play. Besides, it is not expensive to purchase. Even when I advanced in my playing skills, a better trumpet would not cost a fortune.

Reason aside, my passion for trumpet mainly originated in the types of music it can play. Trumpet is also a highlight in jazz music and it can play very intense and sentimental music. I reckon that's why many restaurants would like use jazz music as background music.

When I feel moody, I would play my trumpet. As a friend said, music can bring peace to our mind. I also believed in the mood boosting effect of music. When I play trumpet, the music can also bring back some memorable experience associated with delightful moments in my life.

As a psychologist, I gradually realize the potential of using music to heal people with mental problem or suffer from stress. I also read some research article about music therapy for comfort and relief. Although I don't have the talent or potential to become a musician, I still enjoy tremendous benefits from a playing musical instrument.

必备词汇:

名词

reflection [rɪˈflekʃn] 沉思;反射
relationship [rɪˈleɪʃnʃɪp] 关系
mood [mu:d] 心情;情绪
instrument [ˈɪnstrəmənt] 工具
delight [dɪˈlaɪt] 高兴
perspective [pəˈspektɪv] 观点
trumpet [ˈtrʌmpɪt] 喇叭
impression [ɪmˈpreʃ(ə)n] 印象
routine [ru:ˈti:n] 常规;习惯
halt [hɔ:lt] 止步;停止
melody [ˈmelədi] 旋律;曲子
reason [ˈri:zn] 理性;理智
passion [ˈpæʃn] 热情;激情
type [taɪp] 类型
highlight [ˈhaɪlaɪt] 精彩部分;闪光点
background [ˈbækgraʊnd] 背景
potential [pəˈtenʃl] 潜力
psychologist [saɪˈkɒlədʒɪst] 心理学家
stress [stres] (心理)压力
research [rɪˈsɜ:tʃ] 研究
article [ˈɑ:tɪkl] 文章
therapy [ˈθerəpi] 疗法
relief [rɪˈli:f] 放松;释放
talent [ˈtælənt] 天赋;才能
musician [mjuˈzɪʃn] 音乐家
benefit [ˈbenɪfɪt] 益处;利益

动词

lift [lɪft] 提升
associate [əˈsəʊʃɪeɪt] 联合
boost [bu:st] 促进
originate [əˈrɪdʒɪneɪt] 发源
expect [ɪkˈspekt] 预期;盼望
continue [kənˈtɪnju:] 继续
halt [hɔ:lt] 停止;中止
recall [rɪˈkɔ:l] 回想起
advance [ədˈvɑ:ns] 前进;推进
reckon [ˈrekən] 认为
heal [hi:l] 治愈

形容词

personal [ˈpɜ:sənl] 个人的
effortless [ˈefətləs] 容易的;毫不费力的
attractive [əˈtræktɪv] 吸引人的
comfortable [ˈkʌmfətəbl] 舒适的,舒服的
expensive [ɪkˈspensɪv] 昂贵的
intense [ɪnˈtens] 强烈的;紧张的
sentimental [ˌsentɪˈmentl] 感伤的;多愁善感的
particular [pəˈtɪkjʊlə(r)] 特别的;独有的

moody [ˈmu:dɪ] 情绪化的
tremendous [trɪˈmendəs] 极大的，巨大的
memorable [ˈmemərəbl] 难忘的
mental [ˈmentl] 精神的；心理的

副词

intensively [inˈtensɪvlɪ] 强烈地；集中地
unfortunately [ʌnˈfɔ:tʃənətlɪ] 不幸地
gradually [ˈgrædʒʊlɪ] 逐步地；渐渐地
aside [əˈsaɪd] 在一边；另外
mainly [ˈmeɪnlɪ] 主要地

短词

suffer from 患病；遭受
musical instrument 乐器
in the mid of 半途；中间
come to a halt 戛然而止
cost a fortune 花大价钱

Passage 6 配套单词填空练习

1. Many people a____________ this brand with good quality.
2. I thought he was very a___________ and obviously very intelligent.
3. It will also b_______ our exports of airplanes, machinery and other products.
4. We have a c___________ new residence.
5. Peter's academic success d___________ his family.
6. Where does this doubt and i________ emotional fear come from?
7. You are approaching the problem from a completely different p____________.
8. U______________, I didn't have my credit card with me, or else I would have brought it.
9. My first i_________ of him was very good.
10. What in p____________ did you like about the last apartment that we saw?
11. The game is thought to have o___________ among the native people of Alaska.
12. The painful memories g___________ receded(减弱)in her mind.

13. I felt a t__________ pressure on my chest.

14. Reading from a young age brings many b__________ to children, one of which is good reading skills.

15. Australian students are required to learn at least one musical i__________ since in primary school.

16. Having a daily r__________ means one's life pattern is quite predictable.

17. Dancing to a m__________ is something humans can do even when we are just kids.

18. Machines h__________ suddenly after the thunder hit the factory.

19. Humans are endowed both r__________ and emotion, which are not seen in any other creatures.

20. The visa officer asked me to give her more b__________ information about my past life experience.

21. One of teacher's roles is to help children to develop to their p__________, which means to help them do their best.

22. This article is based on scientific r__________, which makes it trust-worthy.

23. Chemical t__________ is often used to treat cancer.

24. He finally came home safely from his Antarctic adventure, which was really a r__________ to his family.

25. Most children have their own special t__________, only if we can uncover it.

26. There are many days and nights rehearsal behind the ballerinas' e__________ performance.

27. I am longing to make some m__________ trips to foreign countries.

28. Buying an excellent piano sometimes can cost you a f__________.

29. Discussion a__________, we need to put our plans and details in writing.

30. The train suddenly came to a h__________ after a power cut-off.

Passage 7

Screen Time

It is quite common for young people to spend hours on phones or ipads, and this is referred to as screen time.

Recently, screen time has become a contentious topic in many households. Most parents complain that their children spend too much time on screen but too little time on homework. They are desperate for effective ways to eliminate their children's addiction to screens. Conversely, most children think their parents overreact to their behaviors. Unlike parents, most children think time spent on screen is also productive. They often claim that they are inspired to get novel commercial ideas from using apps, and are blessed with an untraditional angle to look at the world.

Young people often blame for generation gap for the misunderstanding between them and their parents. Some children addicted to phone games even confront their parents, which then leads to criticism of each other.

As an equivalent to playing phone games, being constantly active on social media like Wechat or Facebook comes under attack from parents. Social media is the most disturbing concern for parents. They regard those invisible "friends" on the social media as potential risk for their children's healthy growth. Some people on the social media even have a history of criminal offence.

The opposite views about screen time and social media often result in deteriorated relationship between parents and children, the lack of peaceful communication, which even worsens their relationship.

However, as this issue attracts more and more concerns in the society, many schools start to offer relationship counseling service to parents and students. As digital age is inevitable, both parents and children should be equipped with the right way to deal with the negative influence accompanying the digital age.

必备词汇:

名词

topic [ˈtɒpɪk] 话题
household [ˈhaʊshəʊld] 家庭
addiction [əˈdɪkʃn] 沉迷;上瘾
behaviour [bɪˈheɪvjə] 行为
offering [ˈɒf(ə)rɪŋ] 提供
angle [ˈæŋgl] 角度
complaint [kəmˈpleɪnt] 抱怨
reference [ˈref(ə)r(ə)ns] 参考
offense [əˈfɛns] 犯罪,进攻
counselling [ˈkaʊnsəlɪŋ] 辅导;建议
criticism [ˈkrɪtɪsɪzəm] 批评
influence [ˈɪnflʊəns] 影响;影响力

动词

complain [kəmˈpleɪn] 抱怨
eliminate [ɪˈlɪmɪneɪt] 消除;排除
overact [əʊvərˈækt] 反应过激
deteriorate [dɪˈtɪərɪəreɪt] 恶化,变坏
claim [kleɪm] 宣传;声称
inspire [ɪnˈspaɪə] 启发
confront [kənˈfrʌnt] 顶撞;冲撞
regard [rɪˈga:d] 认为;视为
deteriorate [dɪˈtɪərɪəreɪt] 使……恶化
worsen [ˈwɜ:s(ə)n] 使……恶化;变糟糕

形容词

common [ˈkɒmən] 普遍的;常见的
contentious [kənˈtenʃəs] 备受争议的
desperate [ˈdesp(ə)rət] 令人绝望的
effective [ɪˈfektɪv] 有效的
productive [prəˈdʌktɪv] 有成效的
novel [ˈnɒvl] 新颖的
traditional [trəˈdɪʃənl] 传统的 (untraditional 非传统的)
equivalent [ɪˈkwɪv(ə)l(ə)nt] 相等的
disturbing [dɪˈstɜ:bɪŋ] 令人不安的
invisible [ɪnˈvɪzəbl] 看不见
healthy [ˈhelθɪ] 健康的
opposite [ˈɒpəzɪt] 相反的
deteriorated [dɪˈtɪəriəreɪt] 恶化的
offensive [əˈfensɪv] 攻击的;冒犯的
commercial [kəˈmɜ:ʃ(ə)l] 商业的
inevitable [inˈevɪtəbl] 不可避免的
negative [ˈnegətɪv] 负面的

副词

recently [ri:sntlı] 最近

conversely [ˈkɔnvɜ:slı] 相反

短语

be referred to 被称为

addiction to sth. 沉迷于……

be inspired 受到启发

be blessed with 有幸得到

lead to 导致

come under attack 受到攻击 / 批评

result in 导致

the lack of 缺乏

be equipped with 具备

screen time 屏幕时间

generation gap 代沟

social media 社交媒体

spend on 在……上花(时间 / 钱)

Passage 7 配套单词填空练习

1. I have made a c____________ to the police about the noise.
2. We have a d______________ shortage of supplies.
3. He was e____________ in the third round of the competition.
4. She is doing the e______________ job in the new company but for more money.
5. This programme contains language that some viewers might find o__________.
6. My teacher said he should write me a ____________ letter.
7. She has some very c____________ views on education.
8. The c____________ future of the company looks very promising.
9. Octopus is better at defence but not o______________.
10. The political situation in the region has d____________ rapidly.
11. Students with anxiety are encouraged to go psychological r______________.
12. He believes that world war is i___________.
13. Melbourne is commonly r___________ to as the "Art Capital" of Australia.
14. I haven't been p________________ these days; I haven't finished anything yet.
15. Students need an e_______________ way to revise for exams when the

exam period approaches.

16. Many old people's health d_______________ as they getting older and older.

17. Any one can have positive i_______________ on our society as long as they try their best to do good. (do good 短语，以美德行事)

18. Ryan's success in the Australian Junior Tennis Contest has become a hot t_________ at school.

19. Nowadays, almost every h_______________ has a fridge and a dishwasher.

20. A______________ to computer games is quite common among modern teenagers.

21. Sometimes you should look at a social problem from a different a___________.

22. Psychologists offer c________________ services for people who have mental health issues.

23. Students can be i___________ by the ideas in books they have read.

24. Recently, the company Apple was come under a___________ due to data leakage issues.

25. The weather near the sea w___________ as the hurricane approached the coastal line.

26. John's relationship with his mother d________________ since he moved out.

27. Good communication skills are r_____________ as an essential skills for young people.

28. The President candidate c___________ that he would cut tax if he won the election.

29. Some young people c____________ with each other on the street, which resulted in a riot in this peaceful city.

30. Don't o____________! It's just a normal piece of work to finish.

Passage 8

What Is a Text Response Essay?

Most students will be required to write text response essays from year 10. But what is a text response essay? Put it simply, it is a piece of writing that intends to persuade others. In most text response essays, you are assessed on your ability to develop an argument relating to a prompt.

What Is a Prompt?

A prompt is a piece of information that is used to inspire you to develop your writing. Usually you will be given a reading list and the prompts will relate to the titles in the list. The books in the reading list are often referred to as texts in the university entrance exam.

You need to demonstrate your ability to analyze themes, issues and characters in an insightful way, your ability to identify an author's intention, and unpack their narrative devices.

Reading literary works can be tricky for some students, but if you remind yourself that the reason why you are given a particular text is all because it has some complex and thoughtful themes to be explored, then you will be clear what to focus on in your reading. In your essay, you must discuss the text's complexity in a systematic way. You can start with a simple but obvious point, and then gradually build up the progression of thoughts.

Technical Terms

When you write a text response essay, you should use terms accurately. Most literary works have a plot, or a theme. The plot is often built with characters showing the author's purpose of writing that story. The purpose can be criticizing social injustice or applauding the beauty of love or life. The context of the story, or called the setting, is also a crucial element for a text response essay. Students need to sharpen your analytical skills, build up vocabulary of fabulous literary words, and further develop their persuading and reasoning skills.

All in all, simply paraphrasing the author's words in the text is insufficient, you need to grasp concepts of literary device, and use them to explain how the author constructs the story. So, students should spend loads of time on further developing their analytical and argumentative skills instead of making considerable repetitions.

必备词汇：

名词

response [rɪˈspɒns] 反应；回应
text response essay 读后感论文
argument [ˈɑːgjumənt] 议论文；争论
prompt [prɒm(p)t] 提示
title [ˈtaɪt(ə)l] 书名
entrance [ˈentrəns] 入门；进入
character [ˈkærəktə(r)] 角色
analysis [əˈnælɪsɪs] 分析
analyst [ˈænəlɪst] 分析者
concept [ˈkɒnsept] 观念，概念
construction [kənˈstrʌkʃ(ə)n] 建设；构造
explanation [ekspləˈneɪʃ(ə)n] 说明，解释
progression [prəˈgreʃn] 进展
literature [ˈlɪt(ə)rətʃə] 文学；文献
plot [plɒt] 情节
theme [θiːm] 主题；主旋律
purpose [ˈpɜːpəs] 目的；意图
injustice [ɪnˈdʒʌstɪs] 不公正
context [ˈkɒntekst] 上下文；背景
setting [ˈsetɪŋ] 故事背景
element [ˈelɪmənt] 元素
requirement [rɪˈkwaɪəm(ə)nt] 要求；必要条件
technician [tekˈnɪʃ(ə)n] 技师
repetition [repɪˈtɪʃ(ə)n] 重复

动词

require [rɪˈkwaɪə(r)] 要求
intend to 打算；旨在
persuade [pəˈsweɪd] 说服；劝说
assess [əˈses] 考核；评估
relate [rɪˈleɪt] 与……有关
demonstrate [ˈdemənstreɪt] 展示
construct [kənˈstrʌkt] 建造，构造

criticize [ˈkrɪtɪsaɪz] 批评；评论

grasp [grɑ:sp] 抓住；领会

applaud [əˈplɔ:d] 称赞；鼓掌

sharpen [ʃa:p(ə)n] 使尖锐；打磨

paraphrase [ˈpærəfreɪz] 改写；转述

形容词

insightful [ˈɪnsaɪtfʊl] 有内涵的；有深度的

complex [ˈkɒmpleks] 复杂的

thoughtful [ˈθɔ:tfl] 深思的

systematic [ˌsɪstəˈmætɪk] 有条理的；系统的

obvious [ˈɒbviəs] 明显的

crucial [ˈkru:ʃ(ə)l] 重要的

fabulous [ˈfæbjələs] 极好的

literary [ˈlɪt(ə)(rə)rɪ] 文学的

reasoning [ˈri:z(ə)niŋ] 论证的

短语

focus on 集中在……上

put it simply 简而言之

all in all 总的来说

loads of 很多

instead of 而不是；并非

Passage 8 配套单词填空练习

1. Sophisticated statistical a____________ was employed to obtain these results.
2. Many a____________ failed to explain the sudden drop in house prices.
3. It is very difficult to define the c__________ of beauty.
4. The walls are c___________ of concrete.
5. She works in the c_______________ industry.
6. Her work has been c___________ to the project's success.
7. The teacher d_________________ how to use the equipment.
8. It really annoying when a train is late and there's no e______________.
9. Her internationally acclaimed novel has won several l____________ prizes.
10. He's very knowledgeable about German l_____________.
11. The movie's p_______ is very simple.
12. Japan's bad economy has p__________ consumers to cut back on buying cars.
13. Its products met all legal r________________.

14. A t__________ is someone whose job involves skilled practical work with scientific equipment.

15. The novel's central t_______ is the ongoing conflict between men and women.

16. His mother had rarely c__________ him or any of her other children.

17. They have a good g_______ of foreign languages.

18. He could have cut out much of the r___________ and thus saved many pages.

19. To understand the s_________ of a story is the basic thing before you can evaluate the story.

20. Don't just p________________ the words of the author, you need to develop your own thoughts.

21. Sometimes the p____________ of an author is not obvious, and you need to draw it out from how the author tells his/her story with intentionally chosen words.

22. Social i______________ is often seen in countries without stable governments.

23. Students will be a______________ their writing skills at the end of this term.

24. Text response essays require you to writing something to p_____________ your readers.

25. You'd better f__________ on one thing each time.

26. Teachers will teach students to s___________ their writing skills throughout Year 5.

27. Reading is a good way to develop children's i____________ thought.

28. A s_______________ arrangement of exam timetable can help students prepare their exams better.

29. We had a f____________ trip to Europe last year.

30. The boy named Harry Potter is a well-known fictional c_______________.

Passage 9

Different Types of Articles in Literature

In the world of literature, authors use various types of texts to express their perspectives towards life and the nature. Historically, literary professionals classify these texts into following types: novel, fiction, comedy, play, drama, poetry and prose because of their different contents and structures. There are countless titles under each group; students can delve into the ocean of books and discover their "magic books" that inspire them to read more.

Generally speaking, novels and fictions cover many themes; detective novels investigate secret lives and contain numerous twists and turns; romance novels praise the beauty and sorrow of love. Lines of poetry are full of rhythm, and can be read smoothly.

Science fictions are the best for curious souls, whose imagination goes beyond the boundary of the planet Earth even expands to the vast universe. For curious children, aliens from the outer space are not frightening at all.

When you are exploring the books available in your local library, you can read some excerpt from a book and see if it appeals to you. If you are unsure which types of book that set your mind off, you can experiment with some books that are illustrated with interesting pictures. If you choose a thick book only with words, it may put you off because of its lengthy complex expressions.

When choose a book, you can just flick through books that appear interesting to you. If you begin read a book of unfamiliar topic, you can always put it down, and choose another one until you find your "magic book". It will attract you like a magnet. It will make you discover more books, and it will entice you to read more and more.

When you are available, you can go to a library or a bookshop and flick through different types of books. You may just find your magic book there.

必备词汇:

名词

appeal [ə'pi:l] 呼吁,恳求
type [taɪp] 种类
article ['ɑ:tɪkl] 文章
literature ['lɪtrətʃə(r)] 文学
perspective [pə'spɛktɪv] 观点;看法
professional [prə'feʃənl] 专业人士
novel ['nɒv(ə)l] 长篇小说
fiction ['fɪkʃn] 小说; 虚构
comedy ['kɒmədɪ] 喜剧
play [pleɪ] 戏剧
drama ['drɑ:mə] 戏剧
poetry ['pəʊɪtrɪ] 诗歌
prose [prəʊz] 散文
content ['kɒntent] 内容
structure ['strʌktʃə] 结构
beginning [bɪ'gɪnɪŋ] 开始
content [kən'tent] 内容,目录
excerpt ['eksɜ:pt] 摘录,引用
expression [ɪk'spreʃn] 表达
profession [prə'feʃ(ə)n] 职业,专业
rhythm ['rɪð(ə)m] 节奏;韵律
universe ['ju:nɪvɜ:s] 宇宙
soul [səʊl] 灵魂
detective [dɪ'tektɪv] 侦探家
sorrow [saro] 哀伤;忧伤
boundary ['baʊndrɪ] 边界
magnet ['mægnət] 磁铁

动词

discover [dɪ'skʌvə] 发现
appeal [ə'pi:l] 有吸引力
explore [ɪk'splɔ:; ek-] 探索
investigate [ɪn'vestɪgeɪt] 调查;研究
praise [preɪz] 赞美
inspire [ɪn'spaɪə] 激发;鼓舞
entice [ɪn'taɪs; en-] 诱使;怂恿
illustrate ['ɪləstreɪt] 阐明,举例说明
frighten ['fraɪtn] 令……害怕;惊吓

形容词

various ['veərɪəs] 各种各样的
countless ['kaʊntlɪs] 数不清的
numerous ['nju:m(ə)rəs] 许多的,很多的
secret ['si:krɪt] 秘密的;神秘的
familiar [fə'mɪlɪə] 熟悉的
curious ['kjuərɪəs] 好奇的
complex ['kɒmpleks] 复杂的

frightening [ˈfraɪtnɪŋ] 吓人的

vast [vaːst] 广袤的；广阔的

lengthy [ˈleŋθɪ] 冗长的；漫长的

familiar [fəˈmɪlɪə(r)] 熟悉的（unfamiliar 不熟悉的）

副词

historically [hɪˈstɒrɪklɪ] 从历史上来看

短语

delve into 探究

twist and turn 跌宕起伏

flick through 快速翻阅

science fiction 科幻小说

Passage 9 配套单词填空练习

1. They are launching an a________ to raise money for famine victims.
2. Notes on how to use the dictionary can be found at the b____________ of the book.
3. There is no table of c__________ in the book.
4. I looked forward to the e___________ of their theories.
5. Laughter is one of the most infectious e_____________ of emotion.
6. They are already f__________ faces on our TV screens, audience need something fresh.
7. They are still i_______________ the accident.
8. We have discussed these plans on n____________ occasions.
9. You can describe something very beautiful as p__________.
10. The American president p________ Turkey for its courage.
11. He left the teaching p_____________ in 1965 to start his own business.
12. I've got no sense of r__________, so I'm a terrible dancer.
13. Is there intelligent life elsewhere in the u_____________?
14. His confident leadership i_________ his followers.
15. The b_____________ between history and storytelling are always being blurred.
16. Let me give another example to i____________ this difficult point.

17. The project involves a lot of c__________ technical problems.

18. The adverts e__________ the customer into buying things they don't really need.

19. Henry started to d________ _______ the world of insects since he was 10.

20. The d____________ of the wheat pattern on potteries helped to determine the starting time of human society in that area.

21. It is a good idea to f______ ____________ a book to see if it is interesting.

22. After experiencing t________ and t__________ in an young age, Oliver turned out to be a mature man earlier than his peers.

23. The idea of death does not necessarily f___________ everyone.

24. The author i_____________ the complex math formula with a simple illustration.

25. From my p______________, students should not be allowed to bring their phones to school.

26. With a l____________ introduction, the Principal finally started the gist of his Monday speech—student disciplinary actions to be implemented.

27. Articles written in r__________ can be easily read and memorized.

28. The v_________ majority of teachers agree that students should be taught grammar.

29. Many stories are f__________, which means you cannot believe them all.

30. Australia is boasted of n____________ beautiful beaches; this means surfers or beach lovers have many options.

Passage 10

Drawing on Other's Opinions

Reading commentary or opinion columns in newspaper is an efficient way to improve your writing skills. The chief editor of the newspaper is empowered to select the best comments from contributors.

Various kinds of comments can appear on newspaper, some are on fundamental issues occurring in the society, some are on gallery, museum and art exhibition, and some are on enterprises and investments in a global context. Although you can pick up the gist of the news from its headline, but comments are subtle and they deserve your thorough digesting of the entire article.

Opinion writers seek readers' agreement on the issues that are commented. The issues often involve conflict and controversy, while the writers reveal numerous viewpoints on the issues through their comments.

Writers often use various persuading techniques to present readers the gist of the issue under attack. Writers also utilize evidence to support their views. The evidence can be research result or personal witness accounts of the events. No matter what kind of evidence is used, the writers tend to influence readers to accept their point of views. As a reader, it is critical to distinguish what opinions are trustworthy and what are not.

必备词汇：

名词

column [ˈkɒləm] 纵队，列

commentator [ˈkɒmənteɪtə] 评论员，解说员

context [ˈkɒntekst] 环境；上下文

enterprise [ˈentəpraɪz] 企业

exhibition [ˌeksɪˈbɪʃn] 展览

controversy [ˈkɒntrəvɜːsɪ] 争论；论战；辩论

opinion [əˈpɪnjən] 意见；主张

chief [tʃi:f] 首领;酋长
issue [ˈɪʃu:] 问题
investment [ɪnˈves(t)m(ə)nt] 投资
conflict [ˈkɒnflɪkt] 冲突,矛盾
account [əˈkaʊnt] 账户;描述

动词

empower [ɪmˈpaʊə; em-] 授权,允许
digest [daɪˈdʒest; dɪ-] 消化;吸收
reveal [rɪˈvi:l] 显示;透露
distinguish [dɪˈstɪŋgwɪʃ] 区分;辨别
improve [ɪmˈpru:v] 改善,增进
contribute [kənˈtrɪbju:t] 贡献
deserve [dɪˈzɜ:v] 应受,应得
persuade [pəˈsweɪd] 说服,劝说
utilize [ˈju:tɪˌlaɪz] 利用
account [əˈkaʊnt] 认为;把……视为

形容词

editorial [edɪˈtɔ:rɪəl] 编辑的
efficient [ɪˈfɪʃ(ə)nt] 有效率的
entire [ɪnˈtaɪə; en-] 全部的
fundamental [fʌndəˈment(ə)l] 基本的,根本的
thorough [ˈθʌrə] 彻底的
subtle [ˈsʌt(ə)l] 微妙的;精细的
critical [ˈkrɪtɪk(ə)l] 批判的
various [ˈveərɪəs] 各种各样的;多方面的
global [ˈgləʊb(ə)l] 全球的
trustworthy [ˈtrʌs(t)wɜ:ðɪ] 可靠的;可信赖的

介词

on [ɔn] 关于

Passage 10 配套单词填空练习

1. A c__________ is a group of people or animals that move in a long line.
2. A c___________ is someone who often writes or broadcasts about a particular subject.
3. We are doing this work in the c________ of reforms in the economic, social and cultural spheres.
4. The city's transport system is one of the most e__________ in Europe.
5. He'd spent the e_________ journey asleep.
6. Don't forget this is a commercial e_____________; we're here to make

money.

7. The photographs will be on e____________ until the end of the month.

8. Some understanding of grammar is f______________ to learning a language.

9. They did a t_________ search of the area but found nothing.

10. The army is now e____________ to operate on a shoot-to-kill basis.

11. Something that is s_______ is not immediately obvious or noticeable.

12. It often takes a long time to d________ new ideas.

13. There was a big c___________ surrounding the use of drugs in athletics.

14. He was jailed for r___________ secrets to the Russians.

15. The report is highly c________ of safety standards at the factory.

16. He is colour-blind and can't d___________ between red and green.

17. He held the o________ that a government should think before introducing a tax.

18. Within a month, both the texture and condition of your hair should i__________ after you use this shampoo.

19. I believe that each of us can c______________ to the future of the world.

20. The methods to deal with air pollution are v__________.

21. The problems of immigration were not the question at i_______.

22. He said the government must introduce tax incentives to encourage i__________.

23. A g_________ view or vision of a situation is one in which all the different aspects of it are considered.

24. These people d___________ to make more than the minimum wage.

25. There is a c_________ between what they are doing and what you want.

26. We had managed to p____________ them that it was worth working with us.

27. Sound engineers u_______ a range of techniques to enhance the quality of the recordings.

28. Some banks make it difficult for unemployed people to open an a_________.

29. A t___________ person is reliable, responsible, and can be trusted completely.

30. He is the c_____ of the Aboriginal tribe.

Passage 11

A Light Touch on the Australian Political System

Although Australia is an island continent far away from Britain, the framework of Australian political system resembles that of Britain. The parliament is the core of this system. Parliamentary members often debate about social issues and make legislations as well.

Simply speaking, parliament is the place to make laws. If some people break the law or do something illegal, they will be locked in prison and will be judged in courts later. Courts are formal institutions in Australia. There, jury and judges will determine together if some people are criminals or not. Finally, judges will write a judgment for the case. If those people are innocent, they will be released from prison.

Australia is a society with lots of regulations. The Parliament often appoints commissioners as regulators to uphold the law and regulation. The public has to manage their life accordingly; otherwise, they may break the law easily.

For example, if people drive at a speed that exceeds the speed limit displayed on the road sign, they are engaging in an unlawful conduct. Speeding on Australian roads usually triggers a fine; or the drivers will be prosecuted by the police officers in more serious cases.

In most cases, local voters elect leaders from numerous politicians every three years. But all citizens may be asked to do referendum for significant political questions such as founding a republic country. Referendum has only happened a couple of times in the Australian history. But most citizens are active in political matters; they are also members of worker's union.

必备词汇：

名词

appointment [ə'pɔɪntmənt] 任命；约定

continent ['kɒntɪnənt] 大陆

framework ['freɪmwɜ:k] 框架

institution [ɪnstɪ'tju:ʃ(ə)n] 机构

judgement ['dʒʌdʒm(ə)nt] 判断

legislation [ledʒɪs'leɪʃ(ə)n] 立法；法律

referendum [,refə'rendəm] 公民投票权

regulation [regjʊ'leɪʃ(ə)n] 管理；规则

regulator ['regjʊleɪtə] 调整者

core [kɔ:] 核心；要点

commissioner [kə'mɪʃ(ə)nə] 理事；委员

politician [pɒlɪ'tɪʃ(ə)n] 政治家，政客

citizen ['sɪtɪz(ə)n] 公民；市民；老百姓

republic [rɪ'pʌblɪk] 共和国；共和政体

display [dɪ'spleɪ] 显示

conduct ['kɒndʌkt] 行为

动词

appoint [ə'pɒɪnt] 任命；指定

resemble [rɪ'zemb(ə)l] 类似

exceed [ɪk'si:d; ek-] 超过；胜过

trigger ['trɪgə] 引发，引起；触发

prosecute ['prɒsɪkju:t] 检举；贯彻；起诉；告发

determine [dɪ'tɜ:mɪn] 决定，确定

elect [ɪ'lekt] 选举；选择

manage ['mænɪdʒ] 管理；经营

legislate [ledʒɪs'leɪt] 立法

regulate [regjʊ'leɪt] 管理

display[dɪ'spleɪ] 显示

形容词

electoral [ɪ'lekt(ə)r(ə)l] 选举的

innocent ['ɪnəs(ə)nt] 无辜的

parliamentary [ˌpɑ:lə'ment(ə)rɪ] 议会的；国会的

illegal [ɪ'li:g(ə)l] [法] 非法的

formal ['fɔ:m(ə)l] 正式的

significant [sɪg'nɪfɪk(ə)nt] 重大的；有意义的

political [pə'lɪtɪk(ə)l] 政治的；党派的

副词

accordingly [ə'kɔ:dɪŋlɪ] 因此，相应地

Passage 11 配套单词填空练习

1. The school has a____________ three new teachers this year.
2. She had to cancel her dental a_____________, because she could not make it.
3. The c___________ makes up about 35% of the earth's crust.
4. The Mongolian Democratic Party is campaigning for e_________reform.
5. A f__________is a particular set of rules, ideas, or beliefs which you use in order to deal with problems or to decide what to do.
6. He was sure that the man was i_________ of any crime.
7. Harvard University is an internationally respected i__________.
8. I'm going to reserve j_____________ on the decision.
9. The government has promised to introduce l__________ to limit fuel emissions from cars.
10. He used his influence to make sure she was not selected as a p__________ candidate.
11. Some people in the market now want government r___________ in order to reduce costs.
12. An independent r___________ will be appointed to ensure fair competition.
13. Some of the commercially produced venison r___________ beef in flavour.
14. He accepts that he was e___________ the speed limit.
15. Stress may act as a t_________ for these illnesses.
16. The police have decided not to p________ because the evidence is not strong enough.
17. He has the ability to get straight to the c_________ of a problem.
18. He was convicted of i_________ using a handgun.
19. I am the f____________ leader of the project but the everyday management is in the hands of my assistant.

20. Eye colour is genetically d____________.

21. It is a difficult job and they should be paid a____________.

22. I decided to c_____________ an experiment.

23. She believed her job as a p___________ was to represent the views of her party and the people who voted for her.

24. The interests of British c_______ living abroad are protected by the British Embassy.

25. There has been a s_____________ increase in the number of women students in recent years.

26. There are two major p__________ parties in the US.

27. The people of the Philippines have voted to e_________ a new president.

28. A r__________ is a country where power is held by the people or the representatives that they elect.

29. In a busy world, m__________ your time properly becomes increasingly important.

30. Let's d_______ the figures and see what we have.

Passage 12

A Distinguished Author from a Humble Origin (Part 1)

J.K. Rowling, the author of the bestseller books *Harry Potter*, addressed to thousands of young audience on the occasion of Harvard university commencement. In her speech, she shared her thoughts on the importance of imagination.

According to her speech, Rowling comes from an impoverished family, so her parents were desperate for her success after she graduated from university. They hoped she would study a promising area like medicine to make a decent life later. However, she loved writing novels only and she enrolled to study language at university. Language was regarded useless by her parents. Rowling said that behavior disappointed her parents but she did not regret.

She said she knew the taste of poverty, which entails horrible experience, sense of insecurity, and even provokes psychological problems. But she said the power of intelligence and imagination can help us overcome all of those negative things. She said that her passion in writing had led her through ups and downs of life.

必备词汇：

名词

author [ˈɔ:θə(r)] 作者

origin [ˈɒrɪdʒɪn] 起源；出身

bestseller [bestˈselə(r)] 畅销书

imagination [ɪˌmædʒɪˈneɪʃn] 想象力

intelligence [ɪnˈtelɪdʒ(ə)ns] 智力；情报工作

passion [ˈpæʃ(ə)n] 热情

poverty [ˈpɒvətɪ] 贫困；困难

psychology [saɪˈkɒlədʒɪ] 心理学

commencement [kəˈmensm(ə)nt] 开始，发端

success [səkˈses] 成功

insecurity [ˌɪnsɪˈkjʊərətɪ] 不安全;不牢靠
passion [ˈpæʃ(ə)n] 激情;热情
intelligence [ɪnˈtelɪdʒ(ə)ns] 智力;情报工作
medicine [ˈmedsn] 医学;.
behaviour [bɪˈheɪvjə] 行为
taste [teɪst] 滋味

动词

enrol [ɪnˈrəʊl] 登记; 入学
overcome [əʊvəˈkʌm] 克服
provoke [prəˈvəʊk] 驱使;激发
regret [rɪˈgret] 后悔
entail [ɪnˈteɪl; en-] 使需要,承担
address [əˈdres] 演说;处理
graduate [ˈgrædʒʊeɪt] 毕业
commencement [kəˈmensmənt] 开始,发端

形容词

distinguished [dɪˈstɪŋgwɪʃt] 著名的;卓著的;高贵的
humble [ˈhʌmbl] 卑微的;粗陋的
desperate [ˈdespərət] 极度渴望的
promising [ˈprɒmɪsɪŋ] 有前途的
disappointed [dɪsəˈpɒɪntɪd] 失望的
occasional [əˈkeɪʒ(ə)n(ə)l] 偶然的
psychological [saɪkəˈlɒdʒɪk(ə)l] 心理的
decent [ˈdi:s(ə)nt] 正派的;得体的
impoverished [ɪmˈpɒvərɪʃt] 穷困的;用尽了的
negative [ˈnegətiv][数] 负的;消极的

短语

according to 根据
ups and downs 起伏;成败

Passage 12 配套单词填空练习

1. I was d______________ that John was not there.
2. Her mother e__________ her in dancing classes.
3. She's a woman of exceptional i____________.
4. He still misbehaves o________________.
5. We must o____________ our shortcomings.
6. According to World Bank figures, 41 per cent of Brazilians live in absolute p_______.
7. His election success has p__________ a shocked reaction.

C
aeas
10
|
12

8. John received constant physical and p_____________ abuse from his father.

9. It was not until the mid-twentieth century that p_____________ really came into its own.

10. Much to my r______, I am unable to accept your kind invitation.

11. He didn't get a d________ explanation.

12. Such a decision would e________ a huge political risk.

13. She a__________ to the large audience of Royal Academy.

14. Would passengers please turn off their mobile phones before the c___________ of the flight.

15. They both played the game a_____________ to the rules.

16. We need to reduce the burden of taxes that i_____________ the economy.

17. He was a boy who d__________ needed affection.

18. I think he's trying to deal with his fears and i___________.

19. The warm winter has had a very n___________impact on the ski industry.

20. Superior i_____________and the use of language distinguish humans from the other animals.

21. David Williams is one of most favored a______________, because he has written loads of bestseller books.

22. What is the o____________ of those coffee beans, Brazil or Africa?

23. The Australian Prime Minister behaves quite h_____________ in front of the Queen.

24. Although the couple have gone through u_______ and d________ in their life, they still got divorced.

25. A______________ to the *New York Times*, the economy was predicted to go downward in the near future.

26. Many people think property manager is a very p_____________job.

27. My cousin found a job shortly after he g_______________ from the university.

28. Rich people cannot understand the t_____________ of poverty, that is, they

don't know how being poor feels like,

29. Henry dreams to study m______________ and becomes a doctor.

30. The graduation ceremony will c______________ at 10 am next Monday.

Passage 13

A Distinguished Author from a Humble Origin (Part 2)

Rowling unfolded her painful experience of failure in her early writing career before she ultimately presented *Harry Potter* to readers. It ignited the *Harry Potter* phenomenon around the world. It was translated into various languages and was widespread among readers of different ages. The sold volume of the *Harry Potter* books was overwhelming, Rowling's seemingly "useless" study finally brought her both reputation and wealth. She said her talent finally got recognition. Harry Potter books were adapted to movies as well. The film adaptations were very impressive; the imagined settings were made vivid with advanced computer technology. *Harry Potter* films are seriously fantastic.

Imagination is a unique treasure that requires us to uncover with heaps of effort. Imagination not only can transform our life but also can bring triumph to our life. So we should cherish it carefully. However, many educators complain that today's young children are poor at imagining. They say this phenomenon is reflected by the pretending games children play in their early education life. These educators comment that children engage less in pretending games that children played in the past; instead, they would prefer feed themselves with cartoons on iPads or TV. The educators caution that this is a negative trend, because children's imagination will ultimately be worn out by the passive reception of information. That would be an alarming blow to human's culture.

必备词汇：

<u>名词</u>

reputation [repjʊˈteɪʃ(ə)n] 名声，名誉

wealth [welθ] 财富

phenomenon [fɪˈnɒmɪnən] 现象

adaption [əˈdæpʃn] 适应，改编

recognition [rekəg'nɪʃ(ə)n] 识别；承认

triumph ['traɪʌmf] 胜利，凯旋

phenomenon [fɪ'nɒmɪnən] 现象；奇迹

technology [tek'nɒlədʒɪ] 技术；工艺

treasure ['treʒə] 财富，财产

动词

ignite [ɪg'naɪt] 点燃；使燃烧；使激动

cherish ['tʃerɪʃ] 珍爱

transform [træns'fɔ:m; trɑ:ns-; -nz-] 改变，使……变形

spread [spred] 传播

complain [kəm'pleɪn] 抱怨

prefer [prɪ'f3:(r)] 宁可；更喜欢

engage [ɪn'geɪdʒ] 参与；从事

pretend [prɪ'tend] 假装

形容词

overwhelming [ˌəʊvə'welmɪŋ] 压倒性的；势不可挡的

impressive [ɪm'presɪv] 感人的；令人钦佩的

advanced [əd'vɑ:nst] 先进的；高级的

unique [ju:'ni:k] 独特的，稀罕的

humble ['hʌmbl] 谦逊的；简陋的

widespread [ˌwaɪd'spred] 普遍的，广泛的

vivid ['vɪvɪd] 生动的；鲜明的

passive ['pæsɪv] 被动的

pretending [prɪ'tendɪŋ] 假装的

副词

seriously ['sɪərɪəslɪ] 认真地；严重地

ultimately ['ʌltɪmətli] 最终；最后

短语

heaps of efforts 大量的努力

wear out 磨破；消磨殆尽

Passage 13 配套单词填空练习

1. You won't feel the task so o__________________ if you break it down into small, easy-to-accomplish steps.
2. The University of Melbourne has a good academic r___________.
3. These countries have been s____________ disadvantaged by the finan-

cial crisis.

4. How do we t____________ one type of file to another?

5. Economic reform has brought relative w________ to peasant farmers.

6. How would economist explain this p_______________of people investing heavily in houses?

7. Evolution occurs as a result of animals' a___________ to new environments.

8. The bombs i_______ a fire which destroyed 60 houses.

9. He searched for a sign of r__________ on her face, but there was none.

10. It is an i_________ achievement.

11. The course is suitable for both beginners and a_________ students.

12. Each person's signature is u____.

13. All her life, Kelly had been stuck with difficult tasks and challenges, and t________.

14. Henry genuinely loved and c_________ his wife.

15. T_________ is changing fast.

16. The house was large and full of art t________.

17. He gave a great performance, but he was very h_____.

18. There is w_________ support for the new proposals.

19. He sketched the situation in a few v_____ words.

20. Laura p_______ not seeing me when we came across on the street.

21. If you just p_______ involve in the class activities, you can really learn anything. So, you'd better be active.

22. Jim has e___________ in several volunteer jobs, and he has learnt a lot.

23. Which one would you p________?

The yellow one or green one?

24. The woman's patience was finally w_______ _______ by her son's continuous nagging.

25. We will u___________learn how to deal with different people.

Passage 14

Are You Surrendered to Peer Pressure?

When your friends pressure you to go along with something, it is a form of peer pressure. It is OK to feel confused or to struggle with peer pressure. It may be scary, but it just takes practice and courage to stand up to peer pressure. Everyone faces peer pressure at a certain stage of their lives, so no one is really immune from it.

Middle school can be the highlight time of peer pressure. Many students face this issue. Peer pressure can turn out to be moderate to some students but severe to others. It mainly depends on how sensitive the student is. Teachers should observe the conduct of students to discover any victim of peer pressure.

We often see in news headlines that some young people are forced to consume alcohol or cigarette owing to peer pressure. Peer pressure may stir up very fierce inner feelings among students.

Students with soft mind should not remain silent, if the pressure sustains for long time. Instead, they should take actions to resist it, for example, seeking assistance from wellbeing teachers. The resistance helps them to clarify their stance: they will not surrender to the pressure!

必备词汇：

名词

peer [pɪə(r)] 同辈；同龄人

pressure [ˈpreʃə(r)] 压力

peer pressure 同辈压力

form [fɔ:m] 形式

practice [ˈpræktɪs] 练习

courage [ˈkʌrɪdʒ] 勇气

highlight [ˈhaɪlaɪt] 重点；最突出的部分

issue [ˈɪʃu:] 问题

conduct [kənˈdʌkt] 行为

victim [ˈvɪktɪm] 受害者

headline [ˈhedlaɪn] 头条新闻
alcohol [ˈælkəhɒl] 酒
cigarette [ˌsɪgəˈret] 香烟
assistance [əˈsɪstəns] 协助
wellbeing [ˌwelˈbiːˌɪŋ]（心灵）健康
resistance [rɪˈzɪstəns] 反对；阻力
stance [stæns] 立场

动词

surrender [səˈrendə(r)] 屈服；投降
pressure [ˈpreʃə(r)] 施压
struggle [ˈstrʌgl] 斗争；挣扎
observe [əbˈzɜːv] 观察
discover [dɪˈskʌvə(r)] 发现
force [fɔːs] 强迫
consume [kənˈsjuːm] 消费；吃喝
remain [rɪˈmeɪn] 保持
sustain [səˈsteɪn] 维持
resist [rɪˈzɪst] 抵制；抵抗
seek [siːk] 寻求
clarify [ˈklærəfaɪ] 澄清

形容词

confused [kənˈfjuːzd] 困惑的
scary [ˈskeəri] 可怕的
silent [ˈsaɪlənt] 沉默的；安静的
immune [ɪˈmjuːn] 免疫的；免除的
moderate [ˈmɒdərət] 适度的；温和的
severe [sɪˈvɪə(r)] 严厉的；严重的
sensitive [ˈsensətɪv] 敏感的；灵敏的
fierce [fɪəs] 强烈的
inner [ˈɪnə(r)] 内心
soft [sɒft] 柔软的

副词

instead [ɪnˈsted] 反而

短语

go along with 陪同前往；赞同
stand up to 抵抗；抵挡
turn out to be 变成
owing to 由于；因为
stir up 激起
take action 采取行动

Passage 14 配套单词填空练习

1.Not to give in to other’s pressure means not to s________.

2. You don’t need to g_____ ______ ____ anyone’s view, you are an independent person.

3. O______ ____ the technology, people can communicate with friends instantly.

4. The principal's speech has s______ ______ a riot among students.

5. People should t_______ ________ to protect the environment.

6. Sometimes, it is difficult to s________ ______ _____ peer pressure.

7. Employees are p_____________ to work longer than it is normal; otherwise, they may lose their job.

8. Some students may s___________ with reading.

9. My little brother loves to o__________ small creatures in the garden.

10. Some black moles on skin can t_____ _____ _____ ____ the sign of skin cancer.

11. To bake a cake, it is necessary to use s________ butter.

12. Witnessing a car accident may stir up strong i_______ reaction.

13. The storm was f__________ and destroyed many houses.

14. S___________ people usually feel shy to speak to strangers.

15. School may discipline student for their s___________ misconduct.

16. Today's weather is m_________, so we can have picnic.

17. Newborn babies have weak i___________ systems.

18. That movie sounds s________ because of the ghosts.

19. He showed a c___________ expression on his face.

20. Officials should c___________ the recent political chaos.

21. Don't be afraid of s________ help when you need it.

22. The natural resources on the Earth cannot s_________ eternally.

23. His improper behavior r________ for the past year.

24. Nowadays, people c___________ lots of fast food.

25. Sometimes, the yummy fast food is hard to r________.

26. You should be firm about your s_________ even if others do not agree with you.

27. We should look after both your physical health and w__________.

28. Remaining s______ sometimes is not a way to solve the problem; instead, you should speak out.

29. The car accident resulted in many v________.

30. Having c_______ means you are brave to do things.

Passage 15

Electives Offer "Hands-on" Experience

Middle school students are often provided extensive electives, such as biology, chemistry and finance. The formation of atoms and molecules are taught in chemistry, while theory of evolution and genetics are the foundation of biology. Finance may look at the monetary management and investments. Some students may select economy as an elective, though it focuses more on a country's fiscal measures, revenue, and economic landscape of that country.

Take chemistry as an example. When students do experiment in a laboratory, teachers should implement strict safety measures to avoid occurrence of explosion or fire.

Mistakes are inevitable in doing experiment, so students ought to follow guidelines. Diversion from guidelines may result in disasters or catastrophes. For the subject of chemistry, students are required to do heaps of experiment and write a pile of reports. Accordingly, they should record their experiment data accurately. Students should not borrow other's data without their teacher's permission. As maintaining one's own experiment data is relevant to a student's academic integrity, so teachers usually would not permit the sharing of such data. Students need to be aware that an outstanding chemistry experiment report should include such parts as: objective, material, procedure, outcome and conclusion.

必备词汇：

名词

elective [ɪˈlektɪv] 选修课

biology [baɪˈɒlədʒi] 生物学

chemistry [ˈkemɪstrɪ] 化学

finance [ˈfaɪnæns] 金融

formation [fɔːˈmeɪʃən] 形成

atom [ˈætəm] 原子
molecule [ˈmɒlɪkjuːl] 分子
theory [ˈθɪərɪ] 理论
evolution [ˌevəˈluːʃən] 进化
genetics [dʒəˈnetɪks] 基因学
foundation [faʊnˈdeɪʃən] 基础；基石
management [ˈmænɪdʒmənt] 管理
investment [ɪnˈvestmənt] 投资
economy [iˈkɒnəmɪ] 经济学
measure [ˈmeʒər] 措施
revenue [ˈrevənjuː]（财政）收入
landscape [ˈlændskeɪp] 概括；地貌
experiment [ɪkˈsperɪmənt] 实验
laboratory [ləˈbɒrətərɪ] 实验室
occurrence [əˈkʌrəns] 事件
explosion [ɪkˈspləʊʒən] 爆炸
mistake [mɪˈsteɪk] 错误
guideline [ˈgaɪdlaɪn] 指南
diversion [daɪˈvɜːʃən] 偏离
disaster [dɪˈzɑːstər] 灾难
catastrophe [kəˈtæstrəfɪ] 大灾难
report [rɪˈpɔːt] 报告
permission [pəˈmɪʃən] 许可
integrity [ɪnˈtegrətɪ] 诚实
objective [əbˈdʒektɪv] 目标
material [məˈtɪərɪəl] 材料
procedure [prəˈsiːdʒər] 过程；流程
outcome [ˈaʊtkʌm] 结果
conclusion [kənˈkluːʒən] 结论

动词

provide [prəˈvaɪd] 提供
select [sɪˈlekt] 选择
implement [ˈɪmplɪment] 实行；执行
avoid [əˈvɔɪd] 避免
follow [ˈfɒləʊ] 遵守
borrow [ˈbɒrəʊ] 借用
maintain [meɪnˈteɪn] 保持；保存
permit [pəˈmɪt] 允许；给……许可
include [ɪnˈkluːd] 包含

形容词

hands-on 亲身实践的
extensive [ɪkˈstensɪv] 广泛的
monetary [ˈmʌnɪtri] 货币的；金钱的
fiscal [ˈfɪskəl]（国家）财政的
economic [iːkəˈnɒmɪk] 经济的
strict [strɪkt] 严格的
inevitable [ɪˈnevɪtəbəl] 不可避免的
accurate [ˈækjərət] 准确的
outstanding [ˌaʊtˈstændɪŋ] 杰出的；优异的

介词

without [wiˈðaut] 没有

短语

relevant to 与……有关的

look at 看;研究

focus on 集中在……上

take...as an example 以……为例

ought to 应当

result in 导致

heaps of 许多

a pile of 一大堆

Passage 15 配套单词填空练习

1. There are h_______ of fake news online, way too much than it should be.
2. I have organized a p______ of notes before the exam.
3. Students should set up a clear o_______ for their future.
4. The moving of plates of the Earth r______ _____ earthquakes.
5. Citizens o_______ _____ obey laws and rule, which means they have to behave lawfully.
6. What e_________ do you want to choose for Year 11 study along with your compulsory subjects?
7. A country's e_____________ is critical to the wealth of the society.
8. If you want to know how to invest your money, you need to know some knowledge of f______________.
9. I think c_______________ is an interesting subject, because you can learn how things are formed.
10. Sometimes, learning t___________sounds quite boring, but practicing theories out can be interesting.
11. B___________ has become quite popular in school among students who are interested in live animals.
12. The research has l_________ _____ the causes behind some learning difficulties among non-native speakers.
13. The government is responsible for making m_________ measures, namely, policies about money.
14. Company m_____________ is a popular job today.

15. People can win a large amount of money through i________.

16. Students should f_________ ______ revising what they have learned before the exam.

17. Scientists often work in l_____________.

18. The government often i___________ strict laws to not allow people parking their cars anywhere they like.

19. The o_____________ of violent attack on the street caused great fear among the public.

20. Having difficulties is i__________ in the processing of growing up.

21. What p____________ does your company have to protect workers?

22. The e____________ was caused by the leaking gas.

23. D_________ from studying is quite dangerous for students.

24. Can you find any g__________ about how to apply for a bank account card?

25. The last week's camping was a total d_________, because it was raining so hard for the week.

26. The economic loss caused a huge c____________ in small countries.

27. Don't be afraid of making m_____________, it is a natural part of growing up.

28. I have homework of writing a r___________ for my chemistry class.

29. You need to get p___________ before you can park your car here.

30. If you are very careful when recording your experiment data, the data should be a___________ and reliable.

Passage 16

What's Your Family's Magic Recipe?

I guess every family has a must-have dish when there is a special occasion. In my family, my mum's chocolate muddy cake is most favored when our family members have birthday parties.

My mum used to teach me how to bake it. I still can recall that 4 eggs should be added into the mixture with flour and cocoa powder. Cocoa tree is native to Amazon in South America, but now cocoa is prevalent around the world as delicious chocolate. After the mixture is beaten smoothly, it is poured into a cake model for baking.

When the cake is baked into perfectly dark brown, I just need to take it out and let it cool at the room temperature. Then I will melt some dark chocolate in the bath of lukewarm water. And then I spread the gooey chocolate liquid slowly onto the cake. At last, I would add decorations such as sprinkles or icing.

My mum's hand-made chocolate cake is my favorite. Although I know how to make it, but I still reckon the cake made by my mum tastes better. If your family still have not found your own magic recipe, I think it's not too bad to start with this simply chocolate muddy cake.

必备词汇:

名词

magic [ˈmædʒɪk] 魔法;魔术

recipe [ˈresɪpɪ] 食谱

occasion [əˈkeɪʒən] 场合

mixture [ˈmɪkstʃər] 混合物

flour [flaʊər] 面粉

cocoa [ˈkəʊkəʊ] 可可

powder [ˈpaʊdər] 粉末

Amazon [ˈæməzən] 亚马孙

model [ˈmɒdəl] 模型

temperature [ˈtemprətʃər] 气温

liquid [ˈlɪkwɪd] 液体

decoration [ˌdekəˈreɪʃən] 装饰
sprinkle [ˈsprɪŋkəl] 彩虹糖
icing [ˈaɪsɪŋ] 糖衣

动词

bake [beɪk] 烘烤
recall [rɪˈkɔ:l] 回忆起来
beat [bi:t] 打;打蛋
pour [pɔ:r] 倾倒
cool [ku:l] 变凉
melt [melt] 融化
spread [spred] 铺开;传播
decorate [ˈdekəreɪt] 装饰

形容词

must-have 不可缺少的
special [ˈspeʃəl] 特殊的
muddy [ˈmʌdi] 泥泞的
favored [ˈfeɪvəd] 备受喜爱的
native [ˈneɪtɪv] 当地的;土生土长的
prevalent [ˈprevələnt] 流行的;普遍的
smooth [smu:ð] 顺滑的
perfect [ˈpɜ:fekt] 完美的
dark [dɑ:k] 深色的
lukewarm [ˌlu:kˈwɔ:m] 微温的
gooey [ˈgu:i] 黏糊糊的
hand-made [hæn(d)ˈmeɪd] 手工的

副词

perfectly [ˈpɜ:fɪktlɪ] 完美地

短语

used to 过去常常
bake into 烤成了
take...out 拿出来
room temperature 室温

Passage 16 配套单词填空练习

1. Many Chinese love h________________ dumplings that taste better than those bought from super market.
2. Wedding is a unique o____________ for the married couple.
3. My grandpa gave us very s___________ gifts last Christmas.
4. You can buy cake m___________ from the supermarket, and just add water for baking.
5. Many schools offer b_________ classes to teach students to make cakes.
6. F_______is a type of powder made from wheat and you need it to make

bread.

7. My mum has a collection of r__________, from which she learns to cook her favorite dishes.

8. Some young children believe in m_________, like the power Harry Potter has.

9. Chocolate is made of cocoa p__________.

10.Some medicine is made into p__________, so babies can take it easily.

11.My brother's hobby is to collect m_________ cars.

12.Food may go bad at the room t_______________.

13. Water is a kind of l_________.

14. People started to put on d__________________ as Christmas is coming.

15. I love to have s_____________ on my ice cream.

16. I cannot r___________ what my mum told me yesterday.

17. You need to b______ 4 eggs in the cake mixture.

18. The rain is p_________ down, so we cannot go out.

19. Ice in Antarctic is m__________ because of global warming.

20. Bad news s____________quickly.

21. Let the soup c__________ a little bit before you give it to the children.

22. My art homework is to d____________ a big shell.

23. That book is a m________________ if you want to do better in your final exam.

24. The country road became m_________ after it rained.

25. That author writes many fun story books, so he is f___________ by many children.

26. Kangaroos are n_____________animals to Australia.

27. Communicating with friends by social media becomes p______________ around the world.

28. Her trip to Europe went s___________, no bad things happened.

29. It is a p____________ answer.

30. Her d________ skin shows that she loves the beach life.

Passage 17

Will Professionals Be Replaced by Robot?

Many scientists predict that a variety of professionals will be replaced by robots in the near future. Due to the advance in artificial intelligence, robots become increasingly smarter.

Scientists speculate that some surgeons or lawyers will soon be replaced by sophisticated robots. Although these professionals do irreplaceable jobs currently, their jobs are mostly repetitive. A large amount of routine is involved in their jobs. This makes it possible for robots to be programmed to carry out the routine.

While professionals may be replaced, workers in some occupations may remain indispensible. The workers, whose job largely involve comforting people or providing counseling service to people, cannot be replaced, because robots cannot make sensible or empathic response to their clients' emotional outburst.

Those scientists also foresee that novel jobs will be created along with the development of the technology. Accordingly, many educators and schools commence special courses that are expected to prepare the young generation for the future.

I don't know when this revolution will happen, but I think computers and technology definitely gain increasing significance in our life. It will bring forth a great leap in our society, and cause massive changes to how humans communicate. Some people believe we will have robot dentists and solicitors, who can give preliminary advice to their clients. We can even have robot professors who deliver lectures to thousands of student online.

Artificial intelligence is like a driving fleet, which will lead us to a completely novel world.

必备词汇：

名词

profession [prəˈfeʃən] 职业
professional [prəˈfeʃənəl] 专业人士
robot [ˈrəʊbɒt] 机器人
scientist [ˈsaɪəntɪst] 科学家
advance [ədˈvɑ:ns] 进步
intelligence [ɪnˈtelɪdʒəns] 智力
surgeon [ˈsɜ:dʒən] 手术医生
lawyer [ˈlɔ:jə(r)] 律师
amount [əˈmaʊnt] 量
routine [ru:ˈti:n] 惯例；常规
occupation [ˌɒkjəˈpeɪʃən] 职业；占据
counseling [ˈkaʊnsəlɪŋ] 辅导；咨询
response [rɪˈspɒns] 反应；回应
client [ˈklaɪənt] 客户
outburst [ˈaʊtbɜ:st]（感情）迸发
development [dɪˈveləpmənt] 发展
educator [ˈedʒukeɪtər] 教育工作者
course [kɔ:s] 课程
generation [ˌdʒenəˈreɪʃən] 一代人
revolution[ˌrevəˈlu:ʃən] 革命
significance [sɪgˈnɪfɪkəns] 重要性
leap [li:p] 跳跃
society [səˈsaɪətɪ] 社会
dentist [ˈdentɪst] 牙医
solicitor [səˈlɪsɪtər] 律师
professor [prəˈfesər] 教授
fleet [fli:t] 舰队

动词

replace [rɪˈpleɪs] 取代；替代
predict [prɪˈdɪkt] 预计
speculate [ˈspekjəleɪt] 推测
involve [ɪnˈvɒlv] 涉及；包含
program [ˈprəʊgræm] 编程
occupy [ˈɒkjəpaɪ] 占据；占领
comfort [ˈkʌmfət] 安慰
foresee [fəˈsi:] 预见
create [kriˈeɪt] 创造
expect [ɪkˈspekt] 期望；预期
prepare [prɪˈpeər] 准备
commence [kəˈmens] 开始
happen [ˈhæpən] 发生
gain [geɪn] 获得
deliver [dɪˈlɪvər] 送货；上课

形容词

professional [prəˈfeʃənəl] 专业的
smarter [smɑ:tə] 更聪明的
artificial [ˌɑ:tɪˈfɪʃəl] 人工的；人造的
sophisticated [səˈfɪstɪkeɪtɪd]（机器）精密的；（人）老练的

irreplaceable [ˌɪrɪˈpleɪsəbəl] 不可取代的
replaceable [rɪˈpleɪsəbəl] 可取代的
repetitive [rɪˈpetətɪv] 重复性的
indispensable [ˌɪndɪˈspensəbəl] 不可缺少的
sensible [sensəbl] 合情理的
empathic [ˌempəˈθetɪk] 共鸣的
novel [ˈnɒvəl] 新颖的
definite [ˈdefɪnət] 一定的；明确的
massive [ˈmæsɪv] 巨大的；大量的
preliminary [prɪˈlɪmɪnərɪ] 初步的
driving [ˈdraɪvɪŋ] 推动的

副词

increasingly [ɪnˈkri:sɪŋlɪ] 更加；越来越
currently [ˈkʌrəntlɪ] 当前
mostly [ˈməʊstlɪ] 主要地；多半地
largely [ˈlɑ:dʒlɪ] 大量地
accordingly [əˈkɔ:dɪŋlɪ] 相应地
definitely [ˈdefɪnətlɪ] 肯定地

短语

artificial intelligence 人工智能
a variety of 各种各样的
due to 由于
a large amount of 大量的
carry out 完成
along with 伴随着
bring forth 产生；提出
lead to 引领到；导致

Passage 17 配套单词填空练习

1. White-collar workers are also called p______________.
2. R__________ pets are still not popular in Western countries.
3. There are many p____________, you can choose to work in any one.
4. Those whose work is to advance science are called s____________.
5. The a__________ of our understanding of universe enables us to explore the outer space.
6. The i______________ of a person alone cannot decide one's success later in life.
7. Nowadays, many kinds of food contain a__________ flavors other than natural flavors.

8. His dream is to become a s__________ and work in hospital.

9. The a_________ of the salt needed in the experiment is 500 grams.

10.My father has a morning r_________ of running.

11.People work in professional o_____________ earn more than labour workers.

12.That building is suitable for o____________ by old people for aged care.

13. Australian schools provide c___________ service to students who suffer anxiety prior to exams.

14. There is no r____________ from the company after I sent them an email last Friday.

15. The audience had an o__________ of anger after their football team lost the final match.

16. The d__________________ of economy pushes our society forward.

17. The summer English c_________ will begin at 1 July.

18. The birth of the Internet has triggered a worldwide r______________.

19. The s____________ of online safety is still ignored by some parents.

20. S____________ are a kind of lawyer, which also includes barristers.

21. His dream is to become a p______________ at university.

22. The economists have p_____________ the slowing down of economy.

23. What can you e__________ for your trip to Thailand?

24. Some bankers s___________ that the housing price would decrease.

25. Primary school students can learn to p_____________ in their computer class.

26. Many shops are only happy to r_____________ faulty products.

27. The discussion room is o____________, because I can see several people inside.

28. It is not easy to f____________ what the world will become in fifty years.

29. When will the new school term c____________ July or August?

30. Traveling to outer space requires the most s_____________ travelling machines.

Passage 18

Materialism Damages Our Environment

A typical feature of materialism is to satisfy one's material life at all costs. This type of lifestyle has a minimum of consideration of the environment, but maximal or maximum consideration of one's own luxurious life and comfort. An increasing number of people with abundant wealth are the driving factor of materialism. Many international brands have sprawled widely into an empire of luxury, with implication that those brands are a symbol of wealth. However, human's pursuit of luxurious life is a nightmare to the environment. Birds are killed for their fancy feather, while rare animals are slaughtered for their leather or furs.

Many people push their desire for luxury products beyond the boundary of daily necessity, and they choose to sacrifice other creatures. Although some environmental protection institutions advocate to sanction these brands like LV, the preservation of the environment and creatures depend more on ordinary people's conduct. If people's selfish conduct leads to extinction of some animals, these animals will disappear permanently. Accordingly, everyone has an obligation to prevent this striking consequence by not buying products made of rare animals.

Accordingly, it is wise to encourage younger generation to develop the environment-friendly lifestyle. The young people should be guided to pay more attention on their spiritual strength than just owning material products. It is critical to mend the tendency of buying excessive goods by emphasizing the significance of spiritual life.

必备词汇：

名词

materialism [mə'tɪərɪəlɪzəm] 物质主义
material [mə'tɪərɪəl] 物质；材料
minimum ['mɪnɪməm] 最少
environment [ɪn'vaɪrənmənt] 环境
feature ['fi:tʃər] 特征
type [taɪp] 种类；类型
lifestyle ['laɪfstaɪl] 生活方式
consideration [kənˌsɪdə'reɪʃən] 考虑
comfort ['kʌmfət] 舒适；安逸
wealth [welθ] 财富
factor ['fæktər] 因素
brand [brænd] 品牌
empire ['empaɪər] 帝国
luxury ['lʌkʃərɪ] 奢华
implication [ˌɪmplɪ'keɪʃən] 含义
symbol ['sɪmbəl] 标志
wealth [welθ] 财富
pursuit [pə'sju:t] 追求
nightmare ['naɪt.meər] 噩梦
feather ['feðər] 羽毛
leather ['leðər] 皮革
boundary ['baʊndərɪ] 界线
necessity [nə'sesətɪ] 必需品
institution [ˌɪnstɪ'tʃu:ʃən] 机构
preservation [ˌprezə'veɪʃən] 保护
extinction [ɪk'stɪŋkʃən] 灭绝
obligation [ˌɒblɪ'geɪʃən] 义务
consequence ['kɒnsɪkwəns] 后果
strength [streŋθ] 强项；长处
tendency ['tendənsɪ] 倾向性

动词

damage ['dæmɪdʒ] 损害
satisfy ['sætɪsfaɪ] 满足
consider [kən'sɪdər] 考虑
sprawl [sprɔ:l] 扩张；蔓延
pursue [pə'sju:] 追求
slaughter ['slɔ:tər] 屠宰
push [pʊʃ] 推动
sacrifice ['sækrɪfaɪs] 牺牲
advocate ['ædvəkeɪt] 倡导
sanction ['sæŋkʃən] 制裁
preserve [prɪ'zɜ:v] 保护；保存
disappear [ˌdɪsə'pɪər] 消失
prevent [prɪ'vent] 预防
encourage [ɪn'kʌrɪdʒ] 鼓励
own [əʊn] 拥有
mend [mend] 修补；改进
emphasize ['emfəsaɪz] 强调

形容词

maximum ['mæksɪməm] 最多的
luxurious [lʌg'ʒʊərɪəs] 奢侈的

enormous [ɪˈnɔːməs] 巨大的
international [ˌɪntəˈnæʃənəl] 国际的
fancy [ˈfænsɪ] 引人注目的
rare [reər] 稀有的;罕见的
ordinary [ˈɔːdənərɪ] 普通的
permanent [ˈpɜːmənənt] 永久的
striking [ˈstraɪkɪŋ] 惊人的
wise [waɪz] 明智的
environment-friendly [ɪnˈvaɪrənmənt,frendl] 环境友好的
spiritual [ˈspɪrɪtʃuəl] 精神的
critical [ˈkrɪtɪkəl] 关键的
excessive [ekˈsesɪv] 过多的;过分的

短语

at all costs 不惜一切代价
depend on 依赖于
material life 物质生活

Passage 18 配套单词填空练习

1. 21st century is called the century of m____________.
2. The experiment needs several m_________, including water.
3. How to protect the e_____________ has become a hot issue.
4. Everyone can have their own l___________, and ever one can live in different ways.
5. What are the f_________ of ocean mammals?
6. The m__________ ________ should only be a part of our life.
7. Consumers need to c___________ many factors become buying expensive goods.
8. He is a man with w__________, because he has earned huge money when he was young.
9. The publishing e_____________ nowadays are the online publishing companies
10.Choosing shoes with c___________ is more important than their looks.
11. Sometimes it is hard to understand the i____________ behind some political activities.
12. A life of l__________ is desired by most people.

13. The s________ of the school is a lion and an axe.

14. Young children should p________ their dreams.

15. The p__________ of his medical career led to the break up of his family, because he was too busy in working.

16. The days of surviving in a jungle was a n__________ to those participants, and they just want to forget it.

17. The hat with f__________ immediately drew her attention.

18. L__________ goods are very durable, you can use them for many years.

19. Parents should set up the behavioral b______________for young children to minimize their opportunities of getting into trouble of misbehaviors.

20. Air, water and food are n____________ for humans.

21. There are many educational i________________ provide English language course in Australia.

22. The p______________ of animals and plants is a long-term job.

23. Scientists believe the e_____________ of dinosaurs is caused by climate change.

24. Teachers have an o____________ to take care of students in their classes.

25. What are your s_____________ and weakness?

26. The t_____________ of playing phone games is even seen among very young kids.

27. Throwing rubbish away can d___________ the environment.

28. It is very difficult to s____________ customers' needs nowadays.

29. Would you s______________ your social life for better academic result?

30. Regular revision cannot be e___________ too much.

Passage 19

School's Exchange Program

Many high schools offer an invaluable international exchange program to students. It is an outstanding platform for students to familiarize themselves with other cultures and get personal involvement in exotic cultures. Unlike the old term "culture invasion", "culture exchange" becomes prevalent among the younger generation. It is said that the integration of various cultures is the symbol of generation X.

For some students, an oversea exchange program can be a challenge as well as an inspiration. Take Japan as an example, Australian students, who go to Japan for exchange, not only enjoy the spectacular mountain scenery, but also are exposed to the language barrier.

When considering if international exchange program is suitable for you, you need to take into account the expense of the program, the priority of your study, and the period of time you can spend abroad.

Many students who have returned from such a program positively comment the program as very beneficial. They would highly recommend the program to their siblings or friends. They think the experience is priceless, and it can overly compensate the loss of time due to being away from school.

必备词汇：

名词

exchange [ɪks'tʃeɪndʒ] 交换

platform ['plætfɔ:m] 平台；讲台

term [tɜ:m] 说法

invasion [ɪn'veɪʒən] 入侵；侵略

integration [ˌɪntɪ'greɪʃən] 综合；集合

challenge ['tʃælɪndʒ] 挑战

inspiration [ˌɪnspɪ'reɪʃən] 灵感；启发

scenery [ˈsiːnərɪ] 风景
expense [ɪkˈspens] 开销
priority [praɪˈɒrətɪ] 优先
sibling [ˈsɪblɪŋ] 兄弟姐妹
experience [ɪkˈspɪərɪəns] 经历
loss [lɒs] 损失

动词

familiarize [fəˈmɪljəˌraɪz] 使……熟悉
enjoy [ɪnˈdʒɔɪ] 享受;欣赏
expose [ɪkˈspəʊz] 使接触;使暴露
praise [preɪz] 夸奖
recommend [ˌrekəˈmend] 推荐
compensate [ˈkɒmpənseɪt] 补偿

形容词

invaluable [ɪnˈvæljəbəl] 宝贵的;有用的
outstanding [ˌaʊtˈstændɪŋ] 优秀的;突出的
personal [ˈpɜːsənəl] 个人的
exotic [ɪgˈzɒtɪk] 异域风情的
overseas [ˌəʊvəˈsiːz] 海外的
spectacular [spekˈtækjələr] 壮观的
excellent [ˈeksələnt] 杰出的;极好的
suitable [ˈsuːtəbəl] 适合的
beneficial [ˌbenɪˈfɪʃəl] 有好处的
priceless [ˈpraɪsləs] 无价的

副词

abroad [əˈbrɔːd] 在国外
overly [ˈəʊvəlɪ] 极度地

介词

unlike [ʌnˈlaɪk] 不像

短语

culture exchange 文化交流
language barrier 语言障碍
take into account 考虑
be away 离开

Passage 19 配套单词填空练习

1. Before you make a decision, it's better to t________ ______ __________ of every factor.
2. U__________ his little brother, Jane is a book lover.
3. Travelling a___________ requires careful planning.
4. His assistance to us is p_____________.

5. When my mum was a________ for work, my dad took care of me.
6. Reading is a very b___________ hobby.
7. His e_______________ performance won him a prize.
8. The eruption of volcano is a s___________ view.
9. You can choose either time that is s__________ for you.
10.O__________ students need a visa to study in Australia.
11. Travelling in different countries enable you to enjoy e_______ cultures.
12. You should keep your p_____________ information secret.
13. The school principal made o_____________ contribution to the school.
14. Studying in a foreign country is i____________ experience in one's life.
15. The loss of his income should be c____________ by his employer, because he injured at work.
16. That restaurant is highly r___________ by local diners.
17. Children should be e__________ books at an early stage.
18. You should f____________ yourself with the test before you sit the test.
19. Do you have any s_____________, for example, sister or brother?
20. The huge l________ of the company was caused by the unexpected fire.
21. Safety is always the p___________ for outdoor activities.
22. What's your monthly e__________ on clothes?
23. People with good m_________are always welcomed anywhere, because they act themselves politely.
24. Western Australian is famous for its unique s_______ of red earth landscape.
25. Artists can get i_____________ from daily life to create amazing works of art.
26. To read 20 books in a month is really a c__________ for me.
27. A successful man usually has a strong i____________ of skills and knowledge.
28. The i___________ of foreign species caused extinction of some native

Australian animals.

29. Many young people want to have c__________ __________ in other countries when they finish high school.

30. Communicating online is an efficient p__________ for many companies to promote their customer service.

Passage 20

What Makes Australia a Desirable Migration Destination?

For many elite migrants, Australia is one of the most favored destinations to immigrate. One of the reasons behind this phenomenon may be the balance of life and better education offered by Australia.

Independent schools in Australia are renowned for their high quality education. These schools also are equipped with excellent facilities, such as music halls, tennis courses and football fields.

Besides education, the Australian society is very diverse. This means Australians come from various cultural backgrounds but live peacefully together. Most Australians respect the difference between individuals; they believe that all people have right to demonstrate their own personality and characteristic, as long as they do not overstep the boundary.

In addition to the harmonious society, Australians are very creative in terms of jobs. Fantastic musicians compose music and give live music performances regularly. Filmmakers use their lens to capture the touchy moments in people's life. Some movies are made to tell stores from a retrospective angle, so they enable us to understand the Australia in the past.

Furthermore, Australia is proud of its national health care system, which means the Australian Federal government provides health care to citizens for free. Medical professionals are bounded by medical profession's ethics, so their services can be trusted.

In terms of politics, the Commonwealth government and several State governments govern Australia together. Australia is a democratic country, so all adult Australians need to vote for their desired politicians with an interval of every three years.

All in all, Australia offers a good living environment with excellent education and health care. It is no wonder why so many migrants are keen to settle down here.

必备词汇：

名词

destination [ˌdestɪˈneɪʃən] 目的地；终点
migrant [ˈmaɪgrənt] 移民
phenomenon [fəˈnɒmɪnən] 现象
balance [ˈbæləns] 平衡
facility[fəˈsɪləti] 设施
hall [hɔ:l] 大厅
field [fi:ld] ……场；领域
individual [ˌɪndɪˈvɪdʒuəl] 个人
personality [ˌpɜ:sənˈæləti] 个性
characteristic [ˌkærəktəˈrɪstɪk] 特征；特点
musician [mju:ˈzɪʃən] 音乐家
performance [pəˈfɔ:məns] 表演
filmmaker [ˈfɪlmˌmeɪkər] 电影制作人
lens [lenz] 镜头
moment [ˈməʊmənt] 时刻
angle [ˈæŋgəl] 角度
system [ˈsɪstəm] 系统
ethics [ˈeθɪks] 职业道德
commonwealth [ˈkɒmənwelθ] 联邦
adult [ˈædʌlt] 成年人
interval [ˈɪntəvəl] 间隔
wonder [ˈwʌndər] 奇观

动词

immigrate [ˈɪmɪgreɪt] 移民；移居
renown [rɪˈnaʊn] 以……出名
equip [ɪˈkwɪp] 配备
respect [rɪˈspekt] 尊重
demonstrate [ˈdemənstreɪt] 展示；展现
overstep [ˌəʊvəˈstep] 超过；越过
compose [kəmˈpəʊz] 作曲
capture [ˈkæptʃər] 捕捉
enable [ɪˈneɪbəl] 使……能
bind [baind] 约束（bound）
trust [trʌst] 信任
govern [ˈgʌvən] 治理
vote [vəʊt] 投票

形容词

desirable [dɪˈzaɪərəbəl] 心仪的
elite [iˈli:t] 精英的
favored [ˈfeɪvəd] 受人喜爱的
independent [ˌɪndɪˈpendənt] 独立的

diverse [daɪˈvɜ:s] 多样化的
peaceful [ˈpi:sfəl] 和平的
harmonious [hɑ:ˈməʊnɪəs] 和谐的
creative [krɪˈeɪtɪv] 富有创造力的
regular [ˈregjələr] 规律的；定期的
touchy [ˈtʌtʃɪ] 感人的
retrospective [ˌretrəˈspektɪv] 追溯的
national [ˈnæʃənəl] 全国的
federal [ˈfedərəl] 联邦的
democratic [ˌdeməˈkrætɪk] 民主的
keen [ki:n] 热切的

短语

high quality 高质量的
as long as 只要
in terms of 在……方面
all in all 总之
it is no wonder 难怪……
tennis course 网球场
football field 足球场
be bound by 被……约束
settle down 定居

Passage 20 配套单词填空练习

1. Lewis just wants to travel without setting an exact d____________, he will go where his journey takes him to.

2.Most Australians are m___________ from other places, while Aboriginal Australians are the only people who live there for thousands of years.

3. Many guests are waiting in the town h_______ for the Mayor's New Year speech.

4. To keep a b___________ between work and life is not easy for modern people.

5. My school has many first class f_________ such as indoor basketball course.

6. Every i_____________ is different; this means everyone has unique personality.

7. What's the most obvious c______________ of your younger brother? –Outgoing.

8. Our dancing school will give a p_______________at the end of the year.

9. My dream is to be a f____________, because I want to record people's life with lens.

10. The m____________ when my parents heard I won the tennis competition, they felt so surprised.

11. When you write a text response essay, you need to show that you are analyzing an issue from a different a____________.

12. Australia has a democratic political s____________, which is different from that of China.

13. Professionals like doctors and lawyers need to comply with e____________ rules in their professions.

14. A__________ don't need permission to get in, but children do.

15. Australia is a C______________________ country.

16. There is a short i____________ between these two after-school activities, one on each Tuesday and the other on each Friday.

17. The Great Wall is a manmade w__________ in the world.

18. Students need to be e___________ with multiple skills before they graduate from high school.

19. We need to r___________ ourselves, others and the environment.

20. My teacher has d_______________ to us how to solve the complex math problem already.

21. Many parents usually o__________ the mark of supervising their children's homework.

22. Harry Potter has c__________ the most beautiful aspect of magical power.

23. His experience of living in China e__________ him to understand the Chinese culture better.

24. people can't become friends if they don't t________ each other.

25. Many new migrants have s___________ ___________ in Australia in recent years.

26. Students should be taught to develop their i___________ thinking.

27. Australia is proud of its d____________ society, which means different people live harmoniously together.

28. C__________ writing task requires students to create something new in writing an article.

29. I'm a r_____________ customer to that model shop, because I love collecting model ships.

30. That movie tells a story in a r______________ way, which means movie viewers are shown the life in the past.

Passage 21

Traffic Jam and Traffic Accident

As people's wealth accumulate, owning private cars is not without reach. This consequently leads to the increase of traffic jam on our roads. Worse still, the occurrence of traffic accidents also grows annually.

Who are the culprits for the long standstill snakes on our road? I think everyone who chooses to commute by private cars contributes to road congestion. Traffic jams happen when most drivers head to the same direction such as CBD at the same time. This time is also called rush hour. However, instead of saving travelling time, driving private cars to work can extend the travelling time. When drivers get stuck in the long queue of vehicles, some would become impatient or raged, which means they become violently angry.

Once, there was shocking news about the confrontation between two raged drivers in the traffic jam. They even got out of their cars and started violent attack against each other. So I think the government should advocate people to use more public transport. This can alleviate the traffic volume on roads. Accordingly, our roads will become less congested.

Besides using public transport, some Greens have initiated a campaign of cycling to work in Melbourne. Riding bicycles to work not only benefits our environment but also strengthen people's physical health. Although cycling parallel to swift cars can be risky, Melbourne has legislated strict road rules to enhance road safety. These rules require drivers to slow down when they drive past cyclists with a speed no greater than 50km per hour.

Along with the increase of traffic jam, the annual figure of traffic accidents grows quickly as well. It is unclear whether it is a mere coincidence or unexpected correlation between traffic jam and traffic accident. The casualty of traffic accidents has witnessed an appalling growth. As no innocent people deserved to die on our roads, so I think it is an urgent matter for the government to curb the occurrence of traffic accidents.

必备词汇：

名词

jam [dʒæm] 堵塞
accident [ˈæksɪdənt] 事故
culprit [ˈkʌlprɪt] 罪魁祸首
congestion [kənˈdʒestɪd] 堵塞
direction [daɪˈrekʃən] 方向
queue [kjuː] 队伍；队列
vehicle [ˈvɪəkəl] 车辆
confrontation [ˌkɒnfrʌnˈteɪʃən] 冲突
attack [əˈtæk] 攻击
volume [ˈvɒljuːm] 流通量
Green [griːn] 环保人士
campaign [kæmˈpeɪn] 运动
cyclist [ˈsaɪklɪst]（自行车）骑手
coincidence [kəʊˈɪnsɪdəns] 巧合
correlation [ˌkɒrəˈleɪʃən] 相关性
casualty [ˈkæʒjʊəltɪ] 伤亡人数
matter [ˈmætər] 事务

动词

accumulate [əˈkjuːmjʊleɪt] 积累；积聚
commute [kəˈmjuːt] 穿梭；上下班
extend [ɪkˈstend] 延长
confront [kənˈfrʌnt] 与……发生冲突
alleviate [əˈliːvɪeɪt] 缓解；减轻
initiate [ɪˈnɪʃieɪt] 发动；发起
cycle [ˈsaɪkəl] 骑车
benefit [ˈbenɪfɪt] 对……有好处
strengthen [ˈstreŋθən] 增强
legislate [ˈledʒɪsleɪt] 立法
enhance [ɪnˈhɑːns] 加强
require [rɪˈkwaɪər] 要求
witness [ˈwɪtnəs] 见证
deserve [dɪˈzɜːv] 值得
curb [kɜːb] 控制；降低

形容词

private [ˈpraɪvət] 私人的
worst [wɜːst] 更糟糕的
annual [ˈænjʊəl] 年度的
standstill [ˈstændstɪl] 静止的
impatient [ɪmˈpeɪʃənt] 不耐心的
raged [reɪdʒ] 暴怒的
violent [ˈvaɪələnt] 暴力的
shocking [ˈʃɒkɪŋ] 令人吃惊的
congested [kənˈdʒestɪd] 堵塞的
parallel [ˈpærəlel] 平行的

swift [swɪft] 快速的
risky [ˈrɪskɪ] 危险的
mere [mɪər] 单纯的
appalling [əˈpɔ:lɪŋ] 令人震惊的
innocent [ˈɪnəsənt] 无辜的
urgent [ˈɜ:dʒənt] 紧急的

副词

consequently [ˈkɒnsɪkwəntlɪ] 后果是
annually [ˈænjʊəlɪ] 每年
violently [ˈvaɪələntli] 暴力地
once [wʌns] 曾经

短语

without reach 遥不可及
head to 朝……去
instead of 不……
get stuck 被困住
traffic jam 交通堵塞
private car 私家车
rush hour 高峰期
physical health 身体健康
contribute to 贡献;导致

Passage 21 配套单词填空练习

1. Roads become very c__________ particularly on rainy days, because more people choose to drive.
2. Rodney is a famous c__________, because he has won the title of Cycling Tour in France.
3. What is the m__________?
   You looked very worried.
4. Students a______________ knowledge and skills day by day.
5. Do you think there is c__________ between the number of cars on the roads and the number of traffic accident.
6. Police did not believe disappearance of Jimmy is a c______________ with the disappearance of Jimmy's mum; instead, they believed someone had took both of them away.
7. P__________ exercise is important to keep our health.
8. Group work needs every group member to c__________ effort to the project.

9. Travellers had to e____________ their stay in Spain due to the bad weather.

10. Teenagers may easily c_______________ their parents for small issues.

11. Traffic jam has been a_____________ since the construction of two new freeways.

12. Some students at my school i_____________ a campaign of helping the elderly last year.

13. Most employees need to c______________ to work in CBD on every weekday.

14. The new education system will b_____________ most young people.

15. The Victorian government has l_____________ to make it is illegal to smoke in restaurants.

16. Is there anyone who has w____________ the traffic accident on Peel Street?

17. The number of smokers should be c____________, because smoking leads to cancer.

18. You need to keep your personal information p_________; don't give it to anyone you don't know.

19. The train came to s____________ upon arriving to the major station.

20. It's s___________ news! How could people forget to take their babies out when they left their car?

21. I don't often see two trains run p____________ to each other.

22. Can you help me with my application? It is u_______.

23. To dive into the river from the bridge is quite r_______.

24. Cars, trucks and lorries are different kinds of v_________.

25. How about we come to the shop later? There is such a long q____________ outside the shop.

26. The v___________ of information communicated online has increased significantly.

27. No one knows who are the c__________ of pollution, but I think everyone

may have a share of responsibility to mend the problem.

28. Politicians are always ready to hold c___________ for themselves when the election is getting close.

29. Traffic in my city is really poor at r___________hours.

30. Which d___________ are you heading to?

Maybe we can go together.

配套单词填空练习

参考答案

4-6 配套单词填空练习参考答案

Passage 1

1. cozy	2. throw away	3. design	4. favorite	5. fridge
6. grow	7. favorite	8. tasty	9. neat	10. vegetables
11. kitchen	12. order	13. round	14. quiet	15. around
16. stay	17. above	18. rubbish	19. juice	20. against
21. area	22. lovely	23. cupboard	24. free	25. drink
26. tidy	27. table	28. good	29. tall	30. large

Passage 2

1. creatures	2. insects	3. arrives	4. closely	5. curious
6. wonderful	7. fantastic	8. amazing	9. guess	10. idea
11. buzzing	12. enjoy	13. smell	14. spots	15. waves
16. strange	17. children	18. wonderful	19. pretty	20. carry
21. tummy	22. wings	23. heavy	24. fast	25. tiny
26. little	27. lives	28. lives	29. bugs	30. color

Passage 3

1. age	2. renew	3. reply	4. save	5. furs
6. jungles	7. library	8. wait	9. loan	10. stripes
11. condition	12. level	13. frightened	14. huge	15. scaring
16. ending/end	17. picture	18. first	19. spots	20. store
21. soon	22. floor	23. cover	24. cartoon /comic	

Passage 4

1. weekends	2. full	3. during	4. breakfast	5. while
6. pick	7. traffic	8. finished	9. daily	10. next
11. silly	12. funny	13. almost	14. similar	15. clearly
16. fight	17. classes	18. hurry	19. leaves	20. slim
21. early	22. firmly	23. silent	24. Stuff	25. noise
26. drive	27. talk	28. scan	29. fell	30. Share

Passage 5

1. simple	2. short	3. recently	4. backyard	5. plays
6. neighbors	7. good	8. sick	9. soft	10. support
11. represents	12. taking	13. pulls	14. pretty	15. care
16. each	17. wins	18. friendly	19. shadows	20. count
21. tips	22. hear	23. brings	24. front	25. according
26. rest	27. gave	28. middle	29. match	30. tricks

Passage 6

1. well	2. couple	3. announces	4. encourage	5. fair
6. displays	7. costs	8. prize	9. purchasing	10. bargain
11. local	12. available	13. hold	14. whole	15. delving
16. experts	17. price	18. save	19. engage	20. reply
21. club	22. addition	23. behind	24. whole	25. have
26. exciting	27. other	28. world	29. opportunity	30. treasure

Passage 7

1. earth	2. vase	3. types	4. bottles	5. cardboard
6. rubbish	7. find	8. protect	9. happened	10. made

11. figured	12. else	13. jar	14. recycling	15. recycled
16. fill	17. put	18. bins	19. sorting	20. box
21. medals	22. reuse	23. timber	24. cans	25. glass
26. plastic	27. project	28. flowers	29. look	30. guess

Passage 8

1. subject	2. tired	3. quite	4. cold	5. hot
6. noisy	7. attention	8. instrument	9. jumped	10. describe
11. draw	12. ran	13. fail	14. toys	15. large
16. explain	17. building	18. questions	19. bored	20. common
21. folded	22. final	23. help	24. warm	25. circle
26. nice	27. top	28. break	29. brothers	30. divided

Passage 9

1. brilliant	2. action	3. amazed	4. observe	5. went
6. sneezing	7. shake	8. foot	9. finger	10. write
11. comes	12. ankle	13. make	14. himself	15. speak
16. legs	17. think	18. arms	19. chain	20. waves
21. nose	22. leg	23. wonder	24. build	25. hug
26. bend	27. smart	28. kinds	29. breathe	30. waves

Passage 10

1. survive	2. attacked	3. careful	4. tree	5. climbing
6. worries	7. giraffes	8. forest	9. air	10. leaves
11. place	12. chance	13. valuable	14. visit	15. lazy
16. wild	17. efforts	18. swimming	19. hop	20. led
21. danger	22. learn	23. notice	24. chirps	25. extinction
26. change	27. cut	28. elegant	29. easily	30. behind

Passage 11

1. poured	2. chasing	3. presents	4. coat	5. skating
6. harvest	7. allow	8. heavily	9. covers	10. clean
11. bush	12. spend	13. autumn	14. rises	15. thick
16. popped, occurred		17. stuffy	18. looked	19. ripe
20. gloves	21. cool	22. thin	23. walk	24. picnic
25. weather	26. grow	27. temperature		
28. sunglasses	29. sandals	30. sandals		

Passage 12

1. rather	2. license	3. pumpkin	4. accept	5. customer
6. cucumbers	7. salad	8. price	9. owner	10. yoghurt
11. bread	12. supermarket		13. council	14. card
15. fruits	16. shopping	17. displayed	18. products	19. wonderful
20. sorts	21. experience	22. able	23. choose	24. treat
25. set	26. payment	27. fact	28. stalls	29. finished
30. farm				

Passage 13

1. reply	2. forget	3. considers	4. idea	5. gave
6. misses	7. successful	8. curtain	9. closely	10. wash
11. waiting	12. handle	13. knock	14. respond	15. directly
16. calm	17. about	18. suddenly	19. back	20. rush
21. approximately		22. uneasy	23. real	24. weird
25. suddenly	26. note	27. window	28. calling	29. answer
30. believe				

Passage 14

1. prepared	2. office	3. van	4. park	5. safe
6. nearby	7. country	8. demand	9. located	10. opposite
11. police	12. entrances	13. hospital	14. convenient	15. present
16. ensure	17. post	18. pets	19. business	20. space
21. floors	22. cafe	23. hundreds	24. local	25. upper
26. grocer	27. centre	28. town	29. bank	30. chips

Passage 15

1. dine	2. leads	3. unhealthy	4. restaurants	5. pork
6. obesity	7. diabetes	8. yummy	9. gave	10. prefer
11. nutritious	12. fat	13. fast	14. special	15. dishes
16. contain	17. ordered	18. traditional	19. except	20. bill
21. delicious	22. ingredients	23. waiters	24. once	25. signals
26. grandpa	27. obese	28. occasion	29. steaks	30. guides

Passage 16

1. strong	2. seaside	3. bakes	4. jellyfish	5. ruined
6. famous	7. gentle	8. straight	9. holiday	10. light
11. brave	12. hunt	13. pull	14. kilometers	15. hotel
16. passes	17. deal	18. around	19. travel	20. packing
21. rolling	22. unlike	23. sharks	24. difference	25. caught
26. surfing	27. track	28. tide	29. pain	30. flat

Passage 17

1. bit	2. cooking	3. recently	4. force	5. diet
6. articles	7. cookers	8. region	9. meals	10. means

11. wonderful 12. chef 13. attractive 14. actually 15. stay
16. already 17. occasionally 18. bear 19. recipe
20. curry 21. attempted 22. enough 23. balance 24. fan
25. insist 26. insisted 27. host 28. tool 29. smells
30. none

Passage 18

1. slowly 2. outside 3. giant 4. blue 5. valuable
6. adventure 7. result 8. light 9. mark 10. suggests
11. next 12. stand 13. deep 14. low 15. slopes
16. snakes 17. probably 18. dark 19. pirates 20. sting
21. expecting 22. discovered 23. edge 24. northern 25. pretends
26. exciting 27. century 28. across 29. tent 30. insects

Passage 19

1. official 2. participated 3. magnificent 4. laughing 5. manage
6. native 7. languages 8. popular 9. candidate 10. states
11. achieved 12. medal 13. amazed 14. final 15. success
16. regularly 17. fluently 18. collection 19. achievement
20. progress 21. remarks 22. extreme 23. winners 24. outcome
25. definitely 26. especially 27. certificate 28. second 29. minister
30. gradually

Passage 20

1. before 2. like 3. rest 4. choose 5. train
6. though 7. transport 8. passengers 9. imagine 10. late
11. once 12. grey 13. radio 14. attracted 15. stuff
16. company 17. right 18. bumped 19. ride 20. public

21. purchased 22. business 23. announcement
24. station 25. focus 26. operate 27. early 28. fit
29. long 30. miss

Passage 21

1. cousins 2. relieve 3. upload 4. well 5. figure
6. frustrated 7. countries 8. yell 9. relieved 10. loads
11. get 12. previous 13. grownup 14. lost 15. grasp
16. location 17. facilities 18. crowded 19. search 20. unexpected
21. happened 22. annoying 23. seconds 24. offers 25. exclaiming
26. fancy 27. directions 28. separate 29. tricks 30. appears

Passage 22

1. especially 2. recovered 3. diseases 4. calm 5. specialist
6. ideal 7. scared 8. annually 9. medicine 10. regulations
11. cold 12. job 13. review 14. serious 15. dying
16. updated 17. strict 18. sick 19. doctor 20. value
21. minister 22. mental 23. emergency 24. coughing 25. review
26. care 27. types 28. serious 29. cold 30. rescues

7-9 配套单词填空练习参考答案

Passage 1

1.behaviour 2. available 3. Interested 4. adventure 5. curious
6. entrance 7. exhibited 8. arrival 9. disappointed 10. fearsome
11. complete 12. magical 13. scary 14. refreshing 15. offer
16. spoiled 17. guide 18. tasty 19. return 20. fence

21. noisy 22. naughty 23. similar 24. term 25. amazing
26. set 27. seems 28. amazing 29. set 30. parent

Passage 2

1. adopted 2. bully 3. trendy 4. boundary
5. core 6. improper 7. positive 8. acknowledge
9. prohibit 10. session 11. reagard 12. adopt
13. expel 14. dismal 15. cautioned 16. risk
17. access 18. administrators 19. consequence 20. safety
21. otherwise 22. engaged 23. banned 24. aware
25. category 26. wise 27. improper 28. against
29. post 30. banned

Passage 3

1. alter 2. address 3. abuse 4. distinguish 5. nagative
6. bump 7. premission 8. disclose 9. adjusted 10. careful
11. accused 12. stranger 13. expert 14. virtually 15. technology
16. unacceptable 17. footprints 18. accused 19. affect
20. prospects 21. addition 22. ability 23. issue 24. benign
25. cautious 26. permission 27. alternation 28. disclosure 29. separate
30. key

Passage 4

1. hire 2. performence 3. innovative 4. industry 5. agreement
6. yield 7. album 8. fierce 9. bond 10. reflects
11. band 12. typical 13. premise 14. extend 15. appealing
16. local 17. live 18. reality 19. accommodation
20. promoting

Passage 5

1. quoted	2. inspiring	3. discount	4. bargain	5. receive
6. path	7. exposure	8. fantastic	9. encouraging	10. unfold
11. host	12. awaitng	13. tend	14. script	15. delight
16. initial	17. festival	18. annually	19. author	20. surrounded
21. repeat	22. reminded	23. attended	24. give up	25. ambition

Passage 6

1. encounter	2. blast	3. crew	4. mystery	5. elegent
6. shadow	7. touchy	8. bias	9. battle	10. parallel
11. adapted	12. release	13. adapt	14. restrict	15. blame
16. published	17. plot	18. billionaire	19. gunshot	20. enormous
21. astonishing	22. disaster	23. battling	24. intriguing	25. extreme
26. preceding	27. casting	28. director	29. entice	30. picky

Passage 7

1. manufacture	2. gloomy	3. collapsing	4. booming	5. maximize
6. estimate	7. contain	8. crise	9. manufacture	10. resource
11. foreign	12. tough	13. exports	14. recession	15. prospect
16. income	17. reputation	18. vast	19. severely	20. importing
21. gigantic	22. close down	23. spacious	24. resilient	25. mine
26. earn	27. emerge	28. injured	29. budget	30. gradually

Passage 8

1. occupied	2. raised	3. attitude	4. split	5. contribution
6. responsible responsibility		7. commit	8. ensure	9. struggle

10. lifestyle	11. balanced	12. soul	13. handle	14. achieve
15. doubt	16. traditionally		17. managed	18. organize
19. insecure	20. childhood	21. pursuit	22. injured	23. entire
24. particular	25. indispensable		26. opportunities	
27. contribution		28. previous	29. domestic	30. career

Passage 9

1. domestic	2. insurance	3. replacement	4. limit	5. entertaining
6. Charge	7. exceed	8. thief	9. civilized	10. slip
11. radical	12. tragedy	13. obtain	14. valuables	15. set
16. Gap	17. gap	18. book	19 occur	20. destination
21. broaden	22. withdraw	23. fashion	24. penalty	25. vision
26. slip	27. tragedy	28. replacement		
29. extra	30. bear in mind			

Passage 10

1. faith	2. burnt	3. procedure	4. require	5. abide
6. equipment	7. perishable	8. extinguisher	9. wound	10. storage
11. slippery	12. barefoot	13. fetch	14. cope	15. constantly
16. sponge	17. bandage	18. collection	19. order	20. chemical
21. chemicals	22. basic	23. bench	24. goods	25. instruction
26. conduct	27. initiate	28. scalded	29. by	30. tools

Passage 11

1. steal	2. gather	3. pirate	4. declare
5. criminals	6. romantic	7. sailor	8. impressive
9. bunch	10. frightened	11. living	12. pocket
13. cargo	14. robbed	15. essentially	16. spite

17. decade
18. crime
19. millions
20. mysterious
21. chance
22. end up with
23. unscathed
24. definition
25. piracy
26. portraited
27. bet
28. board
29. exist
30 property

Passage 12

1. political
2. several
3. defeated
4. federation
5. candidate
6. efectiveness
7. commenced
8. stadium
9. liberal
10. profession
11. commence
12. religions
13. please
14. opposing
15. democratic
16. conservative
17. state
18. representative
19. freedom
20. national
21. conservative
22. ruling
23. freely
24. automatic
25. voting
26. adult
27. field
28. demonstrate
29. free
30. gallery

Passage 13

1. arose
2. unexpected
3. sweeping
4. executive
5. annonced
6. discharge
7. rescue
8. assembled
9. investigate
10. considerable
11. distract
12. dismissed
13. distressing
14. assemble
15. puffs
16. drown
17. cancelled
18. original
19. apparent
20. distressing
21. normal
22. packed with
23. complained
24. distracted
25. indicated
26. pause
27. rush
28. on scene
29. in time
30. complex

Passage 14

1. appreciate
2. interpret
3. environmental
4. innovative
5. conflict
6. novel
7. accordingly
8. subtle

9. confidently 10. conversation 11. author 12. classical
13. constructed 14. fame 15. collision 16. crash
17. express 18. knowledge 19. unwrapped 20. reality
21. brief 22guideline 23. essay 24. gain
25. comment 26. classic 27. option 28. verbal
29. character 30. follow

Passage 15

1. critical 2. career 3. institude 4. receive 5. training
6. endcavor 7. dctcrminc 8. dominatc 9. strcam 10. training
11. advocate 12. endeavour 13. pursue 14. doubled 15. formal
16. sit 17. handy 18. sharpen 19. held 20. guide
21. regularly 22. receives 23. college 24. sit 25. path
26. diversity

Passage 16

1. crack 2. prioritize 3. concentration 4. sufficient
5. revise 6. timetable 7. treat 8. complicated
9. academic 10. stretch 11. handy 12. stared
13. reward 14. slot 15. stuck 16. slot
17. pile 18. approaches 19. period 20. draw up
21. prioritized

Passage 17

1. capable 2. affluent 3. Agriculture 4. resist
5. promoted 6. Productivity 7. seed 8. technology
9. invented 10. derived 11. draught 12. impact
13. shortage 14. development 15. flood 16. crop

17. invented 18. breed 19. affluent 20. extreme
21. numerous 22. amount 23. harvesting 24. landfall
25. experiments 26. largely 27. climate

Passage 18

1. elderly 2. boosting 3. threaten 4. enhance
5. mental 6. comprise 7. researcher 8. elderly
9. fuel 10. accumulate 11. recommend 12. considerable
13. tension 14. claimed 15. reduce 16. establish
17. daily 18. beneficial 19. possibly 20. hectic
21. area 22. lost 23. harmful 24. comprehension
25. typical 26. slowed down

Passage 19

1. publish 2. advertisement 3. channel 4. platform
5. drawback 6. branded 7. expanded 8. sustain 9. potential
10. sensible 11. widespread 12. powerful 13. ordinary 14. false
15. customers 16. take effort 17. image 18. reach 19. compete
20. compare 21. fans 22. dispute 23. popularity 24. individuals
25. effective 26. via

Passage 20

1. fireworks 2. encourage 3. lobster 4. parade 5. celebration
6. lunar 7. fortune 8. maintains 9. meaning 10. resolution
11. significant 12. hosts 13. status 14. bright 15. wrap
16. Contrarily 17. arrived 18. resolution 19. blissful 20. ideal
21. calendar 22. exchange 23. according to 24. gathering
25. traditions 26. symbol 27. take charge of

28. looking forward to

Passage 21

1. supervise
2. slope
3. revealed
4. sightseeing
5. respected
6. transformed
7. harsh
8. display
9. mining
10. Identify
11. covered
12. intended
13. trail
14. ride
15. commonly
16. field trip
17. mission
18. presence
19. exposure
20. discussion
21. diligent
22. condition
23. underground
24. past
25. diary
26. discovered
27. item
28. pride
29. journey

Passage 22

1. chronic
2. hardship
3. volunteer
4. donate
5. sack
6. disabiity
7. hardship
8. profit
9. strain
10. purchase
11. cause
12. justice
13. strain
14. employment
15. out of fashion
16. once
17. taste
18. tidy
19. sack
20. former
21. instead
22. rejected
23. get involved in
24. suffer
25. as well
26. essential
27. deny

Passage 23

1. shocked
2. refugee
3. competition
4. introduce
5. endure
6. confidence
7. senior
8. hunger
9. fled
10. initiate
11. scholarship
12. enthusiastic
13. vivid
14. drifting
15. hopeless
16. copy
17. definite
18. infinite
19. enthusiastic
20. vivid

Passage 24

1. physically 2. withdraw 3. responsibility 4. responsibility
5. warned 6. connect 7. bossy 8. assured
9. argument 10. behaviour 11. rebal 12. handle
13. uncertain 14. tip 15. extreme 16. argument
17. tip 18. teenager 19. bossy 20. uncertain
21. boundary 22. open-minded 23. responsibility 24. physically emotionally 25. rebel

10-12 配套单词填空练习参考答案

Passage 1

1. absence 2. academic 3. acknowledge 4. adequate
5. accidents 6. announcement 7. anxiety 8. appreciated
9. appropriate 10. approval 11. arrangement 12. capacity
13. circumstances 14. commences 15. depression 16. disciplines
17. divorce 18. exhaustion 19. emotion 20. encounter
21. enhance 22. expand 23. exposes 24. exposure
25. extensive 26. extreme 27. fructrates 28. resilience
29. advice 30. anxious

Passage 2

1. ambassador 2. ambition 3. arise 4. arrival
5. assistance 6. beliefs 7. charity 8. collective
9. conscience 10. conscious 11. consciousness 12. consult
13. consultant 14. contribute 15. definition 16. engaged
17. establishment 18. moral 19. motivating 20. painful

21. sympathy 22. vision 23. vulnerable 24. intangible
25. uphold 26. inherent 27. crucial 28. accumulate
29. alongside 30. amateur

Passage 3

1. alert 2. alter 3. cautious 4. convicted
5. convictious 6. ultimate 7. ensure 8. constantly
9. surrounding 10. suspicious 11. alternative 12. supply
13. potential 14. precaution 15. suffcient 16. wander
17. lighting 18. theft 19. climb 20. securely
21. victims 22. appearance 23. crowded 24. advice
25. survey 26. ultimately 27. constantly 28. zip
29. hang 30. proved

Passage 4

1. abandoned 2. advocates 3. assumption 4. atmosphere
5. carbon 6. combat 7. comprehensive 8. conceded
9. concentrating 10. concluded 11. concrete 12. consistent
13. controversial 14. emphasise 15. emission 16. generated
17. genuine 18. pledge 19. substantial 20. remarkable
21. voluntary 22. resolution 23. consensus 24. corporative
25. tackling 26. phenomenon 27. devastating 28. radiation
29. incentive 30. feasible

Passage 5

1. ballot 2. constitution 3. presenters 4. delegation
5. disclosed 6. enabled 7. exactly 8. delegation
9. procedure 10. candidates 11. essential 12. campaign

13. transparency
14. compulsory
15. interested
16. (is) composed
17. manage
18. showcases
19. elect
20. rewarding
21. smooth
22. print
23. operation
24. position
25. scope
26. framework
27. interest
28. union
29. government
30. reward

Passage 6

1. accociate
2. attractive
3. benefit
4. comfortable
5. delights
6. intense
7. perspective
8. unfortunately
9. impression
10. particular
11. originated
12. gradually
13. tremendous
14. benefits
15. instrument
16. routine
17. melody
18. halt
19. reason
20. background
21. potential
22. research
23. therapy
24. relief
25. talent
26. expensive
27. memorable
28. fee
29. advance
30. halt

Passage 7

1. complaint
2. desperate
3. succeeded
4. equivalent
5. offensive
6. reference
7. untraditional
8. commercial
9. offense
10. worsened
11. counselling
12. inevitable
13. regarded
14. productive
15. effective
16. deteriotate
17. influence
18. topic
19. household
20. addiction
21. angle
22. counselling
23. inspired
24. attack
25. worsened
26. deteriorated
27. regarded
28. claimed
29. conftonts
30. overact

Passage 8

1. analysis
2. analysts
3. concept
4. constructed

5. construction	6. crucial	7. demonstrated	8. explanation
9. literacy	10. literature	11. plot	12. persuaded
13. requirements	14. technician	15. theme	16. criticized
17. grasp	18. reprtition	19. structure	20. paraphrase
21. prompt	22. injustice	23. assessed	24. persuade
25. focus	26. sharpen	27. insightful	28. systematic
29. fabulous	30. character		

Passage 9

1. appeal	2. boundary	3. content	4. excerpt
5. expression	6. familiar	7. investigating	8. numerous
9. praise	10. praised	11. profession	12. rhythm
13. universe	14. inspired	15. boundary	16. illustrate
17. complex	18. entices	19. delve	into20. discovery
21. flick through	22. twists and turns	23. frighten	24. illustrates
25. perspective	26. lengthy	27. rythm	28. vast
29. fictions	30. numerous		

Passage 10

1. column	2. commentor	3. context	4. efficient
5. entire	6. enterprise	7. exhibition	8. fundamental
9. thorough	10. empowering	11. subtle	12. digest
13. controversy	14. revealing	15. critical	16. distinguish
17. opinion	18. improve	19. contribute	20. various
21. issue	22. investments	23. global	24. deserve
25. conflict	26. persuade	27. utilize	28. account
29. trustworthy	30. chief		

Passage 11

1. appointed	2. appointment	3. continent	4. electoral
5. framework	6. innocent	7. institution	8. judgement
9. legislation	10. parliamentary	11. regulation	12. regulator
13. resembles	14. excessed	15. trigger	16. prosecute
17. core	18. illegal	19. formal	20. displayed
21. accordingly	22. conduct	23. politician	24. citizens
25. significant	26. political	27. alert	28. referendum
29. managing	40. determine		

Passage 12

1. disappointed	2. enrolled	3. intelligence	4. occasionally
5. overcome	6. poverty	7. provoked	8. psychological
9. psychology	10. regret	11. decent	12. entail
13. address	14. commencement	15. according to	16. impoverish
17. desperately	18. insecurity	19. negative	20. intelligence
21. authors	22. origin	23. humble	24. ups and downs
25. according	26. promising	27. graduated	28. taste
29. medicine	30. commence		

Passage 13

1. overwhelming	2. reputation	3. seriously	4. transform
5. wealth	6. phenomenon	7. adaptation	8. ignites
9. recognition	10. impressive	11. advanced	12. unique
13. triumphs	14. cherished	15. technology	16. treasures
17. humble	18. widespread	19. vivid	20. pretended
21. passively	22. engaged	23. prefer	24. worn out
25. ultimately			

Passage 14

1. surrender
2. go along with
3. owing to
4. stirred up
5. take action
6. stand up to
7. pressured
8. struggle
9. observe
10. turn out to be
11. soft
12. inner
13. frerce
14. silent
15. severe
16. modetate
17. immune
18. scary
19. confused
20. clarigy
21. seek
22. sustain
23. remained
24. consume
25. resist
26. stance
27. wellbeing
28. silent
29. victims
30. courage

Passage 15

1. heaps
2. pile
3. objective
4. results in
5. ought to
6. elevtives
7. economy
8. inance
9. chemistry
10. theories
11. biology
12. looked at
13. monetary
14. management
15. investment
16. focus on
17. laboratories
18. implement
19. occurrence
20. inevitable
21. procedure
22. explosion
23. diversion
24. guideline
25. disaster
26. catastrophe
27. mistake
28. report
29. permission
30. accurate

Passage 16

1. hand-made
2. occasion
3. special
4. model
5. baking
6. flour
7. recalls
8. magic
9. powder
10. powder
11. model
12. temperature
13. liquid
14. decorations
15. sprinkle
16. recall
17. beat
18. pouring
19. melting
20. spread
21. cool
22. decorate
23. must-have
24. muddy
25. favoured
26. native
27. prevalent
28. smoothy

29. prefect	30. darl		

Passage 17

1. professionals	2. robot	3. professions	4. scientists
5. advance6.	intelligence	7. artificial	8. specialist
9. amount	10. routine	11. occupation	12. occupation
13. counseling	14. response	15. outburst	16. development
17. course	18. revolution	19. significance	20. solicitor
21. professor	22. predicted	23. expect	24. speculate
25. program	26. replace	27. occupied	28. foresee
29. commence	30. sophiscated		

Passage 18

1. materialism	2. materials	3. environment	4. lifestyle
5. features	6. material life	7. consider	8. wealth
9. empire	10. comfort	11. implication	12. luxury
13. symbol	14. pursue	15. pursue	16. nightmare
17. feather	18. luxury	19. boundary	20. necessities
21. institutions	22. preversation	23. extinction	24. obligation
25. strengths	26. tendency	27. damage	28. satisfy
29. sacrifice	30. emphasized		

Passage 19

1. take into account	2. unlike	3. overseas	4. priceless
5. abroad	6. beneficial	7. excellent	8. spectacular
9. suitable	10. overseas	11. exotic	12. personal
13. outstanding	14. invaluable	15. compensated	16. recommoned
17. enjoying	18. famlirise	19. siblings	20. loss

21. priority 22. expense 23. manner 24. scenery
25. inspiration 26. challenge 27. integration 28. invasion
29. culture exchange 30. platform

Passage 20

1. distinction 2. migrants 3. hall 4. balance
5. facilities 6. individual 7. characteristic 8. performance
9. filmmaker 10. moment 11. angle 12. system
13. ethics 14. adults 15. commonwealth
16. interval 17. wonder 18. equipped 19. respect
20. demonstrated 21. overstep 22. composed 23. enables
24. trust 25. settled 26. independent 27. diverse
28. creative 29. regular 30. retrospective

Passage 21

1. congested 2. cyclist 3. matter 4. accumulate
5. correlation 6. coincidence 7. physical 8. contribute
9. extend 10. confron 11. alleviated 12. initiated
13. cycle 14. benefit 15. legislated 16. witnessed
17. curbed 18. private 19. stand still 20. shocking
21. parallel 22. urgent 23. risky 24. vehicle
25. queue 26. volume 27. casualty 28. campaign
29. rush 30. direction